In The Footsteps Of The Kuzari: An Introduction to Jewish Philosophy

Volume 2

by Shalom Rosenberg

In The Footsteps Of The Kuzari: An Introduction to Jewish Philosophy

Volume 2

by Shalom Rosenberg

edited by Joel Linsider
from a translation by Gila Weinberg

ATID
Yashar Books, Inc.
New York, 2008

In The Footsteps Of The Kuzari
An Introduction to Jewish Philosophy
Volume 2

by Shalom Rosenberg

edited by Joel Linsider
from a translation by Gila Weinberg

ISBN 978-1-933143-22-4
Copyright © 2008 Shalom Rosenberg

This book was published in conjunction with ATID, the Academy for Torah Initiatives and Directions. ATID is an independent institution fostering new and significant thought, strategies, and policies for the crucial issues facing Jewish education. ATID's longrange programs include the ATID Fellows, a training fellowship for young Orthodox Jewish educators and future educational leadership, as well as professional and institutional development projects with lead-schools in Israel and the Diaspora, and a research and publishing division. ATID is the parent body of WebYeshiva.org—the world's first fully interactive online yeshiva. Learn more about ATID at http://www.atid.org/.

For information and catalog write to Yashar Books Inc., 1548 E. 33rd Street, Brooklyn, NY 11234, or visit our website: www.YasharBooks.com

לזכרם
המבורך
של הורי
האהובים

אבי מורי
ר' בנציון בן ר' שלום שכנא

ואמי מורתי
מרת גולדה בת ר' מאיר נחום

שלי שלהם

We dedicate this work
to the blessed memory
of our beloved parents

שמואל יצחק בן מנחם מנדל
הכהן בינהקר ז"ל
ורעיתו
שרה בת פנחס הכהן
מבית ברכר ז"ל

אריה לייב
בן חיים ספקטור ז"ל
ורעיתו
שיינדל בת זנוועל
מבית קאופמן ז"ל

Dr. Leo Lyon & Janet
Spector

Dr. Samuel Israel & Sadie
Beinhaker

ת.נ.צ.ב.ה.

Philip Howard & Constance Kaufman Beinhaker

פנחס צבי בן שמואל יצחק הכהן
ורעיתו חנה בת אריה לייב
בינהקר

Contents

Introduction

Professor Shalom Rosenberg's *In the Footsteps of the Kuzari* is much more than a commentary on R. Yehudah Halevi's medieval classic, *Sefer HaKuzari*. Combining a keen sensitivity to the religious dilemmas of our day with the intellectual rigor of the university, this book serves as an introduction to Jewish philosophy, and unapologetically argues that Judaism presents a coherent and sophisticated religious worldview that is as relevant today as it has been for millennia. The book addresses such pressing issues as:

- The sources of the individual's religious experience,

- Religious truth in the context of changing intellectual trends and fads,

- Jewish uniqueness and the nations of the world,

- The relations between the individual and the collective,

- The challenges of educating toward a rich religious life.

Prof. Rosenberg has for decades been one of the leading intellectual forces in Israeli Modern Orthodoxy. As his first major work to be published in English, *In the Footsteps of the Kuzari* will be an important resource for teachers and students of Jewish thought, as well as for English-speaking Jews in search of a rich, sophisticated, and coherent Jewish voice. Readers of Prof. Rosenberg's work will discover his rare ability to use medieval texts to address contemporary issues, without sacrificing an awareness that these same texts are not themselves contemporary. This is not the kind of simple sermonizing that marks so much current writing on Jewish thought, which unreflectively hopes to make older material relevant to today's dilemmas; neither is it academic scholarship which attempts to objectively examine older texts in their historical contexts. Rather, Prof. Rosenberg manages to speak to today without losing an awareness of history, to translate contemporary dilemmas into religious language. He offers a traditional approach, arguing that Judaism speaks to today's readers without kowtowing to this or that contemporary trend.

ATID is proud to publish this book, the second of two volumes, as part of our ongoing work in outlining an agenda for the teaching and study of Jewish thought in Modern Orthodox schools. This is our part of our larger initiative to respond to the lack of accessible materials for the teaching of Jewish thought in English speaking schools.

While all thoughtful readers will find this volume to be stimulating, we believe that it will be particularly useful resource in an educational context—individual chapters or even passages can be used as jumping off points for discussions. The array of issues and challenges that the author outlines in the preface will surely resonate with Jewish educators entrusted with the often daunting task of entering the contemporary classroom. *In the Footsteps of the Kuzari* is something of a series of thoughtful ruminations rather than systematic philosophy, presented in a dialogical tone rather than a polished thesis, and in this sense Rosenberg is borrowing from the *Kuzari*'s own conversational style. The medium is part of the message—abstract philosophy can sometimes miss the connection to life, a connection more readily available in this style.

—Rabbi Jeffrey Saks
Director, ATID

Acknowledgements

In the Footsteps of the Kuzari was originally published in Hebrew as *BeIkvot HaKuzari* (Sifriat Ma'aleh, 1991). It was translated into English by Gila Weinberg and serialized on Yeshivat Har Etzion's Virtual Beit Midrash (www.vbm-torah.org) in 1995–96. Our thanks to Rabbi Ezra Bick, VBM Director, and Rabbi Reuven Ziegler, VBM Editor in Chief, for their assistance and permission to use the translation as the basis for this English-language edition.

The original translation as prepared by Gila Weinberg was revised and edited by Joel Linsider. Dr. Yoel Finkelman, ATID's Director of Research and Projects, ably shepherded the project along while balancing his overall responsibilities for our ongoing work in Jewish Thought.

We acknowledge permission to use material from the following copyrighted materials:

- S.Y. Agnon, *Twenty-One Stories* (New York: Schocken Books, 1979).

- Rabbi Joseph B. Soloveitchik, *Kol Dodi Dofek: Listen—My Beloved Knocks*, trans. David Z. Gordon (New York: Yeshiva University, 2006).

- Rabbi Adin Steinsaltz, *The Tales of Rabbi Nachman of Bratslav* (Northvale, NJ: Aaronson, 1993).

Section 7:
Understanding the
Commandments

CHAPTER 28:
THE COMMANDMENTS

Four entered the Orchard; one looked and expired, one looked and was injured, one looked and uprooted the plants [i.e., became a heretic], another entered in peace and left in peace. Who was he? Rabbi Akiva. The one who looked and expired could not stand the glow of that world, and his body disintegrated. The second went mad and spoke confusedly of divine matters, words of no benefit. The third disdained the practical commandments after having looked upon the higher spiritual spheres, saying to himself: "The practical commandments are merely tools and means which bring one to this spiritual level, and I have already achieved it. Hence, I have no need of the practical commandments." In this manner he became corrupt and he corrupted others, erred and caused others to err. Whereas Rabbi Akiva entered both worlds and left without being struck by calamity . . . and he was the man who, at the moment of his execution, asked his students if the time had come to recite the Shema and he recited it. (III:65).

In Halevi's admirable interpretation of this well known parable, Elisha Ben Abuya represents the philosophical position, which views the commandments merely as a means to achieve intellectual perfection. Rabbi Akiva's personality creates a striking contrast to this approach, for it was Rabbi Akiva who performed commandments even at the exalted moment of sanctifying God's name.

This brings us to one of the central themes in Jewish thought: the reasons behind the commandments (I:79). We will try to understand Halevi's position against the background of other positions. Halevi rejects other possible explanations of the Torah's commandments, and of law in general.

Delving into the reasons for the commandments means trying to understand why we are obligated to perform a particular commandment.

15

We will understand this better in the context of other commandments or obligations. Let us begin this discussion by comparing the commandments to two sorts of action: a soldier wearing a beret and a driver or passenger wearing a seat belt.

The Beret Model: Discipline and Meaning

One approach compares the commandments to the wearing of a military beret. A soldier doesn't wear a beret to protect himself from the sun or the rain. It is rather an expression of the discipline to which the soldier is committed. Similarly, we can describe a philosophical approach which sees the commandments as expressions of the divine will and emphasizes their disciplinary character: "What does God care if [the ritual slaughterer] slaughters from the nape or from the neck?" The meaning of the commandment is discipline. Its significance lies in man's surrender to the King of Kings. Fulfillment of the commandments means accepting the yoke of Heaven, obeying God, and acting in accordance with His word. The content of the commandments themselves is irrelevant, and could easily have been different. But since we were commanded, these commandments became obligatory and may not be altered in any way. This approach views our relationship with God as the relationship with a king, ruler and commander. Man's central difficulty is his position in relation to God, with only two alternatives: acceptance of the Heavenly yoke, or rejection of it which amounts, essentially, to rebellion. According to this approach, the value of the commandment lies in the discipline of accepting it as an order, just as the value of a soldier's beret lies first and foremost in the discipline it symbolizes and not in the practical purpose it serves.

The Seat Belt Model: Law as Compulsory Advice

The second position compares the commandments to the obligation to wear a seat belt. We are legally obligated to wear it. Although the seat belt can be uncomfortable or inconvenient at times, and although we rebel against the punishments meted out to us when we fail to fulfill the obligation, in the final analysis the law is for our own good. It is simply good advice. The law compels us to do what is best for us. In the *Guide*, Maimonides approaches the commandments in a similar vein. His approach stems from a rationalist worldview. The commandments, he claims, have intrinsic value beyond the merit of obedience to the Creator, and one must strive to discover their rational meaning. In explaining the commandments, Maimonides speaks from his own unique philosophical and historical perspective. Although one may accept his opinion in principle, one must not focus on the details of his explanation. His rationalistic students understood him to mean that the human mind—the only judge available to us—is capable of explaining the reasons for the commandments. According to this principle, logic underlies the entire legal system. The sole difference between those laws which we easily understand (*mishpatim*), and those which seem oblique (*hukkim*), lies not in the commandments themselves, but only in our perception of them. These explanations are hidden from us at times, due to certain psychological or sociological circumstances. However, explanations do exist, and our minds are capable of grasping them. The basic model of the rationalist is mathematics, the pinnacle of human intellectual achievement.

Rabbi Sa'adiah Ga'on was among those who developed a synthesis between the various positions. He differentiated between commandments observed because we are told to do so (*shim'iyot*) and those grounded in rationality (*sikhliyot*). These commandments represent, respectively, the first approach and the second.

The seat belt model is an example of the rational position, which reached its height in the writings of Maimonides. He believed that reasons could be given for the principle of each commandment but not for all its details. The details must be seen as arbitrary. This brings us once again to the distinction between obedience-based and logical commandments. The details are obedience based; the principle of each commandment is logical.

The Analogy to Medicine

Halevi presents us with a third position. Rejecting the approach which places all the value of the commandments in human subjugation to the divine will, Halevi assumes that the commandments possess intrinsic meaning, just as there is logic and meaning to the medicines taken by a sick person. What makes medicine unique? To understand this we must return to example of military discipline. Often a new recruit is punished for failing to carry out his commander's directives—failing to stand in line-up precisely as ordered, failing to march in proper time, failing to fold his army blanket properly. Such punishment, however, is completely different from the consequences—the punishment—suffered by a person who uses medication improperly, or fails to take it altogether. In the latter case, the punishment is intrinsically connected to the medication he fails to take properly. There is no need for a judge to punish him for not having used his medication by giving him the disease. This is not something disciplinary and arbitrary. It is intrinsically connected to the person's behavior. This, Halevi tells us, is the case with regard to the commandments.

The medicine model is not appropriate for Maimonides, since he and other rationalists believed that the commandments could be understood and explained logically. Halevi attempts to teach us that there are things in this world that the human mind cannot explain. The efficacy of medication is usually discovered by experience, while its essence often remains a riddle to us, either temporarily or permanently. The effectiveness of the medication does not depend on our awareness or theoretical understanding. It is a reality. A medicine that needs our awareness to function is not a "real" medicine. It works through psychological persuasion. It is actually an illusion. Scientists can study a drug's effectiveness by using experiments and control groups. The testing is carried out using a double-blind method, in which the doctors do not know to whom they are administrating the drug, and the patients do not know if they are receiving it. The drug works even if the expert does not understand it, and even if the patient does not always know that he is taking it. For many philosophers, medicine was the model of a profession which does not always have a theoretical basis to explain its success—yet it constitutes a rational science. Medicine in fact makes use of another method. The effectiveness of certain drugs is ascertained by experimentation, and only afterwards, in some cases, do we reach the stage of understanding why these drugs function as they do. In fact, sometimes we are surprised by explanations of phenomena that had remained mysterious for thousands of years.

The Doctor and the Lawyer

The model of medicine teaches us of the efficacy of human action, despite the inability of the human mind to explain the reality it faces. This approach to the commandments does not accord, however, with the approach based on human subjugation to the divine will, which we expressed in the model of the military beret. This idea will be more clear if we compare the medicine model to another model: that of the lawyer.

Consider the law through the eyes of a "purist" lawyer, zealously advocating his position. The theoretical scientist is successful when he "proves" something in the framework of a theory. The doctor is successful when he cures his patient. When is the lawyer successful? Let us assume that a lawyer is fighting for a client in a certain trial. What is the meaning of success here? It is not to be located in the theoretical heaven of mathematics nor beyond the ocean of empiricism. We must keep the law, but the law is independent. To the extent that the judge—himself another lawyer—rules in his favor, the world will have changed to the lawyer's benefit. Rightfully, the lawyer sees the law that obligates him as a world existing in its own right. What the judges finally decide—after all appropriate procedures—is the truth.

To illustrate, consider a medical exam that asks a doctor how he will treat a particular case. The examiners will assess the diagnosis and course of treatment. A real-life doctor, however, is not being tested by his eminent peers, nor by judges who were appointed by the system. He does not face the judgment of man but the judgment of nature. If he does not succeed, the patient will die—even if medical committees, judges and clerks of the ministry of education decide that he was right. Or consider a more extreme case, in which that someone secretly bribes a corrupt judge, and obtains a favorable verdict. The true culprit goes scot-free. If we compare this to the model of the doctor, we will immediately understand the absurdity. A corrupt doctor can be bribed to move one to the head of a waiting list, but it is impossible to bribe a doctor to succeed, or to lessen the severity of the patient's disease. The judge's verdict creates a legal reality. The doctor's diagnosis, his verdict, does not create reality. It merely describes it. The halakhist is similar to the doctor. He does not create halakhic reality. He merely describes it. Halakhic reality is not the same as the rational reality of mathematics, nor the constructed reality of law. The *halakhah* describes a reality no less real, a reality that includes facts and powers which affect the human soul and the world.

The medicine model expresses Halevi's position. It also opens a pathway to additional approaches similar to Halevi's. The most outstanding among these is the kabbalistic approach, although we must stress that there are significant differences between the two, differences we will explore later on. However, the principle is the same. Man, through his actions, by keeping the commandments, alters reality.

The Sorcerer's Apprentice

Halevi uses the parable of the doctor to clarify his position. The doctor in this parable is none other than Moses, and the later prophets and sages after him. This is the man who receives inspiration from heaven in his halakhic ruling. Our Sages maintained that the Torah is "not in Heaven," meaning that it is interpreted by halakhic legislators who are subject to human fallibility. Yet despite all this the Torah is "from Heaven," and thus every halakhic decision must be directly or indirectly ensconced in the word of God. In our story there is another character, an impostor who pretends to be a doctor (I:79). This character reminds us of the famous legend of the sorcerer's apprentice, a man who learned a few magic words, and begins a process he cannot stop. The sorcerer's apprentice commands the broom to draw water for him, but he does not know the magic words to stop it. Even after he rips the broom to shreds, the pieces continue to bring him water. The doctor's apprentice in Halevi's parable is essentially similar to the sorcerer's apprentice. He is man who learns a little from a doctor and dares to compete with him, without possessing either his erudition or his responsibility. In some cases, the doctor's apprentice will succeed, but in the long term his success will not last, since the apprentice has no access to the doctor's supernatural sources of knowledge.

Often we find living examples of the sorcerer's apprentice, both within Judaism and outside of it. Some religions accept from Judaism the principle of halakhah without possessing the basis to develop this principle. Halevi discusses the status of *halakhah* in the third section of the book.

The Wellspring of Faith and of Heresy

We can now clarify one central assumption that lies at the base of our entire discussion. Rationalism is our sole guide during a significant part of our lives. Halevi teaches us that the Torah addresses us from a vantage point beyond this rationalism. Its source lies beyond logic, and some of its messages cannot be grasped in logical terms. This is the true meaning of the obedience-based commandments. They are not the arbitrary decrees of a capricious ruler. They are expressions of mysteries that the mind cannot fathom.

But while Halevi denies the omnipotence of the intellect, the unchallenged dominion of rationalism, he certainly does not champion all irrational approaches. The *haver* wisely notes that the wellsprings of faith and of heresy are one and the same (I:77). What transcends rationality must not be identified with what is beneath it. Logic sometimes functions as a dam, and man must sometimes open the dam to allow the waters of the post-rational faith and knowledge to flow through. But we must not destroy the dam, lest the pre-rational waters flow more freely than they should, at the wrong time, and in an improper way. Thus, we must carefully stress the distinction between faith on the one hand and astrology, magic, and similar phenomena on the other:

> People behaved in this manner.... They would be tempted by the foolishness of astrology and the opinions of the scientists in their generation, and they would move from one futile doctrine to another.... There are those who viewed the powers of nature as gods, while forgetting the leader and ruler of these powers (I:79).

The source of faith can become the seed of heresy, and in the name of the same deviation from rationality, people find a refuge for many false and harmful superstitions. There is always the danger of drawing unwarranted comparisons, of granting a collective sanction to many "mysterious" approaches that the rational mind refuses to accept. Once again, we see the clarity of Halevi's analysis, an analysis that compels us to distinguish between things that appear, at first glance, to be identical. We must always assess the potential dangers that lurk beyond the boundaries of logic. Despite the blessings of faith in what is beyond logic, we must assess the potential dangers as well.

Commandments and Flowers: A Fourth Model (II:56–58)

We have considered three models for the commandments: berets, seat-belts, and medicine. We return now to the first model, in order to learn about a fourth approach which bears some similarity to it.

The main difference between the beret and the seat-belt is not the punishment. It is the intention of the legislator. Through the beret, the commander sought to establish discipline, to create a symbol for a particular way of life. Through the seat-belt requirement, the legislator attempts to guide man to do what is best for him, even if enforcement through punishment is sometimes needed.

Comparing the commandments to the military beret implies, at first glance, that mankind's principal mission is to submit to the Heavenly command and to do so out of fear. But there is another type of compliance, with a very different meaning: compliance out of love. The human being desires to worship God *li-shemah*, for the sake of the action itself, without thought of reward or punishment. This approach is associated in our generation with the philosopher Yeshayahu Leibowitz, but the basic idea, as we shall see, appears in the Kuzari. Indeed, Halevi himself views certain commandments, or components of certain commandments, in this way. To understand this, let us pay close attention to the background of Halevi's words.

The Sages taught us that there is a need to blend love and fear. When we stand before authority, both love and fear can lead us to deviate from the ideal course. Fear can become hatred of the commandment. Love can cause disrespect for the law. Judaism synthesizes these two elements.

One of the most impressive aspects in of our history in the dark period of the Middle Ages was our ancestors' ability to face the monumental cathedrals, large mosques and impressive works of art and overcome the temptation to be drawn in. They struggled against the pull of a foreign culture, and they succeeded. This was not physical coercion by the sword. Jews faced a different type of coercion, that of a great civilization trying, consciously or unconsciously, to force itself upon them through the power of its imposing presence. The tourist visiting a large modern city has a similar feeling, when he senses his own smallness in comparison to the skyscrapers that surround him. Halevi teaches us that a different type of strength exists as well. Our ancestors' strength was not theatrical. Their mode of worship was not encompassed "in the beauty of the poetic phrase, in sighs, in wails accompanied by the raising of eyebrows and the covering of eyes, nor in speech or gestures unaccompanied by actions." Jews relished something equally monumental: the simple desire of the heart to worship God. Tourists could not capture it with a camera. Yet it is more important and essential than the most monumental edifice.

We must express ourselves differently. This was apparent to Halevi when he passed by the Cordova mosque or stood before the great cathedrals. Christianity itself accepted this idea at a later stage, when the Protestants rebelled against the opulence of the church and sought to return to the simple prayer of the Bible. They perceived the potential emptiness of these theatrics, and realized that when the actor goes home, the show is over.

How do we express what is in our hearts? "These [feelings] are expressed only through actions that are naturally difficult for man. Yet, the worshipper of God performs them with perfect yearning and love." This concept helps us understand another layer of the commandments.

Let me offer an example. If I were to present my wife with a broom or a needle and thread as a birthday gift, she would certainly think I was contemptible. That gift would not be an expression of love, but an instrument for the work which I apparently expect from her. While I could give her gifts that would be useful only to her, sometimes love or friendship is best expressed by a gesture that has no practical use. For example, we often give flowers as a symbolic gesture. This could be a merely theatrical gesture, which only teaches us what price was paid, or displays a stranger's talent for arranging flowers. Judaism wants us to bring flowers to God, but only unique flowers, which we must work hard to discover. We Jews have not expressed ourselves in the Diaspora with the esthetics of flower arrangement. Instead, we have climbed up steep and often dangerous mountains, in order to pluck one flower and thus express our love for God.

When we perform the commandments, heed the advice or take the medicine, we do it for our own good. In a sense, we are bringing a button and needle as a gift so that the recipient will sew our button back on. This is the meaning of reciprocal love: *ani le-dodi ve-dodi li* ("I am my Beloved's and my Beloved is mine"). God gives us advice and we bring him flowers. But when we perform the commandments, we hope not only for a personal divine response. We seek to alter history. We believe that the commandments act upon the world.

The Kuzari king asks the *haver*: "Are you not overwhelmed today by all these responsibilities? What nation could possibly keep such a regimen of commands?" (II:57). Bringing all these flowers seemingly makes life difficult. Just as in the love between husband and wife, however, fulfillment of the difficult obligations protects something far more valuable than what is given up. The true reward in our religious life is our continuous national encounter with God.

Our closeness to God means that Jewish history is not similar to general history. The latter is subject to geographical, economic and sociological laws, but Jewish history is different. Think of a mother who has no time for her children and leaves them with a nanny, while another mother is more connected to her children and gives them her time and her love. She may punish them more often than the successful nanny does, but her children feel her love. The other children's room is more beautiful, but, Halevi suggests, our less elaborate room—the room of Jewish history— enjoys the mother's presence. This is the true meaning of cleaving to God. God does not leave us in the hands of an angel or messenger in the form of normal historical laws. God accompanies us Himself.

According to this approach, when we fulfill rabbinical ordinances, or when we are careful about the details of the commandments, we express our love. We find this idea in Jewish thought throughout the generations. Outstanding in this approach are Rabbenu Yona in the medieval period, and Rabbi Tzadok ha-Kohen of Lublin in modern Hasidism.

The Multifaceted Character of the Commandments

Perhaps all these views are right?

We have examined various schools of Jewish thought, and each offers us a different philosophical approach to the commandments. Could these philosophers have misled us by offering their views as mutually exclusive? Often, we are faced with an approach that is built upon generalizations or an extreme statement that is true in some cases but not in others. Every great philosopher demonstrated the existence of various ways of understanding the commandments. Maimonides, for example, did this is in his *Guide* and in his *Mishneh Torah*. It would make sense to assume that a number of approaches are correct, since the commandments themselves encompass many different principles. In addition, it is possible that certain commandments can be understood on various levels, each of which could have a different meaning. Just as our actions are varied, dictated by various values, so too are the commandments. For this reason we may perhaps accept Rabbi Samson Rafael Hirsch's division, which classifies the commandments according to different principles. Rabbi Hirsch uses biblical terminology to form this division: *torah*, *edut* (testimony), *mishpat* (human ethics), *hok* (non-societal law), *mitzvah* (commandment) and *avodah* (worship).

But the important point here is neither the terminology nor the principles, but, rather, the multi-dimensionality of the principles. For example, Yeshayahu Leibowitz suggests that we read the entire Torah as worship of God, viewing the encounter with the Divine Being as the core of the

Torah, rather than a reason for a specific commandment. We will return to this position shortly. But while this may be true for one group of commandments, which we will call commandments of *avodah*, is not universally true. We must also recognize the existence of *mishpatim*, a system of commandments whose goal is to create a functional society, and of *mitzvot*, a system that develops the individual and obligates him to norms beyond the judicial norms of society. To all these we must add the *edot*, which are a symbolic system, and *hukkim*, which define our ethical relationship to the non-human world. The final element is what the medieval rationalists searched for: the *torot*, a system of commandments that teach us basic concepts in Jewish thought.

Through the *mishpatim*, the *hukkim* and the *mitzvot*, we achieve goodness. Through the *eduyot* [testimonies] we reach truth. Jewish thought expresses the truth, and concretizes it in life through symbolic language. The *avodah*, such as the worship in the Temple, or prayer, constitutes, in Rabbi Hirsch's view, "a departure from the life of action in order once again to comprehend the life truths which we must consider." These truths elude us at times due to preoccupation, illusions, or ordinary forgetfulness. *Avodah* creates a sort of oasis in the desert of life.

We thus see that the commandments express various principles. But perhaps the division ought not to stop at categories of commandments. Perhaps each particular commandment contains various diverse elements as well. To truly understand this idea, we must follow in Rabbi Hirsch's footsteps and explore the position that sees the commandments as messages written in symbolic language. It is that approach we turn to next.

CHAPTER 29:
SYMBOLS AND FACTS

In the preceding chapter, we mentioned R. Samson Rafael Hirsch's presentation of the commandments as a system of symbols. Although the symbolic approach bears an affinity to both Halevi's approach and that of the Kabbalah, it is important to emphasize the differences. There is a fundamental distinction between symbols and facts, corresponding to the difference between a "no-entry" sign and a roadblock that makes entry impossible. The sign is a symbol. It tells us something, but it doesn't act on us or alter our will. A roadblock is something tangible, real. Of course the roadblock can be knocked down, but it still expresses a different dimension of reality than does the sign. It differs from the sign as energy differs from information.

A glance at any car shows us that it comprises two systems. The steering wheel and its accessories determine the direction of travel. The gas and the brakes supply energy and control it. Both systems are necessary. Without gas the car cannot move, but without a steering wheel, it might go over a cliff.

Let me explain the metaphor. If it is true that the commandments are symbols, then it would seem that all they give us is more information—information that could be obtained in another way. However, today we know more about symbols, and this new knowledge allows us to perceive them differently. As we shall see, symbols have a dimension of energy. They act upon us, change our personalities, and, to a degree, change the world as well.

The concept of the commandments as messages written in symbolic language greatly influenced the Jewish psychologist Erich Fromm. All we have learned from modern psychology augmented the importance of the symbol. Man knows much more than he thinks he does. This paradox can be explained only in the wake of the modern discovery of the subconscious layers within man. Man thinks he doesn't understand, yet something within him responds. This modern concept is not at all new to classical Jewish thought. The Talmud speaks of an inner layer in man, which knows and sees things that the conscious self does not recognize. This is called his *mazal* (used here in the Talmudic, not the astrological sense). This hidden knowledge makes its appearance not in man's philosophy, but in the stories he tells on those occasions when he is completely at ease.

We are familiar with many forms of such subconscious activity. The best example is advertising and propaganda. We are accustomed to thinking about messages that are directed towards our intellect, our thought and perception. In contrast, symbols influence deeper layers of consciousness, which are no less important. The language of symbols is a language our intellect does not understand. Yet, something within us does understand it. In his book, *The Forgotten Language*, Fromm illustrates the phenomenon with various examples from both the Talmud and modern psychology. The Talmud in tractate *Berakhot*, for example, informs us that dreams are nonsense, except in three cases. One of these cases is when a person dreams the interpretation of a dream. This teaches us that a conscious person does not understand his dream, but when he is in an unconscious state he understands the dream so well that he can interpret it. This means that there is something deep inside man that speaks a different language.

This idea can be understood from another angle as well. We must distinguish between allegory and symbol. Although both stand in place of something else and describe it, there is a fundamental difference between them. Allegory describes things that could be formulated in a different language, one understood by a person's intellectual side. For example, if I relate the tale of the fox and the wolf, it is clear to me that it is an allegory, because I can interpret it and explain it as the conflict between say, cunning (the fox) and strength (the wolf). In contrast, symbols point to and hint at things that I cannot formulate in my own language. Symbols help me to understand and perceive these things. In order to communicate an emotion, I must use a symbol. I have no other choice.

Music offers a very familiar example of a creation that is written in a language we do not understand but that affects us intensely nonetheless. In this regard music may be compared to the commandments. It may be interpreted as a symbol that describes a different reality. It is written in a special language that has the power to express things that have no other outlet, such as the condition of the human soul. Music becomes a mode of communication. R. Kook suggests that music is not made up of symbols but of very special facts which we do not understand. In any case, a melody can affect us because it speaks to us. The Hasidim claimed that the source of all melody is in the supernal, spiritual sanctuaries that are above the sanctuary of words.

The rationalists erred in thinking it possible to change the nature of man with the help of abstract concepts. They did not sense the fundamental fact that a certain layer of the personality simply does not understand this conceptual language. This is comparable to an excellent lecturer who is speaking to an audience incapable of understanding him. He can speak about philosophy, mathematics, or a complex theory replete with difficult concepts. He may use the technical terminology of differential equations. The lecture may be true and may even have practical application. But the audience does not understand its terminology. Similarly, within man himself there are two audiences. The inner rational audience hears the conceptual philosophical discourse, the ethical arguments. But the inner non-rational audience, which exists along with the rational audience, may not comprehend what it is presented with and is certainly unmoved by it. How does one address this non-rational audience, an audience that has tremendous influence?

But then the situation changes. A new lecturer takes the podium and speaks of soccer, basketball, or other matters not understood by the intellectual elite but understood perfectly by the other audience. The more sophisticated audience does not understand what the simple man understands. Man's inner world is composed of two such audiences, one with rational, sophisticated tendencies and the other with non-rational tendencies. We must reach and influence that inner world, but not through conceptual language. The deep layer of man's personality understands a different language, the language of symbols. Symbolic actions that seem incomprehensible speak to the deep level of the personality, guide it and influence it. Through this medium we speak with our soul in order to alter ourselves.

If the commandments were symbols for rational things, the criticism leveled against them could be justified. But perhaps the commandments are not symbols for rational things. They address a different audience. It doesn't matter if the mind understands or not, because the commandments are not addressed to that audience. There are two levels of irrationalism. One level is beneath the rational, and the other is beyond it.

The Conscious and the Subconscious

It is clear to every one of us that unconscious forces are active within people. Ask a person which finger he uses to type the letter *s* on a keyboard. He will not be able to respond immediately, but he will carry out a simple exercise: He will imagine that he is writing a word containing the letter s, move his fingers as he would to type the word, and then see which finger he used. His conscious mind doesn't know which finger he is writing with, and yet he can type! Man has many internal mechanisms that function automatically, without our conscious awareness. These include not only physical mechanisms but also mechanisms of the soul. If I wish truly to change a person, both internally and externally, I must address him in a different language. Enter the language of the commandments. This idea was expanded on by the various branches of the Musar movement.

We are accustomed to looking up at the sky and seeing infinity spread out before us. But we forget that infinity spreads out endlessly within us as well. We reach into ourselves, as though into a deep sack, and take out all kinds of things, but we must remember that we can only reach as far as our hand extends. But the "sack" is actually much deeper than our hand can extend. The hand is our consciousness, which does not comprehend the ultimate limit of our inner world.

Two important Jewish movements uncovered the subconscious layers of man. One was the Musar movement, headed by R. Israel Salanter. He attempted to solve the riddle of man through the assumption that "dark," subconscious forces are at work within him. Another is Hasidism, and preceding it, the Kabbalah.

R. Aaron Marcus, the Jewish sage who tried to present the philosophy of Hasidism in the language of modern thought, calls our attention to a cryptic passage, a kind of riddle, found in R. Hayyim ben Attar's commentary, *Or Ha-Hayyim* (on Lev. 17). I present it here so the reader can also attempt to interpret it. (Unfortunately, there are various versions of the text, and part of the task of decoding its meaning lies in choosing the correct version. I have including variant readings in brackets, and words missing in some versions are followed by a question mark.)

> And it will be known to the investigator of the inner essence of the understanding of knowledge, that the perception of knowledge will enlighten the intelligence and in his knowledge he will know that the knower of knowledge [?] is bereft of knowledge. And

when he shall succeed in enlightening [explaining] himself to himself, he will know that the knower is informed by a knowledge that not informed by the intelligence.

I will not attempt to interpret the riddle, but the text clearly refers to "knowledge bereft of knowledge." This seems to hint at something similar to the existence of unconscious knowledge in man. This means that he knows things that he doesn't know he knows. As an analogy, consider a man who thinks he has overdrawn his bank account when in fact he actually has more money than he thought he had, and this money earns him interest of which he is unaware.

We need not rely only on this particular text, however wonderful it is. In Hasidic thought we find the concept, *kadmut ha-sekhel*, "pre-intellect." Thus, the *Maggid* of Mezhritch tells us that thought "is comprehended by the person himself, and is not comprehended by others. But the *kadmut ha-sekhel* is not comprehended even by the person himself." The idea was developed further in Habad Hasidism

R. Aaron Marcus was a German Jew who moved to Eastern Europe, and there became a Hasid. He was a student of the *tzaddik* R. Shelomo of Radomsk, and was also connected with Chertekov Hasidism. R. Marcus publicized Hasidism in the West, and wrote a book about it that was translated into Hebrew as *Sefer Ha-Hasidut*. We know that his efforts to identify the authors of various anonymous Kabbalistic works were often incorrect. Still, his book remains important, thought hard to read.

R. Marcus is also an important figure due to his attempt to bridge the gap between Zionism and the ultra-orthodox world. He wrote a letter to Herzl and told him that it was very likely that Hasidism would join forces with the Zionist movement. Unfortunately, history did not work out that way.

R. Marcus was also interested in the meaning of the new archeological discoveries in the Near East. He viewed them as a slap in the face of the wide-ranging speculations of biblical criticism. He also devoted much time and effort to the development of the theory of root words in the Hebrew language. He can be regarded as one of Halevi's modern successors, trying to formulate a middle road to connect Halevi's central ideas to the latest discoveries of historical and archeological research.

To return to our topic, an earlier source for the idea of the subconscious is in the Talmud, in the concept of the *mazal* that we mentioned earlier. The Talmudic *mazal* refers to a basic element of man, which sees, remembers and knows things subconsciously, things that affect him despite the fact that he does not know of their existence.

R. Israel Salanter spoke of the subconscious to teach us an important lesson in his Musar thought. He taught us to look at one of the most difficult problems of our lives: why does man recognize good yet continues to do evil? To take a trivial example, why can't a person stick to a diet that he knows will save him from illness? Why can't a person stop smoking, or why did he even begin this dangerous practice in the first place? This is a philosophical question that has remained with us since the days of Plato and Aristotle.

Plato naively thought that whoever recognizes the good cannot help but do it. In other words, every sinner is misguided. As our sages say, "a person does not sin unless a spirit of foolishness enters him." Though interesting, this viewpoint is sometimes not realistic. It fails to recognize that though we know the truth, there is still a struggle within us. So the question remains: why does man fail to behave morally, even though he knows he should? We could blame our will power. Aristotle indeed spoke of the weak-willed, the weak personalities who cannot resist temptation. He thought we have a way to measure the strength of someone's personality, and that people were born with different amounts of will power. Those whose will power is impaired cannot resist temptation.

Maimonides teaches us that despite the difficulties, which differ from person to person, everyone is capable of overcoming his personality and changing it. This is precisely the point of moral education. R. Israel Salanter added another idea. The reason for the moral failure, in his view, is in the fact that we are not familiar with the field of battle and the fighting forces. This is similar to a strategic analyst who is asked about a particular war when he doesn't know the battlefield or the weaponry to be deployed in the battle. The classic sage giving moral advice does not understand that other forces are at work in man. The mistake occurs when we think that if we understand the rational aspects, we will understand man.

Moral education and self education must touch our subconscious as well as our conscious selves. We often do not understand that we educate through the use of all kinds of conscious and unconscious symbols. We know today, for example, that we indirectly educate people through television, or other means such as advertisements, without the people knowing what is happening. This can leave people open and vulnerable to these subconscious influences. The most extreme form of this type of influence is brainwashing. Then man is not being educated, for even his freedom is taken from him. Judaism believes in maintaining the institution of freedom.

Tzitzit: Symbolic Language

The commandment to wear *tzitzit* (fringes) provides a good example of the use of symbolic language in the commandments. Our sources are full of stories of individuals who were miraculously saved from sexual temptation by their own *tzitzit* which struck them right before their imminent downfall. It seems to me that these stories illustrate the relationship between *tzitzit* and the avoidance of sexual sin. This relationship also helps clarify some of the details of the laws of *tzitzit*. The *tallit* (prayer shawl) and *tzitzit* are symbols for our religious sexual restrictions, a symbol of male sexual purity.

The fringes and knots of the *tzitzit* express this idea through symbols, which we do not consciously understand. The concept is not spelled out in conceptual language. Our Sages did not explain the symbolic meaning of *tzitzit* in philosophical or psychological discourse. Rather, they demonstrated through the stories and legends that they told the effect of *tzitzit* upon the deeper layers of the human soul.

Halevi interprets the meaning of the commandment of *tzitzit* in a similar fashion. "Thus he wears *tzitzit* so that his senses will not trouble him with the interests of the base world, as it is written, 'Do not stray after your hearts and after your eyes' [Num. 15:39]" (III:11).

The commandments are symbols, but they are symbols that have their own powers, symbols which act upon our subconscious, without touching our intellect and consciousness. Accordingly, the commandments touch every area of life. Every area of life has its own Jewish message, which is expressed through the accompanying commandment. Holiness is added to every area of our life, and our inner self incorporates holy values in dress, food, sex and all other aspects of life.

According to this theory of symbols, the commandments and their details do, in fact, alter reality. But the reality that is altered exists first and foremost in man's inner world. The outer world will change afterward. This is the underlying concept of Rabbi Hirsch's symbolic interpretation of the commandments. The Kabbalah teaches that the commandments and the attention to detail, in the laws of Shabbat for example, cause cosmic change. Rabbi Hirsch teaches us that the commandments affect our souls, our consciousness. His successors demonstrated something of even greater significance: the commandments affect what is beneath our consciousness, the deeper levels of our personality that man cannot reach. Logic speaks to the human mind, and indeed, rational claims can impress us very deeply. But, as we learn from the proponents of Musar as well as modern psychology, they do not touch the deepest layers of the personality. The commandments are written in a different language, which penetrates deeply and alters the individual. This power is generated both by the general concepts and the accompanying details of the commandments.

Halevi's Position

This psychological approach to understanding the reasons for the commandments is, of course, a new, reworked version of Halevi's ideas and those of the Kabbalists, and it differs significantly from Halevi's own position. According to the simple interpretation of Halevi's approach, there are several layers of reality. Scientific methods are appropriate for the natural realm. In dealing with that level of reality, the only legitimate tools are those of logic and normative scientific research. But, Halevi claims, beyond normal causality, and beyond the normal rules that govern the natural world, there is another, mysterious system of rules. The commandments are the ways in which we function within the framework of this distinct system, and there are, accordingly, two sorts of causation.

But Halevi's approach lends itself to another understanding as well, one best understood through an illustration. When we implant clouds with silver iodide in order to make it rain, we function within the framework of science and technology. But this is not the entire picture. Rain is not the only substance known to fall from the sky. So does fire. When Elijah the prophet brought fire down from the heavens, it was a miracle. Or, perhaps, one could say that a completely different set of rules was functioning at that point, a system from a different plane. This system is beyond rationality, or perhaps it has its own rationality. Here too, as elsewhere, we must understand that Halevi is trying to build a model using what is familiar to his audience in order to explain something beyond its understanding and perception. One might be a "Halevi-ist" without conceding the existence of two sorts of causation. Some of Halevi's modern successors—most notably, Rav Kook—took that path. Rav Kook's basic assumption on this issue is that the world changes as a result of changes in man. Man serves as a bridge through which the commandments affect the world.

If we return to the previous example, we see three personalities: the technician who implants clouds with silver iodide, the magician who dances his rain dance, and the man who prays for rain. Prayer and commandments fall under a rubric that differs from both the natural domain of artificial rainmaking and the occult occupations of the magician. The difference between prayer and the natural category is obvious. Man, with his rational theories about the efficacy of means and causes, will not assume that mere speech could change the structure of the clouds and transform them into rain clouds. The Torah emphasizes the shift into an area beyond the rational, to something in a different area, but it wants us to understand very clearly that there is a fundamental difference between the wizard and one who prays. The Torah is not magic. Here we must repeat that faith and heresy spring from the same source. Zealots of rational thought view whatever lies beyond it as one homogenous group. We must understand that beyond the boundaries of logic the road forks. One path leads to faith; the other, to heresy.

What is the boundary between Torah and sorcery? It is impossible to distinguish between them simply by observing the actions people do in their name. An external observer of the three rainmakers will be unable to distinguish among them with confidence. This is similar to the weather forecast, which is sometimes entirely inaccurate. Although we instinctively feel that we ought to differentiate between climatological forecasting and astrological forecasting, it is very difficult to formulate this difference in a satisfactory manner. One possibility is to look to science. What the academic establishment decides upon is scientific, although we are not informed why. Halevi offers a similar formal criterion: when one follows the path of the Torah, by definition he is not involved in magic.

This formal criterion is true, yet it does not seem satisfactory. We would like to define the difference between Torah and magic more precisely, for we know that sorcery is both a rebellion against logic and a form of religious heresy. The difference between faith on the one hand and magic or superstition in the other is a significant one, and religious philosophies in each generation should work to discover it. This need has become particularly evident in recent generations. Rationalism has proved itself to be helpless regarding many essential problems, and this lack of success finds expression in the return of the masses to some or another form of magic, idolatry, devil worship, etc. We believe that only faith can stem the tide of this renewed idolatry. We who are the allies of logic, perhaps its only allies, have the power to halt the surge of superstitious beliefs and anti-logical movements.

If we combine these ideas with what we have already seen in our discussion of rational approaches to creation and nature, we will realize once again that Halevi calls the basic concepts into question. We question claims that do not fit in with our basic assumptions. Yet, these basic assumptions, which seem to us to be axiomatic and have no need of proof, are very often merely the result of a social and cultural framework or of a philosophical fashion, which, like all other fashions, has changed in the past and will change in the future. The conclusion that Halevi teaches us is that we must learn to recognize our reality. We are expected to see reality as it is despite rationalist dogmatism, and we must continue beyond it, just as sometimes a taxi or a bus can take us to a certain point, but beyond that point we must continue on foot. Rationalism travels on certain pre-determined "bus lines." There is taxi rationality, which is more flexible, and bus rationality, which is more rigid. But beyond both of these, the individual must continue on foot. Here lies the seed of religious existentialism. Science cannot solve our personal problems, and man must move on.

There is another response, to which Halevi does not subscribe: a response of blind faith that completely disregards the possibility of judging the facts and understanding reality. To explain this, let me refer to a book we will return to later: the book of Job.

God tests Job. Rational philosophy, represented by his three friends, cannot answer his questions logically. The answer lies in faith, in the very encounter with God, in a revelation that goes beyond both scientific and everyday thought. But the book of Job does not end with the description of this meta-logical encounter. It adds a last chapter, which informs us that God restores Job's past. This chapter plants the seed of Halevi's philosophy, intimating that the true answer, the real test of truth, lies in history: history not only of the past, but also as a description of the future. The real proof lies in redemption, in the alteration of the social and natural reality. The real test of truth is an empirical one.

According to Halevi, Judaism proves itself not only through its pure faith, but in its belief in God's kingship which will one day change the world. Faith, despite the suffering and the doubts, was the great Jewish response to the Job-test that has been the challenge of our national history. This was a faith beyond despair, a faith in which the Jewish people had to side against the friends of Job, against those other religions that have tried to prove their own legitimacy through the suffering of the Jews. Their military, political and economic successes seemed to them to be ample proof of the truth of their religions. But the Jewish faith refused to see religious proof in the power of the sword and temporal success. It was sure that history would change, and that the resurgence of the Jews, parallel to the resurgence of Job, heralds the redemption of the entire human race. Thus, the promises of our prophets will be fulfilled. Redemption is the real miracle that holds the key of truth. It is the final outcome of the system of the commandments.

CHAPTER 30:
THE REASONS THAT LIE BEYOND
THE COMMANDMENTS

The Development of Man

We have been considering the reasons for the commandments, but we must now redefine our topic. As important as it is to explain why each commandment was given, the answer must be reached primarily on a different plane. We should not deal merely with why the commandment was given, but with its effect on the human personality. The first approach asks what impelled the commandments. The second tries to ascertain their purpose: what kind of person do the commandments create? How does each commandment alter the individual? The question "Why is this commanded?" can be answered on the assumption that it is a divine decree. But this still leaves room to interpret the results of the commandment.

The effects of the commandments become apparent by examining Jewish history. Our history demonstrates that the commandments have tangible, far-reaching psychological and sociological results. They affect the individual and society. Among their many effects, I will discuss three historical accomplishments of Judaism that are closely tied to three central commandments. Although there have been exceptions to the rule during the course of history, and in certain periods particular commandments took on different casts, it seems to me that they present an accurate picture of historical Judaism.

The most important sociological achievement of historical Judaism was the tradition of peace and nonviolence. Historically, the Jewish people disapproved of and even detested violence, even in those cases when they were compelled to use it. Thus, the king of Aram called the Jewish kings "kings of mercy." The second accomplishment was preserving the value of the family. The third achievement was the avoidance of drunkenness in all its types and forms. In my opinion these achievements

are connected with the laws of Shabbat, *kashrut* (the Jewish dietary laws
—particularly the prohibition of consuming blood) and the laws of
family purity.

In order to understand the meaning of these accomplishments, we
must compare "ghettos." Today there are poor neighborhoods. The common denominator among all the ghettos is the poverty, congestion and tension—and, in some cases, a kind of "apartheid," a separation from the
outside world. But despite the outward similarities, modern ghettos are
very different from the ghettos that our ancestors constructed. Despite the
destructive forces endured by Jews throughout the pre-modern generations, the life of our people was characterized by the sociological values
just noted. This stands in complete contrast to the modern ghetto, in which
internal and external violence, promiscuity, the disintegration of the family, drunkenness and drugs rule with a high hand.

Jewish family values are built upon the laws of family purity. The
tzitzit "tie" the man, so to speak. Our sages teach us that the *tallit* represents Jewish family values. In addition, the laws of family purity create a
holy, constant and continually renewed relationship between husband and
wife. This relationship constitutes the basic building-block of the family,
and consequently has a tremendous impact on the children. In order to
achieve these values, man pays a price, the price of self-diminution. He
imposes the law upon himself. But the benefits to him and his family and
to society in general far outweigh the sacrifice. The existence of the family cannot be ensured by catch phrases and slogans. The family can exist
only through man's self-restraint and development, which are accom-
plished through the framework of Jewish law. Society can thrive only
when its values speak to the depth of man's soul, giving society the power
of influence over its members.

Kashrut: The Jewish Dietary Laws

In his essay, "*Talelei Orot*," Rav Kook explains that the laws of *kashrut*
express the Jews' relationship to taking a life, to the fact that man is nourished by killing animals. Although these are animals and not people, we
must feel some pangs of conscience for causing their death.

Kashrut is, in essence, a war against violence. Judaism has educated
us to a certain attitude towards blood. Blood symbolizes the soul, even
with regard to animals, and therefore we are forbidden to drink it. It

belongs to God. Under certain circumstances we are even obligated to cover up the blood, as a burial of sorts, or to symbolically beg forgiveness for the vestige of sin involved in the taking of an animal life. The best example of the way that the commandments educate is the *shohet* (ritual slaughterer). The character of the Jewish *shohet* is completely different from the character of the animal slaughterer in the general world.

I have no wish to idealize Jewish life in the Diaspora. Life in the Diaspora and in the ghetto had many negative effects upon us. But we must realize that historical Judaism created a tremendous phenomenon, and transformed life in the mire and poverty of the ghetto into a life of benevolence. This is the ultimate expression of the essence of the commandments. This idea is beautifully described in Hayyim Hazaz's story, *Shlulit Genuzah*.

Hazaz tells us a wonderful story about a Jew who loaned money to his friend. While walking in the street, he sees the person to whom he loaned the money coming toward him. He turns into a side street so as not to embarrass his friend and finds himself in an alley full of mud. Just then the town priest drives by in his carriage and offers to give him a lift. The Jew knows that the carriage will drive in the direction of the person who borrowed the money, and he refuses to get in. The priest reacts jeeringly, "The Jews are so primitive, I try to lift them out of the mud, but they refuse to get into my carriage!"

This is the magnificence of historical Judaism. The person looking from the carriage cannot see the great event taking place here—a Jew is choosing to walk in the mud rather than embarrass another person and is refusing to respond to the great modern temptation. The town was muddy, but these were its Jewish inhabitants.

In the modern world, emancipation and Zionism meant escaping from the mud. These processes, however, were accompanied by mass abandonment of the commandments, which in turn led to the destruction of the values that they upheld. With all the achievements of normalization, of getting out of the mud, decadence has invaded modern Judaism. Thus, we see three great catastrophes unfolding before our very eyes: violence, promiscuity and drunkenness are deeply penetrating our society.

The laws of *kashrut* contain a number of intertwined principles. The Torah explicitly informs us of the reason for the prohibition of ingesting blood. Blood represents the soul. In other words, this prohibition applies even to animals. This principle expresses the respect we feel towards animals. Our refusal to consume blood contains a very significant educational message: we are educated to be repelled by blood. The education towards respect for blood, even that of an animal, encourages a non-violent society. Our refusal does not stem from a belief that blood has harmful qualities. The Torah tells us that *helev* [forbidden fat] and blood do not belong to man, but to God. Indeed, when we cover up the blood as required under certain circumstances, we are actually performing a symbolic burial ceremony. We are burying what symbolizes the life of the animal.

The Torah teaches us that Adam was a vegetarian in the Garden of Eden. Rav Kook maintains that in the end of days we will return to vegetarianism. With some exceptions, man is not yet ready for this today. We have a problem, for man is nourished by killing animals, and people who become experts at killing are very likely to develop an insensitivity to life itself. That why the Torah attempts to make the slaughterer into a unique personality. It defines him as a type of technician, a kind of doctor, a spiritual personality. At present, we are in the middle of the road between the unattainable ideal and the cruel reality. The reality is that people eat meat. It is even possible that during certain periods of history, when the secrets of correct nutrition were not yet known, it would have been forbidden to refrain from eating meat. Even today, it is difficult to create appropriate vegetarian nutrition. *Kashrut* is the middle of the road between the ideal and the reality. This experience teaches man, despite everything, not to become a beast of prey.

Violence finds expression even in the act of eating meat. *Kashrut* is a system based on the obligation to respect life. This is also connected to the prohibition of eating meat and milk together. The combination of the two is an expression of sadism. Milk represents motherhood. Through it the mother gives life to her child. The Torah gave us a significant example: "Do not cook a kid in its mother's milk." Through this it expressed the inner meaning of our attitude to the world. Whenever we are faced with a situation of meat and milk, we must imagine that the meat is a kid and the milk is its mother's milk. In mixing the two, man not only steals the kid from its mother and kills it, he also forces the mother to kill her own child. This law is a protest against sadism. There must be a limit to cruelty, even if there is violence that we cannot prevent. The mixing of meat and milk symbolizes cruelty, as though we were forcing someone to kill her child herself. In a certain sense, every time that we separate milk and meat we are protesting against cruelty and trying to limit it. This law teaches us the responsibility to develop the same moral sensitivity which forbids us to slaughter an animal and its child on the same day, or to take away a newborn from its mother before seven days have elapsed. We are taught to respect the mothers of the animal world.

The prohibition against eating certain species is also undoubtedly connected with the question of violence. A beautiful story, which appears in the book *Shevet Yehudah*, describes arguments between the kings of the world and the sages of Israel regarding various details in Jewish law. If we rework this story to apply to our topic, we will be able to understand why certain birds, such as the turtledove and the pigeon, are permitted for human consumption. These are not birds of prey. This is a symbolic expression of our abhorrence for predatory behavior. We do not wish to transfer the characteristics of the birds of prey to ourselves.

All these laws have taught us a central Jewish principle, which differentiates Judaism from Christianity. In a clear attack upon the laws of *kashrut*, the New Testament states that what is important is not what goes into the mouth but what comes out of it. That is, of course, only half the truth. Interestingly, Maimonides, in a similar context explains the verse "He who is careful of his mouth and tongue protects his soul from harm" as hinting at two matters: "mouth" refers to what goes into his mouth, and "tongue" refers to sins of speech, to what goes forth from the mouth. Observing *kashrut* and avoiding slander are both essential! That is the integral approach of Jewish law.

Clearly, food has a powerful effect on man. Harnessing this effect demands refinement in eating—not refinement regarding the taste of the food, but of our own sensitivity. The sensitivity to what one eats is a moral trait of the highest degree. Rabbi Nahman of Braslav teaches that man is beset by the two strongest desires: the desire to live, which is expressed in food, and the desire of our species to exist, which is expressed in sexuality. Rabbi Nahman teaches us that it is not so easy to refine sexual desire, nor is it simple to refine our desire for food, which accompanies us from the moment of birth until the day of death. This is an area of tremendous importance in human behavior, and it cannot be dismissed. In these areas, a theoretical morality can never replace the morality that is put into practice.

CHAPTER 31:
THE HUMAN IDEAL

Captain of the Car

Now that we have covered some of the principles central to an understanding of the commandments, we may step back and survey what may be termed the human ideal. To illustrate, let me again refer to the example of the automobile, a model that seems important both as allegory and as a reality. Philosophers and moralists in generations past often compared man to the captain of a ship, an image we can update by citing the car. The tragic daily reality of accidents brings the dangers of the roads close to home and shows us the need to understand our weaknesses and potential failures. In principle, however, the problems and dilemmas of driving can serve as a model for the problems and dilemmas of life in general. They have much in common. Yet, there is also a fundamental difference between them. The difference between the allegory and its meaning lies in the fact that, to a certain extent, we are actually both the car and the driver.

The first requirement that we must fulfill in order to be able to travel in a car is, of course, that the vehicle be in good working condition, able to move. How may we define this condition? One possible definition—and there are many—is, in essence, a summary of R. Sa'adiah Ga'on's approach as expressed in the last section of his book, *Emunot Ve-De'ot*. Good working condition means that each part of the car is capable of carrying out its particular function in full, and also will limit itself to that function, so that the various parts will function together in harmony. Some of us are all too familiar with a car that spends most of its time being repaired. This is comparable to the state of a person who has not achieved physical or intellectual harmony, or of a person who experiences psychological problems.

Let us assume, then, that a man has reached a minimal state of harmony. Inside the car sits the driver, who provides the right quantities of gas, oil, water, etc. That is the driver's technical responsibility. In the parable, these technical requirements represent the responsibilities of science and technology, which are important but limited in their scope. Thus, the various branches of medicine and psychology can minister to the health of the body and the mind, but beyond these goals lie other questions that they cannot answer. To revert to the parable, the mechanic can give the driver a car in good working condition, but he cannot make the driver adhere to traffic laws. No sane person will ask his mechanic, "where shall I go?" unless he needs the address of a garage. These are questions involving signs and goals, commandments, values and meaning, which are within the authority neither of the mechanic nor of the doctors and psychologists. They are our religious and ethical dilemmas.

These are Halevi's key ideas, as we see in his description, at the beginning of Part III, of the devout Jew. After a man has given each component of his car what it needs, he must define the purpose of the journey: "to adhere to . . . the divine element, which stands above the intellectual degree." This, then, is the divine element. The natural and intellectual elements deals with taking care of the car. The journey's ultimate goal is decided within the sphere of religious faith.

The Mount Sinai Experience

Man's relationship to the purposes of life finds expression, in Halevi's view, in the historical encampment around Mt. Sinai. Mt. Sinai symbolizes the goal. Mt. Sinai symbolizes man's ascent, which takes place when one moves beyond the fulfillment of mere physical needs. To return to the parable of the car, if we recall that the car is actually the individual himself, we can imagine the person who finally acquires a car of his own. He takes care of it, polishes it, washes it. His goal is not to drive the car, but to have a relationship with the car. The absurdity of his behavior is obvious. There must be something else beyond simple maintenance. Knowing where to drive the car represents, in the parable, knowing the goal and aim of our lives. This is the meaning of the Sinai encampment.

Although this parable originated with Halevi, it continued to develop after his time. Maimonides wrote that the ascent to Mount Sinai represents human development. At Sinai, the masses were assigned one location. A higher place was allocated to the priests, a still higher one to Joshua, and the highest location to Moses. Similarly, each individual achieves a different level of development. The parable was further developed by

R. Isaac Aramah in his philosophical commentary on the Torah, *Akeidat Yitzhak*. Aramah teaches that the concept of the center of life and its ultimate goal is symbolized by Mount Sinai and, later, by a new symbol, that of the Tabernacle. The Tabernacle becomes a sort of traveling Mount Sinai that remains with us always.

But the commandment to ascend the mountain is also accompanied by a warning. No one may ascend the mountain of divine inquiry unprepared. This is a common mistake, and it holds within it the seed of ruin. *Harisah*, the Hebrew word here rendered as ruin, in fact has a dual meaning: in biblical Hebrew it refers to the ascent of one who is unprepared. In later Hebrew, it comes to mean the ruin caused by one who does so.

This ruin constitutes the polar opposite of the idea of the burning bush. Maimonides offers a wonderful interpretation of the burning bush, Moses' first vision. But as we shall see when we discuss the issue of prophecy, every prophetic vision contains elements that originate in the imaginative faculty, or in what one might call the subjectivity of the perceiver. Moses experiences no other visions of this sort other than his vision of the crevice in the mountain—which is actually the opposite of a vision. Moses hides his face, refusing to look at the burning bush, because he knows that the vision is tainted by his own imaginative faculty. Accordingly, he merits that his prophetic experience be unique. Maimonides maintains that the prophetic experience descends upon man, but that man apprehends this experience through his own subjective perception, using, among other things, his imagination. His imaginative faculty allows him to receive the prophetic message, but it also distorts the message somewhat. Moses refuses to gaze on the burning bush not because of its holiness or because God was hidden within it, as it were. Rather, he refuses to accept the distortion caused by the imagination. Because he covered his eyes then, our Sages teach us that he merited direct perception of God.

Maimonides gives us a new perspective on opening our eyes, from which we learn an important lesson regarding all the professedly prophetic phenomena about which we often hear. From time to time we hear of a prophet of sorts, who has created a new religion based on a personal revelation. Certainly, supernatural phenomena exist. A heavenly voice speaks out daily and makes announcements, sending telegrams. But people read these telegrams through the distorting spectacles of their imagination. The message they perceive is not at all identical to the message that was sent from on high. The Torah could only be given after the subjective distortions had been overcome.

Given that, we must, alas, deal with truth as we relate to other commodities that are up for sale. We must wave a large banner warning everyone to beware of imitations. But other dangers beset us as well, and Halevi warns us to be constantly on guard against the imaginary realities that surround us. Just as man is sometimes given to hallucinations, so life presents imaginary ideals.

The Human Ideal: The Saintly Person (*Hasid*)

Halevi maintains that the ultimate human ideal is embodied in the saintly person. The model he uses to describe such a person is the model of leadership. The saintly person is the successful leader.

The parable, which has both biblical and philosophical origins, is based on the comparison between man's relationship to himself and the relationship of the leader to the country or the society. Both the Scriptures and the writings of the Sages abound with comparisons between the ruler of a city and the ruler of one's passions. Similarly, the parable of the foolish king and the wise king serves as a common allegory for man's treatment of himself. The classical philosophical source for this idea is Plato's *Republic*.

Plato wished to define the essence of morality. To do so, he moved from the individual to the collective, from man to the republic. His method can be compared to a person who unsuccessfully attempts to read tiny letters. Since he cannot read the writing, he moves on to a different copy, in which the same text is written in large type. The transition from the individual to the group constitutes a kind of magnifying glass. Man's ideal approach to himself will be made clearer if the question is investigated not on the plane of the individual but on the plane of the republic. Justice in the state is parallel to justice in man's treatment of himself. The solution in both cases must be a search for harmony. Man must develop all of his faculties, and not stunt any of them.

The just ruler follows the great principle of justice: "to each what is fit for him." If we transfer the object of the parable from the leader of a country to the individual guiding himself, we find an interesting parallel. According to Judaism, man must give each of his personal faculties its due, and not destroy or blight certain powers in order to develop others, even if the preferred powers are lower and they are developed at the expense of higher powers. The classical tradition encompasses various theories regarding the makeup of the soul. Their common denominator is that the soul is composed of many powers. Some approaches even speak of different souls that coexist in man. As we know, Maimonides came out against this idea in the first chapter of his *Shemonah Perakim*. He concedes, however, that the one soul has many attributes. In every situation, our role remains the same: we must establish a harmonious relationship among these powers.

Halevi maintains that man has various powers. One, shared by man and the animal world, is desire, the demand to satisfy one's basic needs. The second power is anger. The third is intelligence. Halevi claims that higher characteristics exist in man as well, and that one of these is the divine element.

Optimum and Maximum

In his third essay, Halevi begins his exposition of the ideal worshipper of God. Maimonides developed these concepts in his *Shemonah Perakim* and in his *Guide of the Perplexed*. In Part II of the *Guide* (2:39), Maimonides speaks of the Jewish human ideal against the backdrop of the ideals extolled by other religions.

In describing Moses' prophecy and mission, Maimonides writes about the clash between Moses' mission and that of those who presume to be the heralds of a new law or the pinnacle of prophecy. The inner meaning of Moses' mission lay in the fact that his message was God's perfect message. "God's Torah is perfect [*temimah*]." "Perfect" in this context means "optimal"—a concept different from "maximal." The Torah's commandments exist in a state of perfect equilibrium, and any attempt to base a new system on the original represents a deviation that disturbs that equilibrium, either adding to it or subtracting from it. That is how Maimonides interprets the phrase "righteous laws and statutes": they strike the proper balance between opposing forces. The Torah has always stood between two erroneous alternatives. One group errs on the side of excessive obligations, as in the practice of "one who secludes himself in the mountains and abstains from meat and wine and many of the body's needs." The other errs by renouncing obligations, practicing "gluttony and dissipation, to the point that the individual deteriorates in his character and his intellect."

Maimonides here refers to two positions, to two groups. On the surface, he is speaking of the ancient nation of Edom, and of the idolatrous nations that preceded the rise of Islam. But a comparison of this passage to others in the *Guide* suggests he is speaking of Islam itself, in effect characterizing the pre-Islamic idolatrous nations as suffering from the deficiencies he saw among the Muslims of his own time. He used that code for political reasons, since he could not safely disparage Islam directly, but the implication was clear to anyone who had read the *Guide* and Maimonides' other works. This is clearly a part of Maimonides' ongoing dispute with Islam. Although Islam incorporated many of the principles of Jewish lore and law, it worked dramatic changes in those principles, and they underwent dramatic changes in the hand's of Islam's prophet and his successors. The Jewish motifs sometimes remain clearly apparent in Islam but sometimes they are changed so radically as to become unrecognizable.

In light of these realities we can understand the meaning of the statement "God's Torah is perfect." It is very hard to achieve the optimum, and the possibilities for deviation are numerous. Judaism lives between the two extremes and tries to preserve the golden mean.

The Pious Person and the *Nazir*

At the beginning of Part III, Halevi presents us with a conflict of ideals, and he denounces the approach that sought to imitate and "improve" the Jewish halakhic ideal. Conflicts between ideals, Halevi believed, can be explored by focusing on particular points. In the next section, we consider the focal point of love and sexuality. Here, the focal point is that of isolation.

Christianity and Islam both extol the ideal of the person who abandons his society and secludes himself in the wilderness. This practice is particularly common in Christian sects in the East. In the West we find monasteries, but ones that possess their own communal lives as well. In the East, in contrast, we find many more examples of monks who live as hermits, in absolute solitude, and see this as an ideal of devotion to God.

This reality compels us to distinguish between authentic and pathological religious phenomena, between *hitboddedut* (seclusion) and *bedidut* (isolation). The difference between these two phenomena lies in a concept that Halevi saw as central to understanding man and his role in this world. Judaism does not sense any contradiction between this world and the next. On its surface, the Jewish principle that this world is but a corridor to the palace of the World to Come seems to afford this world a secondary status. But if passage through the corridor is prerequisite to entering the palace, the corridor becomes more important. In our case, life within society and community is something man must cultivate to reach his ultimate destiny.

Halevi offers three examples of seclusion, two positive and one negative. Philosophy and prophecy both praise seclusion, but it is a different form of seclusion—not isolation. Halevi sees the ideal example of seclusion in the cases of Enoch and Elijah. They lived and functioned as normal people, reached the highest possible human level, and used their position for the common good. Having completed their walks through the corridor, they had no more need for this world on their spiritual path, and death came to them as a natural continuation of life. Both are portrayed in the Bible as having been taken up by God, meaning they continued to live after death. We see here the biblical meaning of the World to Come.

The second type of seclusion is that chosen by the philosopher, a person who desires to delve into the world of intellectual wisdom, and wishes to remain undisturbed by society. He remains within the community and does not negate society altogether, though he chooses a select community, the society of scholars. Our Sages clearly felt the need to find the synthesis between seclusion and communal life. They expressed it beautifully in the statement, "I have learned from all of my teachers, and from my students most of all." This is precisely the idea of the yeshiva, which, according to Jewish lore, continues to exist in the World to Come.

Halevi next considers, and harshly criticizes, the monk. Halevi maintains that absolute religious isolation reflects arrogance and self-deception. It is the hallmark of the individual who has an inflated view of his own spiritual attainments. Such people strive, in a futile and pitiful manner, to replicate the prophetic phenomenon or re-experience the encounter at Sinai. Still, Halevi's analysis suggests caution in passing judgment. On the one hand, the prophets, though truthful, were seen by their opponents as foolish and deranged. On the other hand, certain people are sometimes viewed as holy, even though their behavior is pathological rather than truly religious. Halevi maintains that the very isolation that some idealize can generate pathological phenomena, which people sometimes perceive as signs of holiness. "Such a person will exhibit the dejection of mental illness, but people will consider this the dejection of humility and submissiveness, and thus he becomes a prisoner who loathes life because he abhors his confinement and his suffering, not because he find pleasure in seclusion." Halevi's discussion here calls to mind some modern psychological experiments, which examine the responses of a person who has been deprived of human contact for an extended time or has been deprived of sensory stimulation. These situations are found to impair psychological health. Halevi suggests that sometimes the psychological criticism of religious phenomena is justified. It is justified with regard to those positions which cause one to escape from life. A religion that encourages this type of behavior is unsound, leading to abhorrence of life. Judaism forges a path between this aberration and the opposite pole, idolatry.

The danger of asceticism is twofold. In itself, it leads one, as Halevi says, to "systematically distance himself from the divine element to which he wished to draw near." But Halevi's far-reaching criticism also heralded the reaction against Christian asceticism, a reaction that led to a return to idolatry and the deification of nature. As Rav Kook realized, the lowest streams of modern idolatry and the appearance of Nazism were also the result of a similar reaction.

Halevi calls our attention to the fact that some types of asceticism and withdrawal from the community are actually manifestations of psychological illness that may be misinterpreted as manifestations of holiness. The prophets were not diseased. They lived within the community. Halevi teaches us that Jewish religiosity does not mean running away from the world, but rather living within it. Mental health is positive. He rejects other religions that have made common cause with mental illness. The Torah is the human ideal, which respects the body and the senses as well as the soul.

The *haver*, the representative of Judaism, is fighting a battle on two fronts. He is battling religious Christianity, but at the same time he is also contending with those who feel that the search for pleasure necessitates the removal of the yoke of the Torah. Paradoxically, the blessings that must be said before partaking of worldly goods, such as food, "bring strength and pleasantness into the life of the pious one, and add pleasure to his pleasure" (III:13). Here, Halevi teaches us a very basic lesson in what one might call the laws of pleasure, and he puts this lesson not in the mouth of the *haver*, but in the mouth of the Kuzari (III:17). Human enjoyment is connected with awareness. If we enjoy ourselves when we are drunk, we do not consider it meaningful or significant. In fact, the opposite is true, and one generally considers that enjoyment as "a loss and not a gain, since these pleasures did not come to him when he was in full consciousness and complete feeling." That is why we attribute pleasure to animals "more than to plants, although the plant constantly receives nourishment" (III:16). Thus, the blessing of *she-heheyanu*, a prayer of thanksgiving to God for keeping us alive until the present time, teaches us to enjoy the greatest pleasure, life itself. The hundred blessings we recite daily compel us to notice, feel and respect what we experience through our hearing, our sight, our speech and our intellectual pursuits.

The Corridor and the Palace

The parable of the corridor and the palace teaches us about the transitory nature of the corridor, but it also shows us that man must pass through the corridor in order to enter the palace, and that he should not fool himself into believing that he can jump directly into the palace without passing through the corridor. Enoch and Elijah are examples of people who made their way to the end of the path. But human life is a fruit that must ripen, and at the end of the path man must have become able to see his entire previous life as mere preparation. That is the experience of the World to Come, and one who reaches that level experiences the World to Come in his lifetime, just as Elijah did. We can illustrate this with the example of dolls and marbles. Clearly, playing with dolls and marbles is very important in the development a child, and it would be a terrible tragedy for a child to have his dolls and marbles taken away. The child then gets older and leaves these toys behind but comes to understand that they served an important function. They were more than a foolish diversion promoted by one's evil inclination (though the evil inclination certainly seems to have been involved, given the way friends battled over a paltry marble or bickered over who won). Maturity is the possibility of seeing the earlier stage as important, but only as a preparation. It may be important to maintain some of the feelings developed during one's childhood games, but to remain at that earlier stage would be infantile. When we are in the midst of a stage, we cannot realize that these things that seem so important are merely marbles. We cannot see this because we must play the game seriously, since that is the essence of the stage—the corridor. But however important the corridor seems at the time, we must remember the palace. Only then will we understand our own true needs.

Later, we will consider the concept of the World to Come. Here, let me emphasize that in discussing the ideal man, Halevi refers to the relationship between this world and the World to Come. Awareness of the World to Come can sometimes endanger the wellbeing of this world. Many injustices are done in the name of faith in the World to Come. Many of the exploiters of this world allied themselves with those who promised a glittering World to Come. This is the essential difference between mysticism and prophecy. We are familiar with the gurus, the great mystics of the Far East who look down at men from the height of their mountaintops and invite them to ascend. They view human struggle and strife, the pains of child rearing, the struggle for food, and other this-worldly concerns, as if they are all a game of marbles and therefore meaningless. Many of these mystics are impostors, who are actually after our marbles themselves. Others are honest people, who promise to redeem us from our troubles by using mysticism to desensitize us to suffering and diminish our love of marbles. But I cannot accept their therapy, and I object to mysticism and spirituality that co-exists with immeasurable poverty, leaving the improvement of society off the religious agenda. The mystic considers improvement of society—healing the sick, housing the homeless, and saving the sufferer—to be worthless pursuits. Prophecy, on the other hand, teaches us that in order to reach God we must tend not only to our personal spiritual exaltation but also to the improvement our society.

Halevi mentions that together with the needs for food, sex and economic activity, one must also involve himself in "the improvement of his home and helping the poor." Economic activity is exalted when one is honest in one's business dealings and uses their proceeds to show love to his children and afford assistance to the needy.

Jewish mysticism always maintained a connection with Jewish law and, in contrast to other mysticisms, did not advocate separation from society. Different groups employ mysticism in many different ways, but the common denominator is the claim that man can enter a different state of consciousness. When we dream, our consciousness is in a different state. We seem to be in a different reality. When we awaken, we return to the "normal" state of consciousness, to alertness. Mysticism is based on the idea that there is another state of consciousness, beyond alertness. It claims that when we awaken from alertness, we will discern the world as it truly is. The mystic claims that another state of consciousness exists and that he has reached it. When man reaches this state he perceives the world differently, he sees the true reality. His experiences are much deeper, and they bring him great joy.

Mysticism exists in Judaism, but it contains both a promise and a danger. As we have seen, the danger is that the mystical inclination often involves an escape from reality. Some ideologues even tried to connect drugs with mysticism—an illusory and deceptive effort. Drugs are one of the greatest dangers threatening humanity. They do not afford a true mystical experience, furnishing only a pale imitation of the real thing. As Halevi tells us time and again, the impostor always builds his ideology using elements taken from the realm of holiness.

The mystics define the perception of the truth as knowledge of the Tree of Life. If we allow ourselves a modern interpretation, we might suggest that the flashing sword of the Cherubim that guard the path to the Tree of Life is none other than the drugs that blind man with their light but do not give him life. Drugs have become a dangerous and destructive pseudo-mysticism.

CHAPTER 32:
JUDAISM AND LOVE

The Golden Mean

Rabbi A. Y. Kook sometimes distinguishes between *da'at E-lohim* (knowledge of God) and *da'at E-lohim ba-aretz* (lit., knowledge of the God on earth). The first concept refers to theology, to an abstract philosophical worldview. The second refers to its worldly implications, its consequences for how we live. Halevi begins the Kuzari with a philosophical-religious confrontation between Judaism and Christianity. To complete the picture, we must add our own discussion of the Jewish and Christian views of the human ideal—one of the most fundamental differences between the two faiths.

Judaism's legal and philosophical distinctiveness finds expression in its attitude toward sexuality. A good example of this approach can be found in our Sages' commentary regarding the wives of Lemekh, an interpretation cited by Rashi as well:

> "And Lemekh took two wives, the first named Adah and the second named Tzilah"—R. Azariah said in the name of R. Judah ben Simeon: This is what the people of the generation of the flood used to do: each of them would take two wives, one for procreation and one for copulation. The one who was for procreation dwelt like a widow, and to the one for copulation he would give a drink that caused infertility so that she would not have children. And she would dwell with him adorned like a harlot. . . . Lemekh clearly was one such, having taken two wives, as it is written . . . "the first named Adah"—she was with child from him (Heb., *adah*); "the second named Tzilah"—because she sat in his shadow (Heb., *tzilo*).

Our Sages thus explain that one wife—the barren harlot—was taken for her beauty, while the other was taken only for childbearing, living the life of a widow. Only one who compartmentalized the "functions" of mother and lover could live that way. Judaism rejects this attitude out of hand.

Although Lemekh and his wives represent the idolatrous position, a similar viewpoint appears, surprisingly, in Christianity. Christianity emphasized Mary's motherhood but negated her sexuality, seeing her as a virgin mother—a miracle that expresses a religious attitude towards women. The approach is grounded in the premise that sex in and of itself is a base, negative thing. On this view, the world is necessarily populated by mediocre individuals, who cannot control their carnal desires.

Jewish law permits us to slaughter a bull but forbids castrating it. This reflects an attitude directly opposed to the attitude of those priests who considered castration—literal or figurative—a holy duty. Sexuality is an integral part of our personality, and it ought to assist us in our development.

Castration was known both in Christianity and in Islam. In the Christian world, priests would castrate themselves in order to worship God. Sadly, children were also castrated, to ensure that young boys' soprano voices would not change and thereby impede their ability to sing. In Islam, castration continued an idolatrous practice in which kings and other wealthy people castrated others in order to create harem guards who would be above suspicion—a practice mentioned already before Islam in the book of Esther. In Christendom, castration served the purposes of religion and art. In Ishmael, it fed the appetites of the privileged few. Judaism forbids it absolutely in any case.

Judaism views the sexless person as a withered tree. Isaiah comforts the eunuchs, promising the God-fearing eunuchs that they will have a remembrance even better than sons and daughters. The Torah, however, blesses man with offspring. Celibacy actually brought about a new Lemekh model. A double standard was accepted. Officially, purity and holiness were affirmed. Behind the scenes, corruption and prostitution prevailed. But the Jewish approach to sexuality is not only an attempt to be realistic. It is the expression of an ideal that occupies the middle ground between celibacy and sexual profligacy. Judaism succeeded in this attempt by emphasizing the sanctity of the couple and the sanctity of the family structure, values which it sees as central.

Maimonides, influenced by Greek thought, comments about the sense of touch:

Aristotle gave a clear explanation in the "Ethics," saying that this sense [of touch] is a disgrace to us. How fine is what he said, and how true that it is a disgrace! For we have it in so far as we are animals like the other beasts, and nothing that belongs to the notion of humanity pertains to it. (*Guide of the Perplexed*, II:36 [Pines trans., p. 371])

But an important work on this subject—*Iggeret Ha-Kodesh*, attributed to Nahmanides—emphasizes that "man should not think that in the proper union there is offensiveness and ugliness, God forbid, for this union is called *Da'at,* knowledge . . . and it is clear that if it did not contain great holiness, the union would not be called knowledge." Following up on this idea, the author of *Iggeret Ha-Kodesh* attacks the opinions of the rationalist philosophers regarding the sense of touch and sexual relations. He maintains that their approach is tied to Aristotle's belief in the eternal existence of the world, which sees matter as an entity absolutely independent of God.

Nahmanides' thinking, consistent with the view attributed to him in *Iggeret Ha-Kodesh*, offers the prototype for the Jewish approach to sex. His position is evident, for example, in his commentary on Lev. 16:18, explaining the ritual impurity associated with the sexual act: "And a woman with whom a man shall lie . . . they shall wash in water and shall be impure until evening." According to Nahmanides, the impurity results not from the procreative sexual act itself, but from the possibility that the emitted sperm will be destroyed rather than resulting in a pregnancy. In effect, the impurity is analogous to the impurity caused by a dead body.

Nahmanides meant to distinguish between pleasure and lust, believing that Adam's sin had converted pleasure into lust, and in a way erotics into pornography: "At that time sexual relations between man and his wife were not a fulfillment of lust. Rather at the time of mating they came together and had children, and therefore all the organs were to them like faces and hands and they were not ashamed of them, but after they ate from the Tree, [man] was granted the choice, and it was a matter of his choice to choose to do evil or good to himself or to others. This is a divine element on the one hand, but bad for man since [man] is [burdened with] . . . desires and lust" (Nahmanides on Gen. 2:9). According to this approach, evil is not connected to sex itself, but to lust, which is sinful, and is at times connected to sex. Before the sin, sex and the accompanying pleasure were simply one of the natural human functions. After the sin, lust became associated with sex. There are thus two types of desire, natural desires on the one hand, and obscenities and perversions on the others.

A passage in tractate *Avodah Zarah* sums up this issue nicely by describing the way the experiences at Sinai remedied Adam's sin, at least until the sin of the golden calf. During that brief period, man was granted immortality. The need for childbearing was over, and yet sexuality and love continued. The Israelites "returned to their tents" and their spouses. Moses, however, remained with God, having attained a different level. He was the sole exception, bearing witness to his unique status as the receiver of the Torah.

Love and Law

Now we can renew our effort to understand the commandments regarding marital relations. Here, too, we are not seeking reasons for the commandments. We are trying to uncover the individual and society that these norms mean to construct. The goal is not theological but anthropological: what human personality does Jewish law envision? The Jewish approach here strives, I believe, to create a system that takes four sets of values into account. The foci of these groups are the individual, the married couple, the family, and man in his relationship with God.

This schematic approach will help us understand the complexity of the problem and its historical development. Sexuality had great, sometimes overwhelming, importance in various areas. The way we live has important consequences. To use a trivial example, in addition to the obvious effects upon the life of the individual and the couple, our sexual lives have a powerful influence upon the existence of the family, the nation, the human race and even upon life on earth. Sexual relationships directly influence the structure of the family and the relations within it. Accordingly, the Jewish system must take into account not only one interest or ideal, but a collage of different ideals that both complement and clash with one another.

It is hard to exaggerate the importance of the family, the basic unit of society. The attempts to create other units to replace the family have failed miserably. The creation of the family becomes possible only when one's sex life is subsumed within a legal structure. Rabbi Sa'adiah Ga'on and Maimonides spoke of this in their respective treatments of the reasons for the commandments. Although Rabbi Sa'adiah, in his *Emunot Ve-De'ot*, includes the prohibition against certain sexual unions among the *mitzvot shim'iyot* (those observed primarily as an act of obedience to God's command), he acknowledges that they encompass "useful details," which he discusses briefly. This is clear with regard to the prohibition of fornication and incest. Divine "wisdom forbade fornication in order that men might not become like the beasts with the result that no one would know his father so as to show him reverence in return for having raised him. [Another reason for this prohibition was] that the father might bequeath unto his son his possessions just as the son had received from his father the gift of existence. . . . As far as the mother, sister and daughter are concerned, since the relationship with them is necessarily intimate, the license to marry them would encourage dissoluteness on their part" (III:2, Rosenblatt trans., pp. 141, 144). Maimonides explains these commandments similarly in *Guide*, III:49. The restrictions upon our sexual lives are not arbitrary. Their purpose is to ensure the existence of various social institutions, with the family at their core. Many of our practices are, clearly, the "burden of inheritance" of religion. They are the remnants of prohibitions which religion placed upon humanity. But this "remnant" is, in fact, a potent social cement, perhaps the only one that protects the social structure from collapse. On another level, what is true with regard to the family is even more so with regard to the nation. The prohibition of mixed marriages is the only guarantee we have for the continued existence of our people.

The Joy of Bride and Groom

We must remember, of course, that beyond the abstract communal needs we have been discussing, there is a real pair of human beings. Remarkably, the seven wedding blessings declare that God causes the bride and groom to rejoice. We know how we, as friends and relatives, enhance the couple's joy through dancing, singing and gifts. But in what sense does God do so?

We have already discussed the importance of the family as a necessary condition for society's survival. It is also a prerequisite to the psychological well-being of every child and adult. The family unit allows the child to develop normally. To grow up in a hospital, an orphanage or some other institution is a psychological catastrophe, if not a health hazard as well. The family, and the daily struggle connected with it, are necessary for growth and success. Were the commandment worded as "be fruitful and multiply in order to have a family," we would fulfill it as we fulfill other religious obligations such as fasting or cleaning for Pesach. We would still celebrate weddings, just as we celebrate completing the study of a tractate of Talmud or writing a new Torah scroll. But God grants a unique gift to the couple who are fulfilling his commandment: sexual pleasure. We must realize that this gift is very fragile indeed, and we must protect it from harm. Judaism sees sexuality as a gift and tries to help us maintain its power and spark.

In the Torah's perspective, sexuality is an aspect of reality through which the individual can attain a deep layer of his own self-actualization, both biologically and psychologically. The divine plan, which finds expression in nature as well, gives man the means to achieve his goals. In the process of man's development, sexual energy plays a significant role. The importance of sexuality can help us understand the prohibition against castration and sterilization of animals, and, of course, of human beings. As already noted, we may slaughter a bull, but we may not castrate it!

Sexual energy is expressed when a couple comes together to form a unit. The basis for this commandment lies in the belief that man and woman are only half of their true selves when each is alone. Love appears beyond the merely erotic. R. Eliyahu Dessler writes about the basis of marriage in his well known work, *Mikhtav Me-Eliyahu* (part one, p. 38), emphasizing that love must transcend mere lust. Of course, physical and biological needs play a large part, but we must change our perception of these needs. R. Dessler writes that our psychological and biological makeup is "the Creator's profound plan for maintaining the existence of the world—just as He instilled hunger within us to ensure the existence of the body." But while this explains the existence of physical desire, it does not account for love between man and woman. Thus love transcends general fraternity and friendship between people "who express mutual gratitude for helping each other fulfill their natural routines." These two types of love are not alike, since "many are ungrateful . . . yet do not lack for sexual love." R. Dessler explains the essence of love through the idea of mutual completion, the return to the original unity: "They *give* to one another and complete one another . . . because one who give loves." Love fades, and problems arise, "when those who joined together to be givers become changed into takers."

Here we find one of the fundamental differences between Jewish law and other legal systems. Jewish law is not solely concerned with the protection of society. Its first concern is to protect the relationship between the couple themselves. It seeks to protect the fragile, divine gift of sexual love. At the same time, it endeavors to create a relationship of loyalty and trust—a covenant—between man and woman.

Maintaining the married couple's relationship is indeed a rational commandment. Marriage is first and foremost a covenant. In the description of the *sotah* (errant woman), the Torah describes the adulteress as treacherous: "should a man's wife err and treat him treacherously" (Num. 5:11). The Maharik notes that the Torah describes the woman's act as treachery towards her husband, not towards God (*Responsa Maharik*, sec. 167), and the Vilna Ga'on similarly says, "It is not written that she acted treacherously towards God, but toward her husband" (Commentary on *Shulhan Arukh Orah Hayyim*). This idea was developed in the responsa literature surrounding the question of unintentional adultery. In addition to the prohibition against adultery, our Sages believed that an additional principle connects the couple, which can be described as a covenant. Thus, adulterous behavior is a breach of this sacred covenant.

Let us now return to our discussion the dilemmas people confront. In considering these dilemmas, R. Sa'adiah Ga'on would examine the full range of alternatives. In the tenth essay of his master work, *Emunot Ve-De'ot*, R. Sa'adiah presents us with various ethical alternatives for "human conduct." The first is *perishut*, according to which one "ought to reject this world, so as not to engage in building or planting, not to marry or beget offspring or dwell among those who choose such activities. . . . Rather should he seek the solitude of the mountains . . . until he dies in sorrow and sadness" (X:4, p. 366). Although much of what they say is true, the proponents of *perishut* "erred in forsaking community and people," for by refraining from marriage, they ensure the ultimate demise of the human race, the very beings for whom the entire universe was created. The other extreme that R. Sa'adiah discusses is homosexual love. R. Sa'adiah was well aware of the Greek origins of homosexuality, and its prevalence among the Greek philosophers. His account is based on the myth cited in Plato's *Symposium*. In contrast to this type of love, R. Sa'adiah presents the ideal of complete love, which is "appropriate . . . only in the relationship between husband and wife. They should be affectionate to each other for the sake of the maintenance of the world" (X:7, p. 377). R. Sa'adiah's picture of the human ideal is that of an individual who is not enslaved to one isolated ideal or value. Rather he integrates all of the various ideals into his life. R. Sa'adiah concludes, "If he encompasses all these actions we have mentioned, he shall be praised in both worlds."

The Yoke of Law

The Jewish strictures concerning sexual relations are no easy matter. We must recognize, however, that the various laws of family purity bind husband and wife in a unique manner. The prohibition against extra-marital sexual activity is not only a social norm; it is also wise counsel. The laws of family purity create a rhythm of renewal in the couple's sexual relationship. They protect the marital bond from internal deterioration. But they also serve as wise counsel from an egotistical point of view, counsel on how to protect the divine gift of sexual love. This is one of the great tests of time that religious marriages have withstood.

We must distinguish, of course, between sexuality, even eroticism, and pornography. Pornography means viewing sex as a market commodity. These ideas were well expressed many years ago by Professor Bonaventura, a religious psychologist who, before the establishment of the State of Israel, was killed in a convoy going up to the university campus on Mt. Scopus. Jewish law tries to build a family life that differs from the one created by the free market. In the free market, a brutal economy rules. The strongest wins and the strongest effects change. The Torah removes sex from the market economy, creating a system that does its best to avoid the rule of the jungle. Pornography is the use of human beings for commercial purposes, a sale of human merchandise. Jewish law tries to limit another element that holds sway in Western society: visual appeal. Good looks are a snare, and judgment of a person on the basis of appearances often works great injustice. In contrast to the attempt to draw attention through sexual attraction, the Talmud stresses the woman's obligation to make herself beautiful for her husband, and the responsibility of the man to please his wife. These are romantic gestures with erotic meaning as well, and Judaism recognizes, and often emphasizes, their importance.

The Talmud states that "twenty is the age of pursuit." As a person matures, he either pursues or is himself pursued. He pursues his goals. He tries to fulfill his ambitions and his desires, and he works to gain respect. He also flees from his fears. When two people form a young couple, they enter into a new stage. Family life becomes a constant struggle, sometimes a battle, a struggle in which there will always be defeats, failures and problems. As a child matures he finds himself in conflict with his parents, with authority. This is the great danger of adolescence. The conflict with one's parents can potentially become a conflict with Judaism. One's father is a Jew, and the rebellion against one's father could become a rebellion against Judaism. But when a man becomes a father and a woman gives birth to a child, they discover another perspective. Things look different from the vantage point of a parent. Responsibility looms large and a person discovers the need to fill his life with meaning. The person may understand that he challenged authority, his father, or his religion in order to achieve independence. Yet, in order to build a home and a society, in order to be a father himself, he has only one choice. He must learn to rely on his Heavenly Father. If the Torah cannot educate, other educators labor in vain.

This reality helps us understand the psychological issues that people must face in order to mature and develop, as well as the need for a legal system. As I heard once from the French-Jewish philosopher Emmanuel Levinas, if there were only two people in the world, love would suffice. Since in the world there are always at least three, law is necessary. Personally, I doubt if any relationship can last long without mutual obligations. Without law, without rules, no process of education is possible.

Taharat Ha-Mishpahah: Jewish Familial Law

To truly understand the laws of family purity, we must consider two separate aspects of the commandment. One involves the actual laws of impurity, while the other involves the effect of those laws on family life and the relationship between the husband and wife. But there is a third aspect as well, reflected in the rabbinic interpretation of the verse "Your belly is a mound of wheat surrounded by a hedge of roses" (Song of Songs 7:3). In tractate *Sanhedrin*, our Sages associate this verse with the laws of family purity. "A hedge of roses" refers to the red barrier of ritual impurity, of menstrual blood. But beyond this obvious meaning, the Sages seem to allude to a broader point, one discussed by, among others, Yeshayahu Leibowitz and Emmanuel Levinas.

Imagine a garden filled with lovely flowers. A person sees these flowers, and wishes to enter the garden to pick them, though they do not belong to him. How do we deter him? We erect a fence, at times even a solid wall, which bars the entrance to the garden. Now imagine a garden which is protected only by a hedge of roses. This is our ultimate goal: we must learn to avoid breaching even a frail hedge of roses.

This is the first and most significant stage in one of the most important concepts in ethics: autonomy. Lack of autonomy constitutes an ethical problem. The law is followed only because an authority enforces it: the police, the courts, the penal system. But Judaism wishes to forge individuals who choose good over evil not because of external causes such as fear of a policeman but because of an internal cause: a personal sense of responsibility, of respect for the commandment and its author. The Talmud explains that the couple who desire each other will keep Jewish marital laws not because of outer pressures but because of their inner convictions. The Torah trusts the couple and does not forbid them to be alone together at times when they may not touch. Someone from outside the system would find this impossible to believe. How can people overcome their greatest desires, and how may we be sure that they will keep these laws in the privacy of their own homes? This is the meaning of the term, "a hedge of roses." That is the highest moral level, in which man's true authority lies within himself, not in the government or police force.

Emmanuel Levinas maintains that this is the central concept of the Jewish religion. The world cannot be improved unless the process goes hand in hand with education based on principles such as these. Jewish law educates man towards self-control. This is the path to improvement of the world under the divine rule. Think of a person walking a tightrope between two mountains, high above a ravine. The primary requirement for success is self-control, control over one's body and over each of its muscles. Similarly, society cannot exist without this sort of self-control. The rational laws and the decrees thus suit two aspects of our nature. The rational laws suit our rational side, while the decrees suit our non-rational side. I educate myself using means that are not merely optional.

The Love of God

The values thus far discussed shape the individual, the couple, and the community. But we are guided by an additional value: the desire to stand before God. We are called upon to overcome our evil inclinations in order to face our Creator.

At the core of all other relationships is the encounter with God, the commandment of love that connects us to Him. Human love must leave some room for divine love. R. Tzvi Hirsch Kalisher, the famed harbinger of religious Zionism, nicely describes the conflict between these two sorts of love, referring to a rabbinic tale:

> Rava brought a gift for Bar Sheshak in honor of his festival. . . . He went and found him sitting up to his neck in roses, with naked prostitutes standing in front of him.
>
> He [Bar Sheshak] said to him: "Do you have such things in the World to Come?"
>
> He said to him: "Ours is greater than this! . . . . Have you no fear of the King?"
>
> He said to him: "What fear of the King oppresses me?"
>
> Just then the messenger of the [worldly] king came and said to him: "Rise, for the king wants you. . . ."
>
> Rav Papa said: "He [Rava] should have answered him from this verse: 'The daughters of kings in your finery, your queen stands to your right in jewelry from Ophir' (Ps. 45:10)."
>
> Rav Nahman bar Isaac said: "He should have answered him from here: 'No eye has seen God other than you, He will act for the one who waits for him' (Isa. 64:3)." (*Avodah Zarah* 65a).

This legend can of course be interpreted on a simple level. Rava and Bar Sheshak seem to be arguing over who can expect the better lot. Is the pleasure of the Jewish World to Come greater than the pleasures of this world which the rich Persian enjoys? Rava demonstrates that Bar Sheshak's hold on life is fragile, and the fear of the king oppresses him.

R. Kalisher offers a more profound interpretation of this story. Bar Sheshak actually prides himself not on the pleasure itself but on the very existence of passion. The pleasure itself cannot exist if desire is lacking. Pleasure is only a function of desire. So he says, according to R. Kalisher's interpretation (*Sefer Emunah Yesharah* [1843], p. 5): "Does there exist a greater passion than I possess now, for my passion is like a burning furnace inside me . . . for the passion of the flesh is greater than the passion of the mind, since the mind does not desire things which are against the will, and the desire of the flesh overcomes the desire of the will." To this, Rava responds: "The fear of the king oppresses you"— "for every material thing has a limit and an end." The obligation to stand before the king caused him to completely lose his passion. Fear overcomes passion.

But, says Rava, there is another passion, the passionate love of God. This is a passion that overcomes fear. The fact of holy martyrdom proves this point, for martyrdom is a situation in which the love of God overcomes the fear of death.

Section 8:
Thinking About God

CHAPTER 33:
THE THEORY OF DIVINE ATTRIBUTES

In previous chapters, we have noted two areas marked by close and rather complex relations between the prophetic and the philosophical traditions. The first is the theory of divine attributes, which Halevi discusses at beginning of Parts II and IV of his book, among other places. The second area is that of miracles. We here consider these matters further, beginning with the theory of attributes.

We will not deal with the philosophical problem in all its depth, attempting instead only to gain an overall understanding of the issue. We start by examining the topic of the divine attributes as presented in the Scriptures—the descriptions, attributes, and names ascribed to God throughout the Bible.

An'im Zemirot

In many congregations, the Shabbat *Musaf* prayers conclude with the singing of "The Hymn of Glory" (*Shir Ha-Kavod*), a philosophical poem, also known as *An'im Zemirot*. The poem expounds upon religious language in general and the divine attributes in particular. The poem refers in particular to the origin of religious language, and to the way in which the Scriptures describe God, both in prophetic visions and in biblical thought and poetry. In essence, this poem is a justification of the use of religious language, a plea for forgiveness for the fact that we dare pray at all. The same message is actually expressed in the Kaddish, in which we state that God's Name is blessed above all other blessings. God exists on a plane beyond the reaches of humanity, yet we desire and continually attempt to surpass our limitations. This is the ultimate goal of the theory of divine attributes, which employed various methods, in the various stages of Jewish philosophy, to teach us how to perform the miraculous act of transcending the limitations of human knowledge and language.

But *An'im Zemirot* teaches us that this is not a purely philosophical issue. We use it to express our feelings—our audacious ambition to comprehend the divine, our yearning to understand what is beyond our reach. Of course we must not interpret the poem's plea "to fathom all the mystery of your secrets" literally. Even in the little that we are capable of understanding, we must be cautious indeed. But another desire underlies the quest for understanding: "my soul longs for You." We pray and speak to God and about God. We weave poems, sing melodies and use religious language, thereby expressing our longing. Behind our desire to comprehend lies a deep and abiding love.

A Child's Question

On Passover, we tell of the four sons. The apt question posed by the wise son can serve to illustrate the theory of divine attributes. We will try to find the answer on our own, but there is much to be learned from the varied —indeed, sometimes conflicting—answers that our Sages have given to these same questions.

We will begin with one of the questions asked by every child: "Where is God?"—or, in the language of the angels, "Where is the place of His glory?" One of the classic answers, originating in the Scriptures, is that God is in Heaven. We will return to this answer shortly. But we must first note the use of the term *ha-makom* ("the Place") to refer to God.

The Sages tried to explain that usage in their cryptic statement, "He is the place of the world, and the world is not His place." This is a philosophical explanation, to which we will return. Its accepted meaning is that God is beyond the dimension of space, and yet He is the One who allows our spatial reality to exist. Various thinkers have related similarly to the concept of time. This idea can be illustrated through the example of a teacher and his classroom. An entertaining anecdote tells of a teacher who dreamt that he gave a class, woke up and found it was true. This description, which is not very complimentary to teachers, demonstrates that we must distinguish between two different situations. Generally speaking, the classroom is the teacher's place. When the teacher dreams of the classroom, however, the relationship between the teacher and the classroom is reversed. The classroom is located within the teacher's mind, but the teacher is not located inside the classroom. In our case, by the use of the term "*makom*," we claim that the dimensions of, and the very concept of, *makom* (place) do not apply to God. On the other hand, we claim that spatial reality, or the concept of *makom* as we know it, is possible only because God exists.

That is the distinctive message of the concept of *makom*. "The heavens and the heavens of the heavens cannot contain You" (1 Kings 8:7). Yet, despite all this talk of God being beyond the confines of space, the Scriptures refer to "the heavens" as the divine abode: "And You will hearken from the heavens" (1 Kings 8:32). What does this concept of heaven mean? To explain, we must first examine two other concepts, both of them encountered in various guises, both philosophical and scriptural. In philosophical terms, we speak of immanence and transcendence; in scriptural terms, of *kavod* (glory) and *kedushah* (holiness). The concept of *kedushah* creates for us a sense of distance. In an interpretation accepted by the philosophers, our Sages read the angels' cry, *kadosh, kadosh, kadosh* ("holy, holy, holy"), as describing our journey through each of the spiritual worlds, in search of God. In each world, we inquire if God is to be found there, and each world answers *kadosh*—God is beyond me. This is transcendence. God is beyond. But the angels also cry: "The world is filled with his glory." The concept of glory (*kavod*) creates in us a feeling of closeness, a sense that God is near. This is the concept of immanence. God is transcendent, yet the world is suffused with His glory.

One of the great Hasidic masters, R. Tzadok ha-Kohen of Lublin, used these principles to explain the beginning of the Talmudic tractate Eruvin. The Talmud wrestles with two terms: *mikdash* (temple) and *mishkan* (sanctuary). The two terms correspond to the two ideas noted above. In the *mikdash*, God is transcendent. In the *mishkan*—which means "a dwelling place with them"—He is immanent. These two perspectives of distance and closeness express a central religious assumption. Every blessing we recite is on the model of "Blessed are you God . . . Who sanctified us . . . ." At the beginning of the blessing we refer to God in the second person, and at the end we refer to Him in the third person. These are the two aspects of our relationship with God.

This interpretation can help us understand why we refer to the heavens as God's abode. Perhaps when we say that God is in heaven, we mean that He is above us, He sees us, and we do not see Him. The concept of a God in heaven expresses the experience of a transcendent God.

Hasidism and the Existential *Makom*

Hasidic legend relates that when R. Menahem Mendel, the Kotzker Rebbe, was asked "Where is God?" he replied, "Wherever he is allowed in." Though well-developed in Hasidic thought, this idea originates in the Scriptures themselves: "God is near to all who call Him, to all who call on Him sincerely (Ps. 145:18). This is a different concept of closeness. God is close to whoever calls on Him sincerely. This is not an objective place, but a place in the heart. This is beautifully expressed in the writings of R. Nahman of Braslav. R. Nahman used the medium of a tale to express the complexity of the concept of *makom*. He relates the story of seven maimed beggars who tell wondrous stories. The blind beggar presents the secrets of time, and the hunchback presents the secrets of place—*makom*, expounding the mystery of *tzimtzum* (divine constriction). He explains the paradox of the smaller vessel containing the larger one. We often find such paradoxes in the writings of our Sages. For example, they write that the pilgrims to the Temple "were crowded when they stood yet could bow down comfortably . . . and no one ever said 'it is too crowded for me to find a place in Jerusalem'" (*Avot* 5:7). Another example is the paradox of the tiny land capable of containing the entire nation of Israel. These strange statements imply that some things are not measured by miles and appear to exist in another dimension.

The child's question—"Where is God?"—is really a metaphysical, philosophical question, inquiring about God's concept of space. But Hasidism is interested not only in metaphysical questions. It is more interested in human existential questions. R. Nahman's story certainly has a metaphysical interpretation, but R. Nahman's student, R. Natan, revealed the existential meaning of the story, showing that mystery of *makom* differs from what we thought it was. Our Sages said, "there is no man who does not have his hour, and no thing that does not have its place [*makom*]." To understand this, we must recall another adage, "Do not judge your friend until you are in his place [*makom*]". In other words, the true *makom* is each person's subjective location. Every person looks at the world from his place, from his perspective. Every point of view creates a world, and if we change the point of view, the world changes. Our subjectivity is our inner perspective, from which we look at the world around us. This perspective does not permit us to correctly judge another person, who sees his problems from his own point of view. We cannot enter the subjective *makom* of another person, his perspective, his intimate inner world. Do not judge your friend until you reach his place, his subjectivity. We call God *ha-Makom*, the Place, because He is with every person in his place. He alone can judge me from within my subjectivity, because He alone is with me in my internal world. God is the world's place, meaning that he looks at every situation and every problem from the subjective perspective of each of us. In every child's development, he reaches the Hasidic stage, when he moves beyond metaphysical questions and deals with existential questions. At this point his central interest shifts to the inner, personal issues.

"The World Is Not His Place"

We return now to the philosophical question. When we refer to God as *ha-Makom*, the Place, we express a central idea in Jewish philosophy: the rules that apply to us do not apply to God. The strictures of time and place do not apply to Him. As we shall see, this is the meaning of what the philosophers termed "negative attributes." But, here too, the philosophers used their own language to express a basic biblical principle.

The Scriptures combated the use of a human model to envision God, an opposition that formed the source for the traditional objection to what would later be termed anthropomorphism. The Scriptures impress this upon us in various ways. For example, they teach that sexual identity, one of mankind's central and defining characteristics, does not apply to God. God is neither male nor female. Idolatry projected human experience onto the divine and created gods in human form. The mythological system is based upon the concept of gods and goddesses who have sexual relations. Judaism completely eradicated this concept from its creed.

This fact is of paramount importance, particularly since we attribute grammatical gender to God, referring to God as "He." But God is not a he or a she, for He is beyond this distinction. We use the masculine form in prayer, for Hebrew grammar has no neuter form, and even neuter objects are assigned a gender. Hence, God's grammatical masculinity is a "historical accident" that ought not to affect us. But the Kabbalah does not believe in historical accidents. It sees meaning in language, perceiving it as a vehicle for the expression of mystical wisdom. Certainly, Judaism has a tradition of referring to God in the feminine gender as well, as the *Shekhinah* (divine presence). We must be wary of referring to God exclusively in the masculine form, for God is neither one nor the other.

The Kabbalah ascribes both masculine and feminine attributes to

God. They are symbolically represented by Hebrew letters. In the Tetragrammaton, the letter *yod* is masculine and the letter *heh* is feminine. Similarly, in the structure of the *sefirot* (divine emanations), *hokhmah* (wisdom) is masculine, while *binah* (understanding) is feminine. *Tiferet* (glory) and *yesod* (foundation) describe God's masculine attributes, and *malkhut* (sovereignty) describes God's feminine side.

I do not mean to enter here into the world of the Kabbalah. R. Kook wrote that entrance into the world of Kabbalah must be preceded by spiritual and intellectual cleansing in the manner of Maimonidean philosophy, just as all of a surgeon's instruments must be sterilized before an operation in order to avoid infection. Without this spiritual cleansing, entry into the world of kabbalistic mystical images would be dangerous indeed. But for our maximally abstract and dematerialized concept of God, we might come to believe absurdities through a simplistic understanding of the kabbalistic texts. Therefore, religious philosophy teaches us that God is utterly beyond sexual identification. The kabbalists agree with this assumption, but they argue that if we must speak of God, the language we use must incorporate both sexes. Just as we represent the attributes of *hesed* (lovingkindness) and *gevurah* (might, restraint) as being on the right and the left, we must represent the divine attributes in general in masculine and feminine form. The *Zohar* states, for example, that man was created "in God's image (*tzelem*) and in His form (*d'mut*)"—"His image" is masculine; "His form" is feminine. The kabbalistic solution to the problem of an accurate expression of the divine attributes is to view religious symbols as both masculine and feminine. Interestingly, the transcendent and immanent experiences of divinity are represented in the Kabbalah in terms of sexual identification. The *shekhinah*, represented by the *sefirah* of *malkhut*, refers to God's immanence, while the sefirah of *tiferet*—regarded as masculine—describes the transcendent God. Mankind comprises two sexes, and we must never regard only one of them as having been created in the divine image. Only in unity between the two sexes can humans achieve the image of God. Therefore, the Bible states, "And He called *their* name Adam."

Holiness

Some people have an intuitive sense of holiness. They perceive it as though it were a sort of electric current to be found in certain places, things or situations. Is this an accurate description of holiness? What is the

meaning of holiness in Jewish thought? What do we mean when we speak
of the holiness of the Land of Israel?

(a) Holiness and the Commandments

Let me begin with an approach represented in our times by the late
Yeshayahu Leibowitz. This viewpoint maintains that the Jews are holy by
virtue of their obligation to perform the commandments. It strips holiness
of its independent character, making the concept of holiness dependent on
the more fundamental concept of the commandments. Holiness means
sanctification through the commandments.

It is important to note, however, that Jewish law distinguishes between
holy objects and objects simply employed in the fulfillment of commandments. A Torah scroll and *tefillin* are regarded as holy articles, while a
lulav is an article used in performing a commandment. After the *lulav* has
been used and is no longer needed, it may be discarded (though not dis-
honored). It no longer has independent value. Not so holy articles, which
retain their status and may not be discarded. If we apply this distinction
here, we may say that the commandments are instruments that serve other
goals, while holiness characterizes the values that have their own independent worth. The concept of human holiness, for example, teaches us
that we may not use people as raw material for industry. When we speak
of the Land of Israel as a holy land, we mean it is not merely an instrument, a neutral base for a Jewish state, but that it has its own value. On
this explanation, holiness means that the holy entity has its own independent value and purpose.

(b) Holiness and Encounter

What is the meaning of the term "Holy Land"? We previously spoke
of the meaning of the Land of Israel. We now return to this issue only from
the perspective of the concept of holiness.

R. Nahman Krochmal discusses this question in the context of his
effort to understand the meaning of holiness. If indeed, "the whole world
is filled with His glory," what is the difference between one place and
another, one thing and another? This paradox was well expressed by
R. Nahman of Breslov. As his student R. Natan put it, this is the difference
between *tzitzit* and *tefillin*. A person may enter a filthy place (such as a
privy) wearing *tzitzit* but may not do so wearing *tefillin*. God's presence is

everywhere, yet holiness exists and one place differs from another. Krochmal explains that God's presence, though pervasive, becomes more transparent at particular times or in particular places or situations. Man's vision of the divine presence in the world is clouded. In the Sages' words, we perceive it *be-aspaklaria she-einah me'irah*—through a cloudy glass. When we perceive reality more clearly, we experience holiness. We differentiate between days in which the encounter with God is less and more apparent. In Part IV (16, 172), Halevi presents this idea with reference to the distinctions among the holy names, a distinction to which we will return later. He compares them to the various appearances of light to the human eye. Under certain circumstances the light is refracted, in others it is reflected, while in still other situations it is obstructed. We perceive the light from above in a similar range of ways. The clear light represents the "divine principle."

(c) Holiness and Religious Sentiment

This approach brings us back to the intuitive approach considered earlier. Imagine that you are walking in a dark place and suddenly experience an intense fear of something you cannot see and cannot exactly define. We have all experienced this emotion at some time or another. A similar emotional response exists, in which one is conscious of being in the presence of something not threatening but holy. One feels that he is in the presence of a Being that is beyond all that is ordinary, everyday and human.

Imagine a man walking with a compass. The compass will always show him which way is north. In close proximity to a strong magnetic field, however, the compass will begin to behave in strange ways. The theory of holiness assumes that man is sensitive to the encounter with that which is beyond nature. This reality explains the surprising fact that religions appeared all over the world. If we investigate and study all the religions, we will discover that they all bear the marks of this same basic feeling. All religions contain the joy of apprehending immanent divinity on the one hand, and the religious awe of transcendent divinity on the other.

(d) Holiness as the Ultimate Goal

Each of us performs many actions during the course of our lives. We must ask ourselves why we do these things. Maimonides reminds us that many of our actions are actions of folly, meaning they have no real goal.

A person is often caught in the trap of acting hastily without asking himself what his ultimate goals really are. He is so busy with the intermediate goals and the problems of making a living that he never reaches the question of "what is it all for?" This is similar to a person who spends his whole life repairing a car, never driving it.

Holiness, in essence, means the locus of our ultimate goals. If a person's goal in life is making money, then he worships money. That is his holiness, because everything else serves this end. He makes money holy, and by doing this profanes holiness.

(e) Holiness as Moral Perfection

Another concept of holiness applies to one who has moved beyond the "war against the evil urge." That battle is waged within each and every one of us, but some may achieve a state of perfection that places him above and beyond the fray. This, according to Lubavitch Hasidism, is the difference between a *beinoni* (an ordinary, "intermediate" person) and a *tzaddik* (a righteous person). A *beinoni* is one who fights the inner battle and wins. A *tzaddik* has moved beyond the battlefield.

(f) Holiness as Pursuit of the Realm Beyond Human Experience

One might say that Nahmanides originated this concept of holiness. All the relations between man and his fellow man are based on Jewish law. Beyond this, we have commandments that are based on the principle of "you shall do the just and the good." Just as there is permissible and forbidden behavior between man and God, so are there permissible and forbidden behaviors among people. But beyond this legal reality lies the realm of holiness. The prohibition of drug abuse, like that of alcohol abuse, stems from the category of commandments founded on the verse, "you shall be holy." (Lev. 19:1) When using drugs, man loses his humanity and his freedom. Thus, drug abuse is a desecration of holiness. The idea of holiness allows us to broaden the concept of commandment, and it serves to expand the sphere of our religious behavior.

CHAPTER 34:
ATTRIBUTES AND ARCHETYPES

During the Middle Ages, the theory of divine attributes was associated with interesting logical and philosophical issues, some of which we will discuss later on. To do so, we will have to categorize the various types of attributes, an effort in which we must recognize that our religious language in general, and our language of prayer in particular, is based upon the Scriptures. In *An'im Zemirot* we say, "Through the hands of Your prophets, through the mystery of Your servants, You have portrayed Your glory." Our religious language is rooted in the prophetic vision, and we must return to the prophetic vision to gain a deeper understanding of it.

We begin with the most basic of divine attributes, those that depict God in human terms. Imagery of this sort is termed "anthropomorphism."

Anthropomorphism

Anthropomorphism, as noted, depicts God in terms that pertain to human beings. The terms may be physiological or psychological. We find references, for example, to "the eyes of God" and to "God's anger." Of course, these divine attributes are not to be interpreted literally. As our Sages put it, "the Torah speaks in human language."

This phrase is important, but it does not say enough. The *Kuzari*, and Maimonides in its wake, taught us that this phrase is only the opening for a discussion of biblical language. First of all, it is worth noting the position of Abraham Joshua Heschel. He maintained that the Bible contains no real anthropomorphisms, but only His apparent emotional response to our actions. This distinction helps us understand the importance of the "psychological" attributes, such as the statement that God "loves the convert" or "abhors evil." These phrases explicitly direct us to their ethical meaning and rule out anthropomorphic conclusions.

Given this background, we ought to take note of the interesting paradox brought to our attention by Benno Jacob, a modern Bible commentator. As we, the readers, proceed through the Scriptures chronologically, we notice that the anthropomorphisms become more pronounced. The reason is simple. We must be wary of anthropomorphisms when they pose a danger, when people are liable to be misled by them. But when people attain a degree of distance from corporeal representation of God, use of the wording associated with it becomes less of a challenge. Use of anthropomorphic imagery then becomes more acceptable, if it helps us express what we cannot express directly in words. That is why the prophets used human language much more freely. If we combine these two statements, we will better understand Maimonides' guiding principles in this area, which we would do well to follow. They are as follows:

1. The Scriptures do not take anthropomorphisms in accord with their simple meaning.

2. We must closely examine the anthropomorphic image, taking account of all options for understanding it.

Why Use Anthropomorphisms?

Maimonides fought stubbornly against anthropomorphism. His great achievement, however, was not his rejection of the simple meanings of these attributes but his wonderful explanation of why anthropomorphisms are used in the first place. He explains that the goal of all Scriptural descriptions of God is to convey a sense of God's flawlessness. When alternative descriptive options exist, the Scriptures choose the one that best conveys that flawlessness. Wanting to impart the concept of an utterly perfect God, the Torah uses terms that imply perfection, even though they do not accurately describe God.

For example, the Torah depicts God in terms related to the human senses. God is said to have sight, hearing and even smell. By speaking in these terms, the Torah aims to teach us that God is familiar with and interested in mankind, and responds to man's behavior. But the Torah does not refer to all five senses. Terms connected with touch and taste are entirely absent, an omission that appears to be intentional. The sense perceptions that the Torah attributes to God are those that can operate at a distance. People can hear, see and smell without being close to the object perceived. That is not the case with respect to taste and touch. The Torah wished to convey the sense of God's presence and watchfulness while

avoiding the potential pitfalls of an anthropomorphism that suggests proximity. Idolatry succumbed to that pitfall, for its intimate anthropomorphisms gave legitimacy to the belief in physical relationships between the
gods and their human subjects.

Anthropomorphism in Language

We can attribute characteristics to God, because we use various indirect
linguistic and poetic forms of language, such as metaphors. There appear
to be two types of metaphor. One type is the intentional use of a word to
evoke associations from another area and apply them to the area under discussion. For example, one might say, in reference to a politician, "So-
And-So is a real snake." We describe a particular situation in the social or
intellectual sphere by using terms taken from the world of the jungle.
There the snake is the wily, slippery trickster. We mean to say that this particular person demonstrates characteristics similar to that of the snake. We
borrow a word from one domain and move it to another, bringing its connotations along. Another type of metaphor would be the use of a word in
order to apply only one narrow aspect of it to our situation. For example,
when we say that we have completed "the lion's share" of the work, we
do not mean to allude to all of the lion's qualities. We refer only to the
large size of the lion's share. In general, the metaphors used in describing
God's attributes are of the second type.

Holiness

Thus far, we have considered the building blocks of anthropomorphism.
We must now consider the matter more broadly. Let me illustrate with a
prayer we recite, in one form or another, every day. When reciting the
Kedushah, we join with the angels in fundamental pronouncements,
derived from the visions of Isaiah (chap. 6) and Ezekiel (chap. 1). These
prophets respectively heard the angels proclaim: "Holy Holy Holy" and
"Blessed is the glory of God." We refer in this prayer to heavenly beings
called *ofanim* (celestial wheels) and holy *hayyot* (beasts), but what do
these terms mean? Every child asks this question upon reading this prayer,
yet we quickly set the question aside with all our other unanswered
queries. We therefore fail to grasp the depth of these concepts. Let us
attempt now to do so, following Maimonides' approach to the matter.

The description of the *hayyot* and *ofanim* originates in Ezekiel's
famous vision of the heavenly chariot. Maimonides explains that this

vision is a depiction of the relationship between the world, including the angels, and God. This vision expresses the impenetrable barrier between the two spheres. Without delving into the issue of the celestial beings, we will assume the existence of spiritual entities above man, just as we know of beings that are beneath him. Using the image of the distance between the rider and the chariot, the prophet first describes the impassable chasm between the Creator and the world. He then proceeds to illustrate the gap between God and the angels. The chariot is composed of beasts, a type of horse, and of technology. The most significant and revolutionary technological element of the chariot is the wheel, or what the prophet calls the *ofan*. The image of the chariot conveys the sense that the components of our world are merely an insignificant cog in the machinery. The *hayyot* appear in the vision in place of the horses drawing the chariot, except that the image is augmented by an additional element. These beasts differ from their earthly counterparts, for they are composites of various animals. The angels are not described as additional passengers in the chariot, but as the *hayyot* and *ofanim* that pull it. They are merely a part of the chariot's mechanism, while the distance between them and their passenger remains constant and unbridgeable. In the vision, a kind of platform is described, which separates the chariot from everything beyond it. This platform symbolizes the heavens, which in turn illustrates the unbridgeable gap between the Creator and all His creatures. God is symbolized by the man in the chariot, but we must remember that the human form is one of the faces that appear among the *hayyot*.

Let me note another detail, related to a point made earlier. In describing the *hayyot*, Ezekiel says that "their leg was a straight leg." This is the position we adopt during the *Kedushah* and *Amidah* prayers, when we stand with feet together. But the use of the singular means that the angels have only one leg, which implies that they are beyond division into sexes. How much more so is that true of God.

This description of the chariot illustrates the full meaning of the barrier that separates the creature from its Creator. The prophet uses physical representation, but the vision is carefully constructed and is actually a statement opposing any physical representation of God. The utter gap between the creature and the Creator is expressed in the fifth of Maimonides' thirteen principles of faith.

Do the angels belong to a sphere beyond our own? This question is disputed among Jewish thinkers. But the premise that angels exist means that just as there are distant galaxies in the natural world, there is a spiritual reality beyond our thought.

Taking a kabbalistic perspective, Rabbi Abraham Ben David of Posquieres (Ra'abad) objected to some aspects of Maimonides' approach. We have seen, for example, that when the Scriptures say "the eyes of God," we take human reality and try to apply it in the expression of religious ideas. But there are two ways to understand this type of interpretation—the philosophic and the kabbalistic. The difference is related to the difference between allegory and symbol. After the allegory is written, it can be interpreted. One may write, for example, "divine providence" in place of the "eyes of God." As the philosopher sees it, the eye is merely an allegory. Kabbalists, however, say just the opposite: the fact that man has eyes is not coincidental, and all of our earthly reality is a reflection of an archetype in the spiritual world. The symbol is not a mere linguistic invention. It is an expression of the relationship between our everyday reality and the spiritual world. This does not mean that God has eyes, but that divine providence possesses a characteristic that is expressed in the eye. The eye is a symbol, much more closely connected to the object symbolized than is the allegory to its interpretation. The philosopher argues that the use of the term "the eyes of God" is meant to explain the spiritual reality to people in terms they can understand. This is anthropomorphism, the use of human language. For the Kabbalist, the vector is reversed. The lower world is simply a model of the spiritual reality of the higher world. In a similar vein, some doctors and healers claim the ability to discover diseases through an eye examination. A doctor of this type does not use eyes as an allegory. He sees them as intrinsically significant and necessary, for his method is based upon the assumption of a parallel between the state of the eye and that of the entire body. The Torah uses the language of symbols.

The Kabbalah perceives everything in our world as a distorted, imperfect reflection of the upper world. Man has two hands that function differently, one hand being stronger than the other. This asymmetry reflects the asymmetry in the upper world between the divine elements of Law, symbolized by the left, and of Mercy, symbolized by the right.

One final example. The lowest *sefirah* is called *malkhut* (sovereignty). It is symbolized by the Hebrew letter *dalet*. That letter, in turn, symbolizes *dalut* (poverty), that is, passivity. The *sefirah* of *tiferet* symbolizes activity. It is represented by the Hebrew letter *vav*. The connection between them is, in essence, the connection between the giver and the recipient of charity. This is symbolized by the graphic connection between the letter *vav* and the letter *dalet*, which together from the letter *heh*, the symbol of true sovereignty. According to the Kabbalah, this connection is reflected on every plane. Thus, when a person gives charity, he gives to the *dal*, the needy, and forges a connection between the *vav* and the *heh*.

This compels us to see the larger picture in a different light. Take the example of the word "book." We can view this word as a pointer referring to all books. In this simple approach, the written word, made of letters, suggests the reality. However, this is only half the truth. The Kabbalists claim that reality itself is composed of letters. In other words, our reality is also a written text, which suggests the existence of something deeper than itself. It would be a mistake to think that our perception of reality is the end of the analysis. Reality itself is a text, which hints at a deeper reality.

God's Voice and the Archetypes (I:88–91)

In the course of discussing revelation as the basis of the Jewish faith, Halevi touches upon the problem of physical descriptions of God. How do we reconcile the concept of revelation with our basic belief in God's incorporeality (I:89)? We will consider the question and its fundamental implications before moving on to Halevi's theory of divine attributes (presented at the beginning of Part II).

As we have seen, many of the physical descriptions of God are merely turns of phrase. Their meaning is tied to the structure of the language. In these instances, religious language approaches the language of poetry. But other expressions—those tied to the prophetic experience—compel us to seek other sorts of explanation. What, for example, was the voice of God heard at Sinai or by the prophet in his vision?

All that the text permits us to say is that we hear God's voice. This was indeed a unique voice, mysteriously described in Scripture as "all the nation saw the sounds." In other words, the Israelites perceived an auditory stimulus through their sense of vision. Although the verse may be interpreted in accord with its plain meaning, as Ibn Ezra attempts to do, our Sages emphasize the unique quality of this "voice." Though not as problematic as references to "seeing" God, the use of the term "voice" is still difficult. When we speak of one's voice, we refer to a quality of his, or even to a particular physical function through which his body creates the sound of his voice. Even if we disregard the mechanism and argue that the presence of a voice does not imply that God possesses an "anatomy," we must still question the meaning of the term "voice of God." Jewish philosophers have answered the question in various ways, related to each thinker's approach to prophecy in general—something to be discussed below.

The Archetypes

Before turning our attention to the possible answers, we must reiterate one of Halevi's important principles: although various options are plausible, the important element is not the answer itself but the direction in which it points. The answer itself is merely scaffolding on the building of understanding, a help to our ascent:

> We do not know how the spiritual element became physical and became an audible voice. And we do not know if at that time God created something that had not previously existed or if He used for that purpose something that had been in existence, seeing that God does not lack the ability to do either of these things (I: 89).

Halevi teaches us that various models exist to explain the phenomenon, and we are free to choose among them. Maimonides also adopted this principle.

Both Halevi and Maimonides accepted the possibility that prophecy might be explained by the theory of glory (to be described presently), but they both offered alternative explanations as well. In summary, we are faced with three possibilities. The prophetic vision may be:

1. A phenomenon that takes place on a separate stage, one that differs from the usual media studied by physics and chemistry.

2. A phenomenon that takes place within the prophet's soul.

3. A deeper view of reality.

The Theory of Glory (*Kavod*)

The first answer is known as "the theory of glory." It has taken a number of forms, and Halevi discusses them. The classic answer speaks of "the created voice," a concept used by Onkelos in his Aramaic translation of the Torah. A contemporary person may regard it as similar to the synthetic voice generated by a computer. A person, whom we will call Moses, can speak by typing on the computer's keyboard. This voice is Moses' voice, but not in the true meaning of the word. We can thus speak of "created voice" and "created light." These are the realities that God creates and utilizes, which do not express His essence, but constitute a mode of communication with the prophet.

To explain this approach, R. Sa'adiah Ga'on and others taught that the prophetic vision takes place not in the space-time reality, and not in the prophet's psychological world, but in a distinct reality, which Sa'adiah termed *ha-avir ha-sheni* (literally, the second atmosphere). Think, for example, of a hologram, a sort of picture that seems to hover in the air. Were I to attempt to touch it, I would discover that I was faced with an optical illusion. I cannot touch it, yet it exists. In R. Sa'adiah's view, prophecy is a kind of unique hologram that affects the prophet and has objective existence. In another sense, however, it differs from a hologram. The prophetic picture appears before us, but it is not located in the atmosphere. There is another reality beneath the physical atmosphere, a kind of "second atmosphere." It is generally closed to our eyes, but can open at particular times. Nahmanides' version of this approach brings us closer to the second answer. Nahmanides accepts the possibility of seeing angels, since they can take on a physical form, but their "physicality" differs from the one studied in physics.

Halevi accepts this approach in principle but does not try to build theories on it, as Sa'adiah does. He presents the problem in a larger context, and offers a surprising answer: in essence, even Moses' real voice is not his real voice. A good analogy might be the voice heard through a telephone receiver—amazingly similar to, yet not actually, the speaker's real voice. The speaker's actual voice does not travel across the telephone lines. It is coded, passed on in a completely different way, and deciphered. Only afterwards do we perceive the new synthetic creation. Halevi teaches us that the same process occurs when a person is standing before us and talking to us. Here too, encoding and deciphering are the essential tools of communication. The paradox which we posited regarding God is true of each and every person. We do not commit a new "sin" of personification when we ascribe a voice to God. We have committed the exact same sin by ascribing a voice to Moses. Halevi writes:

> For what does Moses use to speak to us, teach us and guide us? It is not his tongue, not his heart, nor is it his mind. All these are but tools for Moses, while Moses himself is a soul with the power of speech and consciousness, which is not a body and has no special boundaries (I:89).

Further, a person's actual appearance differs from what we see when we look at him. His body is a vessel, a sort of computer, which synthesizes voices in a marvelously accurate fashion. This is a process whereby the hidden thought, which is beyond our comprehension, is transformed into an audible voice. The essence of this process is unknown to us. Behind the scenes hides "the real Moses." Behind the brain is the brain's owner. There is a hidden being here, which for simplicity's sake we will call the soul. This is a being which does not exist in space, and it does not push aside other things that share its space. It does not exhibit the characteristics of physical objects. The opposite is true as well: "The thing would not be strained if the form of all the creatures in the world were contained in it." It creates a space of its own, and can contain an entire world within itself.

The Psychological Theory

As we have seen, Halevi's approach encompasses that developed by Sa'adiah. According to the "theory of glory," the prophet does not see a reality that is inside himself, but a different, incorporeal reality, created for him. This is a kind of private screening presented by God, not part of our daily reality. This reality of prophecy is not physical, yet the experience is real.

Another option is presented by Halevi at the beginning of Part IV. It can be understood in two different ways. According to one interpretation, prophecy does not occur in an external reality, but in a sort of personal psychological screen belonging to each prophet. This would later become Maimonides' approach. According to another interpretation, the prophet sees the true reality which hides behind our daily experience. In order to understand these approaches, however, we need a brief philosophical introduction, and therefore we will return to this discussion only after we have finished presenting the theory of divine attributes.

CHAPTER 35:
RELIGIOUS LANGUAGE

The Classic Theory of Divine Attributes

The theory of divine attributes was of crucial importance not only in medieval Jewish philosophy but also in Kabbalah and other literature. The roots of this debate can be traced to the Scriptures themselves, translations of the Scriptures, and the writings of our Sages. For example, Maimonides notes the story in tractate *Berakhot* about a person harshly criticized by R. Hanina for applying extra descriptive terms to God. In rabbinic writings we find ample analyses of the divine attributes and their meanings. For example, our Sages discuss the attributes of divinity as derived from the scriptural use of the divine names. This discussion is reflected in the *Kuzari*.

The theory of divine attributes reached its peak in the Middle Ages. Clearly, the sages of the period wished to underscore the battle against anthropomorphism, but this was not the central issue. Although Maimonides writes much about his objections to physical descriptions of God, he stresses his principal concern is not with an issue already raised and satisfactorily resolved, as in R. Sa'adiah's *Emunot Ve-De'ot*. In Maimonides' view, the problem lies not in the physical descriptions of God, but at a higher level. These descriptions or divine attributes must pass philosophical muster. Perhaps even more sophisticated terms such as wise, capable, living, omnipotent and omniscient also describe a human reality, albeit not as obviously. In fact, the wording and formulation of the divine attributes creates more complex religious and theological problems.

What can we say about God? This question addresses the essence of the theory of divine attributes. What led philosophers to take such extreme positions on this issue? We will focus our attention on one of the many pertinent factors: the idea of divine unity.

Divine Unity

Maimonides writes that the concept of divine unity is the axis of our faith. All of the Jewish religion revolves around this idea. The centrality of the commandment to declare God's unity, in the phrase "Hear O Israel, the Lord our God the Lord is One," illustrates and emphasizes the religious significance of this concept. The concept of divine unity can be interpreted in four different ways.

1. *Cardinal numerical unity.* God is one, not two or more.

2. *Ordinal numerical unity.* God is first, a point stressed in philosophy and paralleled in Scripture by the statement "I am first and I am last."

3. *Indivisibility.* Medieval philosophy emphasized the indivisibility of God, a focus that had powerful effect on the development of the theory of divine attributes. Unity means something that is not a composite. There is no compositeness in God's essence, and therefore physical representation of God is absolutely forbidden. The belief in God's unity compels us to read the biblical text more accurately and honestly, and, at times, to depart from its simple meaning. But the belief in divine unity not only forbids us to assume the existence of a divine anatomy, such as eyes and hands. It also prohibits the assumption of philosophical complexity. The culmination of this position appeared in the argument that no statement containing a subject and predicate may refer to God. If we claim that God is wise, we have given Him a particular quality. Philosophical thought struggled with the problem of creating a religious language without violating this principle. This philosophical problem is the source of the statements that God's wisdom is not separate from His essence, or that His wisdom is not additional to His essence, or that His wisdom is of a different genus than our own, or that He and His wisdom are one. (The danger inherent in the attributes was realized in Christian philosophy, which used them to justify the doctrine of the trinity.)

4. *Uniqueness.* Central to Maimonides' thought is the idea that God's oneness is absolutely different from any other. Unity becomes uniqueness. We may not attribute to God a quality used to describe a created being.

Halevi and Maimonides

To understand the approaches of these two great philosophers, we must first create a kind of catalogue, defining what may be said about someone or something, about a person or an object. Various philosophers, such as Maimonides, have used this approach, and each had his own manner of classification. We will briefly describe the various categories defined by these philosophers. They cover the following range of possibilities: accidental attributes, essential attributes, relational attributes, behavioral attributes and negative attributes

Accidental Attributes

To understand this concept, we will compare these qualities to their complement, essential qualities. We may say that John is blond or tall, but we can imagine John undergoing an operation and no longer being blond or tall. These qualities change in any case during the course of one's life. They are accidental attributes that do not define John's essence but merely attach themselves to it. To borrow again a phrase from Yeshayahu Leibowitz, we could say that to speak of the accidental attributes of a particular being is like speaking about its anatomy.

Essential Attributes

This is a much more limited group of attributes that actually define John. If one of these attributes were altered, the person before us would no longer be John. For example, if we were to change the fact that John is a rational, thinking being, he would no longer be John.

Philosophers agreed that accidental attributes could not be attributed to God, for those attributes imply the compound nature of the entity being described. On the surface, there seems no reason not to attribute essential attributes to God. Yet, as Maimonides argues, we cannot use essential attributes so easily because we are impaired by the limitations of human knowledge. This fact is expressed in the classic medieval adage *lu yeda'a-tiv, hayyitiv*—"if I understood Him, I would be Him." In other words, if I knew God's essence, I myself would be God. Only God can know His true essence.

When we objected to literal interpretations of the physical descriptions of God, we argued that God was beyond the perception of the senses. When we begin to doubt the possibility of knowing God's essential attributes, we are saying that God is beyond human perception and understanding. In the words of the religious poem, *An'im Zemirot*, "I speak of Thy glory, though I have not seen You; I imagine You, I characterize You, though I do not know You."

Relational Attributes

Relational attributes are beyond essential attributes. For example, if we say of John that he is a grandfather or an uncle, it is possible that a nephew was born to him without his knowing of it. It is therefore difficult to say that he has changed since becoming an uncle. We can posit relational attributes for God, but here again Maimonides objects. He maintains that any relationship between A and B necessarily implies that A and B share a common quality.

Attributes of Action

An'im Zemirot continues: "Your greatness and might are indicated by the power of Your actions. You have been imagined, though not in accord with Your essence; You have been described in accord with Your actions." The essential attributes ("in accord with Your essence") are inaccessible to man, but another path is open. God's attributes of action—"according to Your actions"—can be perceived. They are supplemented, as we shall see, by the negative attributes.

When describing attributes of action, we speak not directly about God but about His actions. This may be compared to our use of electricity in our kitchens. When it flows through various appliances, such as the oven and the refrigerator, it either heats or cools. We can learn many things about electricity, such as its magnetic and chemical effects, but we still do not know anything about its essence. Most of the biblical accounts of God describe His behavior, not His essence.

Negative Attributes

In speaking of negative attributes, we deny the possibility of ascribing attributes to God. Here, too, Maimonides has much to teach us. He argues that the very denial of divine attributes is itself informative. As an analogy, consider the game in which one player leaves the room and the others choose a concept. The player who left must identify a concept by asking a set number of questions. Even if he receives a negative answer to each question, he may still be able to identify the concept and win the game.

How is this possible? It resembles the statistical method known as lion trapping. We choose a continent, and divide the area into two parts. The lion must be in one of the halves. We determine in which half the lion is *not*, and again divide the remaining half into two parts. If we repeat the division many times, we will eventually "catch" the lion. The principle here is that we can use the negative attributes to gain knowledge. If we know where the lion is not, we will advance toward our goal.

What Is Negation?

Halevi nicely defines negation in his explanation of its use as a divine element. We use negation in everyday language. For example, we speak about a person as "intelligent" or "unintelligent." Of course, this negation is completely relative. Linguistic negation does not describe absolute negation in reality. The possibility of formulating things using opposites such as these teaches us that negation in and of itself does not express any absolute value. Negation is merely a linguistic form that can be used to create one term on the basis of another, in order to express the absence of a quality.

In many cases we use negation in a straightforward way. For example, we say that a person "does not see," meaning that he lacks the attribute of vision. At other times, however, a grammatically positive term conceals a negation within it. The word "blind" is a good example of this. It does not describe a positive quality. It actually points out the absence of a quality, the lack of the ability to see. Maimonides notes that many philosophers have fallen into this linguistic trap. For example, the Muslim theologians, whom Maimonides often disputed, made this mistake and lost sight of the difference between negation and positive description.

In addition to the negation of a possible situation or trait, there is another type of negation, which we will call, for now, infinite negation. This sort of negation does not assert that someone or something lacks a particular quality. Instead, it denies the very possibility that the quality might ever be applied. For example, when we say, "The wall can't see," we don't mean that the wall is blind and lacks a particular quality. Instead, we mean that the concept of seeing is wholly inapplicable to the wall. We can illustrate this with endless examples, in which the question itself becomes absurd. What is the color of the musical tone C? What is the sound of the cold? Although there are people who would use such imagery in their poetic language, we would argue simply that the property of color does not apply to sounds. We must develop the awareness that there are things to which we simply cannot apply certain paired descriptions such as hot and not hot, tall and not tall. Sometimes this is obvious. Still, we may be deceived and must use all of our intellectual powers to avoid falling into this trap.

Infinite negation, then, does not indicate that something is lacking; it is absolute negation. We must use this type of negation when talking about God. Here, however, we must apply another principle, that of value. If we say that God is alive, we seem to be describing God using a concept from human experience. Yet we do use this term, says Halevi, because we use it as a negative attribute. This description negates the application of the very human pair of words, life and death, to God. Halevi writes:

> When you say, "The stone is not wise," it does not follow that you would describe the stone as foolish. It is at too low a level to be described either as wise or foolish. So too, the Divine Being is too elevated to be described by the terms life and death. God is beyond these qualities, just as He is beyond light and darkness. If we were asked "Is the Divine Being bright or dark?" we would answer metaphorically: "Bright!" (II:2).

The complete, complex answer to the question—which really ought to be given—is that God is beyond all description but religious language points in a direction that leads us to choose, from each possible pair of words, the term denoting the higher value. Since we instinctively feel the superiority of light to darkness, we use metaphor and say that God is bright. The *haver* continues and explains that we would refer to the divinity as "bright," due to a

> fear that the questioner will think that whatever is not light is darkness. In truth, we ought to have responded: light and darkness apply only to physical bodies, but the Divine Being is not a body. Therefore, He should not be described in term of light and darkness except as a metaphor, or in order to negate an attribute that we consider a deficiency (ibid.).

To understand the meaning of negative attributes, I invite the reader to join me on an imaginary journey within the warm room which he currently occupies. We will there take a fresh look at the objects in our daily lives, while wearing unique glasses, earphones, scientific clothing and gloves that will present the world in accord with the theories which we study in physics, chemistry, etc. This unique garb will also enable us to grow and shrink, like Alice in Wonderland, in order to reach these otherwise invisible worlds. The only condition of this trip is that we take what we learn there seriously.

If we look through these glasses at the table, at the chair, etc., we will begin to see a strange world. Instead of objects we will see strange structures, until we reach the chemical elements and begin to see molecules, atoms and then a dense forest of sub-atomic particles. As R. Sa'adiah Ga'on expressed it, we reach a reality that is "finer"—less robust—than reality as we know it. In other words, on the way to these strange worlds we lose what we call the "physicality" of our concrete everyday world. In the room we hear sounds and see colors. On our journey we will discover that the harmony between the various sounds is merely a function of the relationships between the lengths of various sound waves, and that color is merely a different wavelength of light. The concrete world is merely a surface layer, and whenever we dig into it and go deeper, we lose more and more of our basic intuitions.

To illustrate, assume that we have shrunk to the point that we can travel on an electron. As noted above, our trip takes place in a warm room. We measured the temperature before setting out, and now that we have reached one of the electrons of the table, we will measure the temperature again. What result will we get?

Of course, we will get no result at all. Not because we do not know how to measure, but because the concept of temperature in that world is meaningless. Temperature describes a particular phenomenon in a world that contains molecules in perpetual movement, as we learned in physics. When we speak about a single sub-atomic particle, temperature has no place. The concept of temperature cannot be applied there. But this should not surprise us, since on this trip we have lost our sense of touch, our ability to discern color and virtually all of our conventional perceptual abilities. We have reached a state in which all of our normal frameworks of perception have disappeared. We might well be persuaded by that great early twentieth-century mathematician, Henri Poincare, who argued that particles are merely holes in absolute nothingness, holes filled with mathematical formulas. That is a disturbing thought, but is it more disturbing than colors being reduced to mathematical abstractions describing waves?

Is our perception incorrect? If we are mistaken, where is our mistake? Various philosophers try to save the warm room in which we began our journey, but we promised to be loyal to the scientific theories we learned in high school. These theories teach us, among other things, the negative attributes of many objects whose existence we never dreamed of at first. This is both the blessing and the curse of science. Science begins from the world close to us, from the world of the simple honest man, who believes in realism and plain logic, and ends in abstractions and theories that are far removed from our original perceptions. We encountered this reality in our search for scientific truth. How much more so is it present in our search for God. This feeling is expressed in our use of negative attributes in relation to God. God is distant, perhaps infinitely distant, from our perceptual channels.

What do we accomplish with the application of negative attributes? Maimonides teaches us that we create a system of negative attributes, which does not only concern itself with the neutralization of attributes, but also creates a certain concept of God, as a Being which is beyond the assignment of these attributes. Let me give you an example involving the concept of time.

What do we mean when we say that God is eternal? Of course, on a basic level we mean to teach that God has existed forever. He did not come into existence at a particular time. He has no biography as people do. That much is clear. But Maimonides teaches us that we must reach a higher level in order to understand that the category of time does not apply to God at all. God is beyond time. This understanding that God is beyond time entails tremendous effort and intellectual development. We may come to understand the full meaning of this statement through an examination of man. Man's body exists in space and time, while his soul does not exist in space, but only in time. Emotional episodes, such as fear or joy, can be "located" in time, but not in space. We could say that the fear preceded the joy, or that the joy preceded the fear. However, since our spiritual life does not exist in space, we certainly cannot say that the joy is to the left of the fear. This is an example of a reality that stands outside a certain category. God is likewise beyond the categories of space and time. Incidentally, this understanding helps us deal with the question of divine foreknowledge and free will. From the divine perspective, our future is in essence an eternal present.

Divine Perfection

Finally, we will discuss an attribute to which philosophers of all generations have been sympathetic, the attribute of perfection. We can think of
God as the ultimate, perfect being. Maimonides referred repeatedly to this
divine element, particularly in his thirteen principles of faith. In his *Guide*,
Maimonides explains that we choose the attributes we are willing to use
in reference to God first and foremost based on a desire to lead people to
recognize God's perfection. This teaches us that, in Maimonides' view, the
attribute of perfection is a psychological and pedagogical attribute.

The Doctrine of Divine Attributes Today: The Language of Religion

Is the theory of divine attributes relevant today? Surprisingly, the philosophical discussion of the theory of divine attributes has shown much
more vitality than other philosophical discussions. One factor contributing
to that trend is the modern interest in the linguistic aspect of philosophy.
Philosophy today is more and more aware not only of issues related to
proving claims and constructing systems of thought—its classic goals—
but also of the language used to formulate these arguments.

This linguistic trend reached its zenith (or what some would call its
nadir) in the argument that philosophy's only role is to clarify the language
used to formulate statements in various fields. Philosophy of science, for
example, deals with scientific language. These preoccupations had a
destructive effect on some areas of philosophy, but they taught the importance of taking note of religious language. In that context, the theory of
divine attributes developed into a way of understanding the language we
use to speak about God and how that language differs from, say, scientific
language.

We spoke earlier about divine unity as the dividing point between the
Creator and His creatures. Many discussions in medieval Jewish philosophy revolved around this point. Thinkers were divided into two camps:
those who spoke of polarity and those who spoke of analogy. The first
group maintained that the difference between the Creator and His creatures
was absolute, and no divine element may be ascribed to His creatures. The
second group argued that the creatures had characteristics bearing "fingerprints" of God, and we may therefore speak of analogy between them. To
describe this analogy, medieval philosophers used the term "relation"

(*yahas*). We use these attributes to compare human wisdom to divine wisdom, but we continually point out the tremendous gap that must necessarily exist between them. That gap may be viewed in two ways. The first is that the very relationship between the Creator and His creatures produces the divine "fingerprints," and that is all we can say. This was the view of Gersonides (Rabbi Levi ben Gershom). The second possibility is that the relationship between the Creator and His creatures is comparable to the relationship between the infinite and the finite. This was the view of Rabbi Hasdai Crescas.

Gersonides

We can explain Gersonides' approach with a simple example. Imagine that you are looking at a painting in an art gallery and hear the person behind you say it is "a sad picture." This demonstrates that we can use the word "sad" in two ways. The picture may be sad, but it is sad in a different way than is the person looking at it. We ascribe to the picture a quality it certainly does not possess, for the qualities of pictures can be described in terms of perspective, color and other physical realities. Still, it is not absurd to attribute "sadness" to a picture. What we mean, though, is that the picture creates a sad response in us. Similarly, we can attribute wisdom to God. We mean that He is the ultimate source of human wisdom, though that source itself is so exalted that we cannot describe it in our language.

Crescas

R. Hasdai Crescas likewise believed in analogy, but he argued that the concept of the infinite is at the center of the analogy. Infinity has various meanings. It is a basic kabbalistic concept, expressing the idea that God is beyond any characteristic within the sphere of human comprehension. In this sense, the Kabbalists are more extreme than Maimonides. Nevertheless, these same Kabbalists maintained that we can and must create a religious language. They did so using the doctrine of the *sefirot*. (The kabbalistic approach itself is beyond the scope of our present discussion.)

Crescas bases the difference between divine attributes and human attributes on the unbridgeable gap between the finite and the infinite. He argues, in effect, for a sort of mathematical proportionality: Man's wisdom is to God's wisdom as the finite is to the infinite.

The Indigent's Song: Our Religious Language

> Bring my multitude of songs near to You
> And my prayer shall come close to You.
> May my praise be a crown of glory for Your head
> And may my prayer be accepted as incense.
> May an indigent's song be as precious to You
> As a song sung over Your offerings.

These final passages of *An'im Zemirot* can be understood in accord with its simple meaning but can also be interpreted mystically. On the simple level, our song is the "song of the indigent," for the Temple has been destroyed. We nevertheless plead that our poor song be accepted just as God accepted the song of the Levites in the Temple.

However, the passage has mystical significance as well. The indigent's song is the song sung in man's own poor language. The entire philosophical endeavor is an indigent's song that can never succeed in describing reality. This idea is expressed in parallel in the writings of three of modern Judaism's most profound thinkers: Rabbi Nahman of Breslov, Rav Kook, and Martin Buber. Each one independently claimed that the construction of all of these theological concepts is only a temporary stage, and when man reaches a higher level of development, he will abandon these interim concepts as overly corporeal. This was expressed by Rabbi Nahman of Breslov when he said that in the future we will repent over our repentance. From our loftier perspective, we will look at theological intellectual definitions as the creation of teenagers who investigated the issues on a superficial level and created a philosophy for adolescents. When all is said and done, this is the deeper meaning of the final sentence of *An'im Zemirot*, in which we ask God to excuse our use of our religious language, for we use it only to express our love for Him: "May my speech be pleasant to You, for my soul longs for You."

CHAPTER 36:
THE PRINCIPLES OF FAITH
(*IKKAREI EMUNAH*)

David Kaufmann, a leading nineteenth-century Jewish scholar, showed that as as part of his discussion of prayer, Halevi also developed a system of principles of faith (III:17). The principles are described and affirmed in the prayer that follows recitation of the *Shema*: "After this [reciting the *Shema*], the pious ought to recite the principles through which the Jewish faith will be perfected." Juxtaposing extracts from the prayer and the principle each affirms produces the following list:

The Prayer	The Principle
1. "Truly, You are the Lord our God"	Acknowledging God's sovereignty
2. "Your Name has existed forever"	His eternal existence
3. "[You have been] the support of our forefathers"	Providential guidance of our forefathers
4. "Happy is the man who obeys your Commandments"	He is the giver of the Torah
5. "Truly You redeemed us from Egypt"	The Exodus from Egypt as proof of this

Rabbi Isaac Aramah similarly saw the prayers between the *Shema* and the *Amidah* (the Silent Devotion) as a summary of the principles of faith. These truths form our response to the divine message of the *Shema*. We will not elaborate on this idea here. Instead, we will return to principles two through five in Maimonides' classic formulation, which provide an excellent summary of the basic elements of the theory of divine attributes. Maimonides thirteen principles (except for the fifth) can be divided into three definite sections:

1–4: God and His attributes.

6–9: The Torah as divine revelation.

10–13: Reward, punishment, and redemption.

The fifth principle, as we shall see, is actually an independent section, constituting a sort of practical-pragmatic definition of the essence of the individual's faith.

The First Principle: God's Necessary Existence

We will explain the first principle in accord with Maimonides' ideas in his *Code* (*Sefer Madda*) and in his *Guide*. We have already noted Maimonides' opposition to the use of positive attributes in relation to God. Nevertheless, Maimonides allows for use of one very important positive concept that conceals a negative concept within it: God's existence is necessary.

I will attempt to explain this concept with a simple analogy. Recall how we explained the concept of creation through the analogy of a film, and think of us as creatures projected in a film onto a screen. On this model, our world is a three-dimensional film, not the two-dimensional ones we are used to. We can learn much about the world from this comparison. We, the protagonists of the film, are trying to understand our reality. We develop science, history, psychology, etc., in order to become familiar with the world of the film, which is our reality. But even if we succeed in developing these fields, our perception of reality will be incomplete if we do not realize that there is someone or something "outside" of our film which is projecting us onto the screen. We must realize that even if we are capable of action, and can choose to change the screenplay (in other words, have "free will"), our existence will still be dependent upon the person activating the projector. We will never truly understand our reality unless we realize that our existence is secondary compared with the existence of the person activating the projector. If we were to imagine that this person died or that the projector broke, we would disappear. Yet nothing that occurs in the film can harm the projector.

This relationship differentiates between two types of existence: the world, which is contingent, and God, Whose existence is necessary. That our world is contingent means that our world is a reality which does not have its own independent existence, and it requires something outside itself to make its existence possible. Through this analysis, we understand something of the philosophical significance of the Tetragrammaton. This name teaches us not only the eternal nature of God as existing concurrently in the past, present and future. It also teaches us the true essence of God's statement, "I will be what I will be," which means that His existence is enough to sustain Him. He does not require anything outside of Himself in order to exist.

This concept is described in various forms throughout Jewish philosophical literature. In Hasidism, we find the astute observation that our existence resembles the spoken, rather than the written, word. If the writer of the word disappears, the word remains, but the spoken word exists only as long as the speech continues. Even if the speaker were to draw out the word for a long time, it would only exist for as long as he was speaking. R. Israel Ba'al Shem Tov applied that interpretation to the verse in Psalms "Forever, O Lord, Your word stands in the heavens." The heavens exist only because they are a manifestation of the divine Word. The existence of the heavens is thus similar to that of the spoken word. This interpretation also uncovers a deeper meaning in the blessing, "Blessed are You . . . our God, at whose word everything came into being." The divine speech that created our reality did not cease with the completion of creation. That original speech continues to exist through every object and organism in our world.

All existence is a chain. Each link is a stage dependent upon a previous stage. But the links, however many, do not account for the fact that the chain remains suspended and is not falling. It remains suspended only because it has an outside support. The chain is contingent and its supporter is God, Whose existence is necessary. The proof that something must exist outside of the chain to support it is, in essence, the proof of God's existence.

Another version of the same idea is found in the writings of R. Hasdai Crescas. Consider again the analogy of film, which emphasizes that God's relationship with the world is not expressed solely through the creation of the world at one point in history. Rather, God is the reason for the world's continued existence. The film does not become an independent entity after the projectionist begins to project it onto the screen. It must continue to be projected in order for it to continue to exist. The explosions in the film are not dangerous to the viewers. In essence, what we are describing here are two levels of existence. The entire world, with all its physical and spiritual components, needs God in order to exist.

The Second Principle

Our belief in divine unity finds expression in the second of Maimonides' principles. As we have seen, this principle has various meanings. Maimonides stresses that unity does not mean only "uniqueness" (one as opposed to many). It also means "oneness" (unity as opposed to complexity). If we carefully examine this principle, we will discover that God is the only "one" that exists.

Let us set out on a journey in quest of oneness. We will soon find our mission is fraught with difficulties. True, many things in our world are called one. For example, we speak of one humanity, but humanity, of course, is composed of many individuals, of many people. In other words, the unity of humanity is abstract and conceptual. A person visiting a school enters a room and is told that he is observing one class. The unity of the class is not in the children. It is in our mind. We create unity by projecting our thoughts onto the world. We could easily divide the class in half, according to reading levels, or those who wear glasses and those who don't, light-haired and dark-haired students, etc. The reality would have remained the same. Yet, the unity about which I spoke earlier would disappear. This is the unity of species and types, which Maimonides declines to classify as true unity.

The foregoing instances have involved abstractions, but the situation is no different when we consider objects that appear to be a single unit. We see a single human being standing before us. There is unity here, but is it perfect unity? This is doubtful, since the unity is composed of such immense complexity. Is man indeed one? No, because man has an anatomy. We can speak about his limbs and organs, his cells, his molecules, etc. The problem does not lie only with man's complexity. Assume a chemist were to present us with one unified block of pure and totally homogenous chemical material. This pure chemical body can also be divided. All physical bodies have the capacity for division, as a result of our presence in space. Geometry allows for infinite divisions.

In other words, whatever we observe can be magnified into larger and larger categories, or can be divided infinitely into smaller parts. As early as Greek times, people spoke about the atom. The etymology of the word atom is "not subject to division" (*a-tom*). Yet science divided the atom, each time discovering more elemental particles, which are of a divisible character in three different ways: there are many particles, they have many characteristics, and they are themselves, perhaps, complex. No one knows the limits of the process. Are there particles that cannot be divided? Perhaps. But even if they exist, they are not unitary; they are complex. They have a mass, an electrical charge, momentum, etc. If that were not enough, recent research has discovered other characteristics, called "color" and "taste," that are beyond our comprehension. There are particles that are identical in all their recognizable characteristics, and yet they behave differently. These theories suggest that additional characteristics exist which we cannot perceive.

Thus, we see that in our world there is no unity. We have the unity of the number one, but that unity also is abstract. When we create one from many, we ourselves are combining disparate elements. We are placing all these parts in imaginary brackets in our mind, creating compartments and groups. They exist only in an abstract sense. We view them as unitary, but there is no true unity in the world. It is just one of the conceptual constructs that we create in our minds.

Maimonides' conclusion is interesting. Our recognition of God as One is enough to make Him completely different from anything else that exists in the world. The trait of unity is attributable to God, and to God alone.

R. Bahya ibn Pakuda also develops this concept in his book *Hovot Ha-Levavot* (Duties of the Heart) in the section entitled, "The Gate of Unity." He distinguishes between "passing unity"—that is, the quality of something that is unitary only on the surface—and true unity. Maimonides accepts this idea but goes further. As we have seen, he emphasizes the concept of God's necessary existence, in contrast to the contingent existence of all else. The two approaches differ in their views of which divine element is most basic. According to one view, we say, essentially, that "God is one," meaning God equals one. According to the other view, the elemental attribute is that of existence: "I will be what I will be." God's existence is necessary.

The Third Principle: Negation of Corporeality

Maimonides' third principle of faith negates the possibility of divine corporeality, but this principle must be elaborated on. Maimonides teaches us that God is neither a physical body nor a physical force. In this way, he seeks to warn us against pantheistic views that connect God with the world. Some philosophers perceive God as the soul of the world, but

Judaism is built on the premise that God is absolutely outside of the world. He does not need the world, and He is not connected with it. We must not relate to God as a kind of magnetic field. This pantheism is sometimes expressed in a very innocent way, by those who speak of God in terms of nature, a cosmic force, etc. Thus, for example, in the movie *Star Wars*, the hero saves the world, using the powers given him by a mysterious power that he calls "the Force." Man must achieve a kind of harmony with it, and then he connects with the Force. The premise in the movie is that there exists in nature a force in addition to the electro-magnetic, a force that we can perceive. That approach reflects a particular idolatrous tradition.

Although Kabbalah and Hasidism speak of a God who is present in the entire cosmos, these positions are not identical. Hasidism wishes to teach that there is holiness in nature, but not that nature and holiness are identical. Habad Hasidism, for example, teaches that God fills all the worlds, but He also surrounds all the worlds. In other words, holiness finds expression in nature, but there is holiness that is absolutely outside of nature. This principle serves to deter us from following mistaken views.

The Fourth Principle: Eternal Existence

We have already discussed negative attributes at some length. The best example of a negative attribute is that of eternity. In Maimonides' view, God's eternal existence does not mean that He exists in time but is immortal rather than mortal. It means, rather, that God exists outside the realm of time altogether, that time has no meaning for Him. This concept is related to the age-old question of foreknowledge and free choice, an issue we will discuss later on.

The Four Elements

The four divine elements—existence, unity, non-corporeality and eternity —are interrelated. The philosophers saw their interrelationship as analogous to that of mathematical statements linked in a ring of equivalence. Statement one can be proven on the basis of statement two, but statement two can then be proven on the basis of statement one. This proves that they are expressions of the same truth. It follows that the four attributes are really one.

This idea is parallel to R. Sa'adiah Ga'on's central claim, that the multiplicity of divine elements is a result of the problems of human language. The limitations of language cause us to use various words, such as alive, willing, and capable. If we were of higher intelligence, we would be able to say alive-willing-capable in one word. For, in truth, God has only one attribute.

The Fifth Principle

Maimonides' fifth principle is essential to our understanding of monotheism. This principle teaches us that our relationship with God is not only intellectual. It is, first and foremost, a relationship that finds expression in action. Assume the existence of superhuman creatures or spiritual beings. Does that possibility pose a danger to monotheism? The fifth principle explains the boundaries of faith in this area. Simply asserting that such other beings exist does not necessarily constitute idolatry. It depends on how man perceives these beings and on the practical ramifications of that perception. Jewish monotheism means that we do not worship any other element in the cosmos. We do not worship any creature. We worship the Creator. In the final analysis, the issue of worship is what defines monotheism. Idolatry can be based on a very spiritual and abstract idea, which was nonetheless drawn into practical idol worship. The most outstanding example is Buddhism. The Buddha's philosophy was extremely abstract. In a sense, he could even have been accused of atheism. Yet, his approach created a new paganism. People who are unaware of the very abstract philosophy of the religion's originator will enter a Buddhist temple and see statues and sacrificial rites. Thus, a very abstract, philosophical religion, containing definite elements of truth, may be expressed in practice through idolatrous decadence. This is typical of many Eastern religions. It echoes in the voices of the meditation masters who demand a sort of symbolic sacrifice while at the same time denying any element of idolatry in their practices. Their intentions may be good, but their consequences prove that without the fifth principle, extreme abstraction encourages paganism. (I:96–97)

We will return to the fifth principle when we discuss the phenomenon of idolatry. Now, however, we must focus on an incident connected to this—the sin of the golden calf.

The Dangers to Monotheism

The sin of the golden calf impaired not the first principle but the fifth. Monotheism constantly faces two dangers. The first is idolatry, paganism: "You shall have no other gods before Me." The second can be termed fetishism: "You shall not make for yourself any statue or graven image."

This analysis is the basis for the Halevi's interpretation of the sin of the golden calf, which requires portraying the sin in a way that differs from first appearances. This portrayal is now a popular one, but that is thanks to the *Kuzari*. The sin, says Halevi, is not rebellion against God or an attempt to revive idolatry. Indeed, from a subjective point of view, from the perspective of the people, the nation did not sin. Rather they tried to worship God in this manner. Yet, despite this positive desire, the action they took contains an objective mistake, perhaps even a sin. The sin of the golden calf should be understood as an offense against the fifth principle, a sin of fetishism. This was not a betrayal of the God who took us out of Egypt. It was a transgression of the prohibition against making idols, idols that—whatever the intention—fail to represent God and constitute, instead, different, improper forms of serving Him.

The Kuzari's position is clearly the obvious interpretation of the text, since it points to the essence of the calf as a sort of throne for God. The golden calf is parallel to and contrasting with the Ark. The Ark and the cherubs constitute the true throne, which symbolizes God's continued accompaniment of the Israelites on all their journeys, even after they left the place of revelation, Mount Sinai. But despite the structural similarity between the calf and the ark, they remain very different. The calf contains an element of paganism, a remnant of a world that the liberated nation ought to have left behind. None of that is present in the Ark and the cherubs.

The Essence Of The Sin

Interpretations of the golden calf episode fall into three broad categories:

A. The people sinned because they were unable to accept an abstract form of divine worship, one divorced from physical images and symbols. In their minds, these symbols constituted giant magnets attracting positive divine influences. Sometimes man sins out of love, like a bull that enters a china shop to buy a gift for his beloved. It is the folly of the person who, though guided by good intentions, does not know how to express them appropriately.

B. The sin is the result of not fulfilling the divine command. The Israelites did not follow the divine instructions. The essential difference between holiness and defilement lies in the faithful fulfillment of the divine command.

C. The Israelites transgressed a commandment that is, in fact, grounded in reason. This idea is also expressed in Halevi's parable about the doctor and his impersonator. We must recognize that there are connections and interactions in reality that man cannot rationally understand. We cannot rely simply on untested or unexamined assumptions that come from common sense. With openness and humility, we must face facts and discoveries that alter our perceptions. In retrospect, we will recognize that our previous positions were not rational but rather a result of our imaginative faculties.

These three principles were developed by different commentators. The first approach was developed thoroughly by R. Ovadiah Seforno, who saw the sin of the golden calf as a fall from abstract consciousness to a need for tangible symbols. According to this explanation, the Tabernacle and the worship focused therein were not part of God's original plan. Originally, God distanced the Jewish people from any relation to a tangible, physical symbol. Now, after the sin, the Jewish people evidenced a need for the physical and tangible in divine worship, and God provided them a way to meet that need. This approach may reflect the opinion of Maimonides.

The second position is formulated in principle by various commentators, who emphasized that the essence of keeping the Torah lies only in performing the will of God.

The third opinion is represented by Halevi, who reiterates it later on (III:23). The tabernacle and the cherubs represent a different causality, not a natural one. This position would later find expression in kabbalistic literature as well. Halevi writes:

> All this came to them at the advice of the magicians and talisman masters among them, who thought that the worship that they worshipped based on their imaginations was actually close to the true worship. But their path was truly that of the simpleton we mentioned earlier (I:89) who entered the physician's pharmacy and killed people with the same drugs that formerly had cured them. (I:97).

The fact is that divine commands are not arbitrary. The apparently meaningless command entails a deeper meaning that cannot always be understood. When a person disobeys God he not only commits a sin.

He also destroys a reality that he cannot properly understand. Halevi formulated this difference succinctly when he said that "the source of faith is the source of rebellion."

The Eternal Covenant

The sin of the golden calf stands at the center of the debate regarding the eternal or transient nature of the covenant. This issue lay at the heart of all our religious polemics. Christian theology, and, to a certain extent, Muslim theology as well, claimed that the Jews were chosen by God but then rejected by Him because of their sin. Halevi teaches us a paradoxical truth. It is the sin of the golden calf that teaches us the eternity of the covenant. It was a horrible sin. Our sages see it as an appalling betrayal, immediately following the establishment of the covenant. Nevertheless, the covenant was not annulled, and God forgave the Jewish people. The very intensity of the sin shows, oddly enough, the eternity of the covenant.

CHAPTER 37:
SCRIPTURAL SEMANTICS:
THE DIVINE NAMES (IV: 1–9)

In the fourth section (IV: 1–9), Halevi interprets the various divine names used in the Bible.

E-lohim (IV:1)

We begin, as did Halevi, with the divine name E-lohim. This choice is not arbitrary. This name expresses the concept of God that man may discover not through prophecy but through the application of his logic and intellect, without direct divine assistance. As already explained on many occasions, man may reach God in two ways: through logic, which Halevi calls *hakashah*, and through intuition, which he calls *ta'am* (IV:17). This refers to a direct human experience, as opposed to an indirect, logical conclusion that God exists. *Ta'am*, of course, pertains to prophecy, but it is not limited to the prophetic sphere. Halevi explains that this experience occurs at the encounter between the simple, humble individual and the prophet. "Their souls find repose in their complete faith that they received from the prophet. Yet the masses are not drawn after [the philosophers] . . . seeing as the truth had been revealed to the masses as a sort of prophetic vision" (ibid.).

The terms *ta'am* and *hakashah* originate in the Hebrew translation of the Kuzari by R. Judah Ibn Tibbon. R. Judah Ibn Samuel, in his translation, uses the words *hush* and *hekesh*. The terms used in classical translations of Jewish texts often have become an integral part of the Jewish philosophical tradition.

The term E-lohim can help us pinpoint the difference between "the God [E-lohim] of Abraham, Isaac and Jacob" and the "god of Aristotle" (IV:16). The great philosophers in their investigations achieved the perception of God as E-lohim. But this understanding was also reached by all nations, from the most primitive to the most sophisticated. The recognition of a higher power is a universal phenomenon, common to all places and periods, since the beginning of human existence. However, this universal character also teaches us much about how the concept is understood. The pagan idol worshipper achieved some understanding of what exists beyond his sensory perceptions. Yet, he did not actually reach a perception of God. This is demonstrated by the fact that the pagan never discovered the unity of the Creator. The pagan searched for God, but he found His servants and was content to look no further.

The name E-lohim is applied in the Bible to mundane figures as well, such as the ruler or the judge. That is because they are individual instances of a larger principle denoted by E-lohim, namely, power and sovereignty, particularly powers we cannot perceive with our senses because they exist in a realm beyond our palpable reality. Thus, this name is an instance in which we use one term to express a number of ideas. In this case, we apply the semantic principle known in Jewish thought as *bi-khlal u-ve-yehud*— a generalized or a particular meaning of a word. The word E-lohim refers generally to the powers that operate in our world, and refers in particular to the ruler of the entire world. A neutral term like "E-lohim" makes our relationship with other cultures possible. How, then, do we explain how we differ from pagan idolatry and other religions? We share a common, almost neutral term, E-lohim, which we all use. But like a person returning to his home on a stormy day, we must be careful not to track into the house the philosophical mud we have contended with outside.

Pagan idolatry recognized the forces of nature and enslaved itself to them. Much of pagan mythology is merely the anthropomorphism of natural events, such as climatic phenomena. The death of Tammuz or of Adonis represent the change of seasons and the withering of plant life. The same is true of the other forces of nature. This anthropomorphism is retained in abstract Greek philosophy. In Aristotelian philosophy, we find an explanation of the migration of the stars, or, more specifically, the spheres in which, according to the theory, the stars were located. According to the Greeks, the explanation was that every star has a force, a soul or intellect, that propels it. These are the souls of the separate spheres or intellects of medieval philosophy.

For Aristotelian philosophy the concept E-lohim became identical with the concept of "unmoved mover." Philosophy inherited the pagan perceptions and retained them in the post-pagan cultural world, while giving them a philosophical interpretation. The common denominator between the philosophical and pagan models is that they both recognized the existence of super-human forces that rule the world.

The philosopher who speaks at the beginning of the Kuzari believes without a doubt in the oneness of God. This is a legacy from the philosophical-religious synthesis created by Alexandrian Jewry. God is part of the scriptural heritage. Indeed, without the Scriptures, the philosophical development of the world would have been drastically different. If we delve into the philosophy of Aristotle, for example, we will notice that despite the special place reserved for the concept of E-lohim, his identification of E-lohim with the unmoved mover actually means that the existence of many gods is possible. Each god is in charge of one sphere and the star or stars inside it. These are clearly mythological remnants that have penetrated into the most abstract Greek philosophy.

Halevi relates to this question in Part V:

> What led the philosophers to the premise that divinity could be divided into many levels was their investigation of the movement of the heavenly spheres, which they counted and found to be over forty. . . . They came to the conclusion that these movements came from free will, and this proved that each of them came from a soul, and that every soul's origin is in an intellect, and this intellect is an angel, separate from the material, and these intellects they called gods (V:21).

Classic philosophical thought was founded upon the Greek principles of physics and mathematics. They are characterized by the absence of any concept of inertia. This early physics offered no explanation of why an object in motion, like a sphere or a star, continues to move. There was a need to posit a constant reason for the movement. Today, we explain continued movement through the principle of inertia, but Aristotle did not recognize this principle and therefore assumed the existence of souls that propel the heavenly bodies. These souls are guided by tendencies which can be termed "intelligent." This is the origin of the system of the souls and the incorporeal intellects.

Halevi's view, and Maimonides' thereafter, teaches that philosophy became idolatry. Halevi felt that all the theories about the angels and the constellations were merely "intricacies that help to sharpen the mind, not to recognize the truth, and the one who is enticed in the end becomes a heretic" (V:21). Maimonides also thought that this was the way humanity moved away from belief in one god to idolatry. It is interesting to note that this was also the position of Aristotle in one of his lost dialogues, a book that was not known in the Middle Ages. He perceived paganism as the remnants of a philosophy that had developed in an earlier civilization before it was destroyed. But we can construct an opposite model. It was the pagan heritage which caused Aristotle to formulate laws of movement according to which the planets move because gods move them. The monotheistic philosophers thought that the movers were merely angels.

Aristotle's cosmic approach was overturned with the advent of new physics, and the discoveries of Galileo and Newton. Since then, the astronomical system has been perceived not as a system of living bodies, but as a very complex system similar to the inner workings of a complex clock. As Newton explained, this system makes sense only if we assume the existence of a superior watchmaker who wound it up in the first place.

But Newton's revolution is also outdated. Relativity and quantum physics inform us that the truth may be much more complicated, and the watch model is not at all satisfactory. Now it seems possible that human awareness may have an effect on the "winding up" of our world.

Thus we see that the unity of God was a problem in the Aristotelian philosophical system. Later, at the beginning of the fifteenth century, R. Hasdai Crescas expressed his firm conviction that there is absolutely no possibility of proving divine unity as a matter of philosophy. He bolstered the view expressed by Halevi here. The concept of divine unity comes from faith, the very content of the *Shema* prayer.

As Halevi implies, from the philosophical position it would be easy to reach a kind of aristocracy of gods. What was missing here was the concept of a highest god, or "God of the gods." The name E-lohim allows us to formulate our conflict with paganism. The nations of the world use the name "gods" when they speak of the powers that rule the world, but their perspective is always specific. Each god is a partial power, an expression or an explanation of a particular natural phenomenon. They saw the gods in the phenomena, for they perceived each phenomenon as itself and not as an expression of its source. We can assume that if the idol worshippers had known about electromagnetic fields, there would have been enough people to worship them. They certainly would not have felt that what they saw was only part of the whole system, and that God must be sought outside the system as a source for the entire system. This is the "God of the gods," the source of all the forces. The belief in divine unity compels us to look for the source of the entire system, but that source lies outside the system—as distinct from the view of the idol worshippers who believed that one could worship the forces and affect them magically. In that way, the forces of nature became gods for them.

There are two ways in which the use of language permits us to emphasize the differences between our own view and views we oppose. The Scriptures use both:

1. We use the name E-lohim because it is true that there are forces in nature beyond the phenomena. Nevertheless, we believe in one God, who is behind and beyond all phenomena. He is the E-lohim, or, if you insist, "the God of gods."

2. We give a new meaning to the collective term E-lohim. Let me give you an example to explain what I mean. Reuben and Simeon are arguing about the origin of a certain object. Reuben claims that a group of people manufactured it. Simeon knows that not to be true, for a single individual, Judah, is responsible for the object. When Judah approaches, Simeon says to Reuben, "Here comes the group." The Scriptures took a term that was originally collective and transformed it to the representation of unity, a unity that supersedes all the forces in the world. The word underwent a transformation, which made its use possible by monotheists as well.

The Tetragrammaton

The essential quality of the name E-lohim is its generality. The main difference between it and the Tetragrammaton (usually rendered in English as "Lord") is comparable to the difference between a proper and a common noun. This distinction is not merely grammatical. It also has an emotional impact upon us. We can relate in all kinds of ways to strangers that we happen to see on the street, but the central expression of our acquaintance with them and the prerequisite for verbal contact is that we know their name. Of course, we can speak to them as a passenger speaks to a driver or as a cashier to a customer, but that type of interaction is not what one would call personal acquaintance. Learning the other's name is akin to the transition from speaking about someone far away, a "he," to speaking to someone close, a "thou." The phrasing of the blessing, "Blessed are you, Lord" expresses the creation of a personal relationship and direct connection with God. The prophet, in contrast to the philosopher, knows Him directly. The knowledge of God is one of the marks of the Jewish nation, and it allows for the calling of God's name, for prayer, and for the hope of divine response.

In his *Sefer Ha-Shem* ("Book of The Noun"), R. Abraham Ibn Ezra analyzed the differences between proper and common nouns. He also demonstrated that the Scriptures were careful to preserve these distinctions. For example, common nouns are never preceded by the definite article. In Hebrew, it is correct to use the term "the E-lohim," but "the" can never precede the Tetragrammaton. A proper noun is not subject to declension, nor does it take the plural form.

Medieval grammarians compared the relationship between the Hebrew consonantal alphabet and the supplementary vowel markings to the relationship between bodies and souls. This is because one written word may potentially have a number of meanings, depending on the vowels affixed to the letters. A word without vowels is like a body without a soul. It is not yet alive. But the letters of the Tetragrammaton, Halevi teaches, are themselves like souls. Halevi adds a trifling but very important point. We are forbidden to pronounce the Tetragrammaton, and its expression was always a unique one. That is because the Tetragrammaton is made up of a combination and arrangement of letters that are quite difficult to pronounce together. In addition, the appropriate vowels for the Tetragrammaton are unknown to us.

We can now return to the difference between the two types of nouns through a different analogy. A blind man tries to master the streets of the city in which he lives. With great effort, he will succeed in doing so perfectly or almost perfectly. Nevertheless, there remains a difference between the blind man and the man who sees the city with his eyes. That is the difference between the philosopher and the prophet. As philosophers, we grope in the dark and attempt to construct a map of the city. We have reached the conclusion that God exists, but as philosophers we cannot know God personally and directly. The blind philosopher knows God in the general sense represented by the name E-lohim. The direct address to God of the sighted prophet, the unmediated encounter between God and man, finds expression in the Tetragrammaton. The God of the Jews is not the God known to the blind philosopher: "All those who walk in the path of the divine Torah are drawn after those who have the prophetic *vision*" (IV:17).

There is yet another component to the difference between prophecy and philosophy. The blind gropings of the philosopher, though usually successful, inevitably lead to the trap "that produced heresy and worthless [religious] approaches." The examples are many and as varied as the history of ideas. We will mention only two, both cited by Halevi. The first is the mistake of the dualists, those who believed in the existence of two gods, such as the Persian religion and later the Gnostic groups, who believed in the existence of two divine entities. The second is the error of another group, the Jahariya, who believed that God exists but only as a physical force, bringing us back to the third of the thirteen principles. These are pitfalls in the path toward finding a logical solution to the eternal questions. Of all the human attempts to find God, the finest of all was the philosophical way. It was powerful, logically consistent and very careful to avoid errors. In fact, it did reach the truth, though not the whole truth, for the philosophers sometimes reached partial and incorrect conclusions. As we have already seen many times, the god of the philosophers does not know, and is not interested in, man. The adherent of the philosophers' beliefs therefore has found neither religion nor existential meaning. Here we return to the Kuzari's response to the philosopher's presentation at the beginning of the book. The importance of truth is measured by its ability to create devotion. "This intuitive knowledge [*ta'am*] leads one who experiences it to [be willing to] give up his soul and die for his love, [while] the logical knowledge [*hakashah*] of God demands only an obligation to raise God up as long as it does no harm and one does not suffer from it" (IV:16). The final test of truth lies in the sanctification of God's name in its two senses: sanctification by man, in his willingness to suffer for his beliefs, and sanctification by God Himself, through the final redemption.

The Power of Language

We have spoken of prophecy as a way of arriving at the knowledge of God, but there is another way to do so. It is through the received tradition, by accepting the testimony of one who has attained prophecy. This indirect encounter with prophecy can indeed provide man certainty in his knowledge of God. This phenomenon is most evident in the "secondary" phenomena that accompany prophecy. If we think of prophecy as a fire, then these phenomena are the smoke that informs us of its presence. These phenomena are known to us by various names: *Kavod, Shekhinah, Malkhut, Eish,* and so on. These were supernatural phenomena that appeared when the divine presence alit on a person.

As we have already seen, the theory of *Kavod* suggests that the prophetic vision takes place on a different level of reality. It may be understood as a hologram that exists in some other atmosphere. They are seen, but they are not real in the physical sense of the word. An audio tape or a video camera could not record them. Still, they exist and bear witness to the existence of prophecy. Prophecy itself is entirely spiritual, but it leaves a trail that we can perceive.

This perceivable trail relates as well to language. Let me note an important semantic phenomenon. Often, when the Bible relates to the Tetragrammaton, it omits the actual subject of the sentence. This occurs, for instance, in the passage beginning "when the Ark was carried" the phrases "arise, Lord" and "return, Lord" must be understood as "arise, Ark of the Lord" and "Return, Ark of the Lord." It is forbidden, indeed impossible, to relate phrases such as these to God. God does not sit or stand, arise or return. These phrases refer to the Ark, but the verses are written elliptically. In other examples, words such as "nation," "covenant" and "Torah" are elided. This elliptical style is used because the text is referring to phenomena that are specific to God. Thus, when we say "the nation of God" we refer to the Jewish nation, which is consecrated to God, a nation which is different from the rest of the world. We describe this connection grammatically through the connection to God's name.

I Will Be What I Will Be

Now we turn to the name God chooses in order to "present" Himself to the people in response to Moses' request for such a name. The divine name *Eheyeh asher eheyeh* ("I will be what I will be") is clearly related to the Tetragrammaton, having the same root (*h-w-h*). But the meaning of this name must be understood in context. Moses asks God for the divine name to be used in presenting God's message to the Israelites. Of course, Moses was not asking merely for a name. He was asking for a definition of God's essence. God answers with one word: *Eheyeh* (literally: I will be). Man cannot attain an understanding of God's true essence. The investigation of God's essence is completely beyond man. Nevertheless, it is possible to submit to the dangerous illusion that man is capable of comprehending God's essence. The true meaning of this name lies not in philosophy, but in history. God accompanies the Jewish people throughout its history. This is the meaning of the name "I will be what I will be": I will be with the Jewish nation whenever they turn to me.

It is on the stage of history that we feel the presence of God.

A-donai

We now reach the last divine name, the name depicting God's lordship: A-donai. (We are speaking here of A-donai as a written name, spelled *a-d-n-y*, not as the contrivance used to avoid pronouncing the Tetragrammaton.). Halevi's interpretation is innovative and interesting. A prophetic vision entails standing before some being or apparition, but it is not these phenomena that we address. Rather we address God, Who is concealed behind them. To understand this, we must point out a common, but significant semantic phenomenon of using one word when we mean another. For example, we speak of a person "without a roof over his head" when we mean a homeless person. We say "the White House" when we mean the President. Although the terms are not identical, there is a connection between them that allows us to use one term instead of the other.

Halevi illustrates this by using the phrases which are connected to the Hebrew word *lev* (heart). When we say *vayit'atzev el libbo* (He was saddened in His heart) or *amarti be-libbi* (I said in my heart, i.e., to myself), we do not mean to refer to a specific organ called the heart. We use this term in order to create an image of the world inside us, as though in this organ our souls, minds or feelings are reflected. Therefore, when we say "heart" we mean our souls, minds or feelings. Of course, we cannot really allude to the intellect by speaking of an organ, since it is not located in a specific place. But our feelings are expressed through the heart, and we can say that the heart feels. The soul exists or acts throughout the entire body, but we associate it with the heart.

Halevi distinguishes between two sorts of actions and events, depending on the immediacy and directness of the encounter with God. God affects many things indirectly. On a deep level, it is God Who made the car I see before me. But I can form an illusion that the car was man-made. Man is a link in an immense chain of causation that brought this car into being. With regard to other things, however, such as the heavens, the chain is much shorter. The cosmic phenomena are not in our hands. They are in the hands of God. Because of the immediacy and directness of the relationship between God and the heavens, we use the term "God in heaven," or, to use Halevi's excellent example, "fear of heaven." Here is another example of the way language expresses an idea through a related word. We appeal to the heavens, but of course we are actually appealing to God. We do not fear the heavens; we fear the One Who rules over them.

In the Bible, the use of one word to represent some other concept is a process that can work in both directions. As noted, we often speak of the heart when we mean the mind, but we may also speak of the mind and mean the heart. Imagine a surgeon who jokingly tells his patient before open-heart surgery or brain surgery that he is going to operate on the patient's "intellect." Halevi illustrates this phenomenon with the help of the phrases "a seeing eye" and "a hearing ear." These phrases are literally absurd, because the eye itself does not see. Rather, the soul that uses the eye sees, just as it is not the violin that plays, but the violinist. When we say that the eye sees, we are transferring the traits of the one using the eye to the eye itself. In the same way, we transfer traits of God to the things we see. This is the linguistic device of inserting the cause into the effect. This holds true for the symbols in prophetic visions as well, such as the pillar of fire. People bow before the pillar. Yet, they are really prostrating themselves before the One who commanded the pillar to come into being.

Halevi uses this concept to explain the term *Ish E-lohim* (Man of God). People who attain a certain spiritual level become God's messengers or agents in this world. They are vessels in God's hands, following all his commands and disregarding their own personal desires and interests. A person who achieves this level merits the title *Ish E-lohim*. He has reached the highest level a human can attain. God uses him as an agent and messenger, and the divine traits apply, or are passed on to him as well.

This may help explain an ambiguous biblical narrative. When the angels appear to Abraham (Genesis 18), Abraham says, "My lords (Heb: *a-donai*), please do not leave your servant." Interestingly, the Hebrew vowels used for the word A-donai imply that the word refers to the divine name, and not to the visiting angels. This can be interpreted in many ways.

Our Sages explained that Abraham asked the divine presence (which had appeared to Abraham in verse 1, before the separate appearance of the angels in verse 2) to wait while he fulfilled the commandment of greeting his guests hospitably. Rashi raises the possibility that Abraham was speaking to the senior-most angel, but that explanation does not explain the implication of the vowels. Halevi presents a third possibility: the visit of the angels is actually a prophetic vision. Since the angel is a messenger of God, the vowels imply that Abraham is indeed experiencing a prophetic vision.

When discussing the divine names, Halevi returns to the topic of the angels. He explains the phrase "the image of God" as the image of the angels. The element that people and the angels have in common is their rationality. Moreover, an angel is a messenger, a role played by prophets as well, who act as God's agents. There are two additional concepts which can help us understand the angels. The angels are phenomena of *kavod*, a concept we have referred to earlier. These are phenomena that the prophets see in their visions. There are also angels who are spiritual beings. In the first sense, the angels are beings whose presence is transient, for the vision exists only for a short time. In the second sense, the angels are spiritual beings who exist on a higher plane than mortal man; they are a part of "the heavenly assembly."

When viewing the prophetic vision, the prophet uses the divine name A-donai, for behind the vision is God. Similarly, we use a number of phrases that imply that God is in a particular place, although in reality He is beyond all locations. Since many prophetic phenomena occur in the Temple in Jerusalem, we describe it as God's dwelling place.

Kadosh

The word *kadosh* describes the concept of transcendence. *Kadosh* literally means "separate." God is "separate," that is, He is beyond the domain of human comprehension. As *An'im Zemirot* states, "I will tell of your glory yet I have not seen You; I will compare You, name You, yet I do not know You." In human speech we use words as tools through which we perceive things. We use our words like missiles, trying to hit our target. We are often successful, and the missiles reach their target. Sometimes, however, this is an impossible task, for we aim to hit something far and transcendent, which is beyond the range of the missiles of words and thoughts.

Human thought cannot grasp or explain God; he is *kadosh*. God is "too lofty and sublime to be described by humans in their terms."

God is sublime, but not only to us. It is interesting that Isaiah hears the angels incessantly calling *kadosh*, *kadosh*, *kadosh*. According to Halevi, the thrice-repeated formula expresses the idea that the angels repeat their statement infinitely. It is analogous to our use of "et cetera." The angels' cry teaches us that God is higher than everything. As the Kaddish prayer puts it, He is "above all blessings and song, all praise and comfort that we express in the world." Halevi's interpretation is repeated in the writings of Rabbi Soloveitchik. If we consider the context in which Isaiah hears the angels saying *kadosh*, *kadosh*, *kadosh*, we can consider the full breadth of the account. Isaiah sees God sitting "on a high and lofty throne." The throne is another expression of the idea that God is beyond our understanding. But the phrase "and its edges filled the hall" teaches us that despite the high and lofty throne, the divine presence is in the hall, in other words, on the earth, and essentially in the entire cosmos. God's presence is the *kavod*: "The whole world is filled with his *kavod* [glory]." If we look closely, we will see this glory not only in extraordinary events such as prophecy, but also in the ordinary events of life. Thus, Rabbi Soloveitchik teaches us that one can translate the angels' statement into a philosophical creed: "Transcendent, transcendent, transcendent is the Lord of Hosts; the entire world is filled with His immanence."

An initial reading informs us that God is separate even from the angels. Isaiah proclaims that He dwells within a nation of defiled lips. He is present within the impurity. As a response to this, the angels proclaim that God is exalted, and that we, the people, cannot taint Him with our impurity.

The concept of *kedushah* (holiness or separateness) teaches us something else. There is no doubt that the soul is spiritual, in the same way that the angels are spiritual. But the soul is an interesting example of a reality that has been an enigma to the human intellect from ancient times until this very day. The soul is not physical, yet it is clothed in a physical body. Thus, it is possible for spiritual phenomena to be clothed in a physical sheath. This is what distinguishes man from God. God is purely spiritual; He has no physical raiment. This lack of physicality is *kedushah*. This explanation recalls the viewpoint, mentioned by Halevi, that there is a connection between God and the cosmos. Such a connection is an expression of the attempt to clothe God in physicality, which detracts from God's *kedushah*.

Kedosh Yisra'el

The foregoing suggests that the phrase *kedosh yisra'el* (Holy One of Israel) is paradoxical. Halevi tries to solve this paradox. On the one hand, God is "separate." On the other hand, He is connected to the Jewish people. This is not the physical connection that ensnared the Christians. It is a paradoxical connection. To describe one's relationship to the *kadosh* is a paradox, as though we had said "my distant one." We know what distance is, but what is "my distant one"? This is an expression that only a prophet can use. For a prophet, the distance remains even though the relationship is possible. We cannot say "my *kadosh*" or "my distant one" unless we use the language of prophecy. Now perhaps we can shed more light upon our understanding of the divine presence in our world. It is the relationship with Someone Who is shrouded in the distance. What is dear to us is far away, and yet we manage to establish a relationship with it, an emotional-spiritual connection, through the letter He sent to us, the Torah. It is the Torah that makes the paradoxical relationship possible.

On the basis of these ideas, we can try to understand the meaning of the word *kedoshim* when it is used to refer to the Jewish people, particularly in the context of the commandment *kedoshim tiheyu*, you shall be holy, or separate. The commandment *kedoshim tiheyu* is based on the principle of imitating God. From our perspective, the *kedushah* is both the distance that separates man from God as well as the relationship with Him expressed in prophecy, and to some extent, in the nation led by God. This type of closeness, called "closeness of leadership," is the bond through which the Jewish people were given commandments, guidance and providence, which entails the possibility of being punished for sins. This accounts for Jewish history and its tragic component. Other nations are within the natural system, but we are distanced from it by providential guidance. This is the type of closeness which, despite all the tragic events in our history, will ultimately bring about our redemption.

Chapter 38:
The Sub-Sensory Realm:
A Chapter in Metaphysics

Another Look at the Theory of Attributes

We will now return to the problem of the numerous divine elements, which Halevi resolves by way of an analogy to the sun. The sun is far away, but it is reflected in many different houses. There is only one sun, but its rays are numerous. Imagine different houses with different colored windowpanes. The one sun will be perceived differently in each location. Analogously, God has one name, just as there is only one sun. The many variations are the result of our different perceptions. Although the thing itself is one, everyone sees it differently. Similarly, we attribute many attributes to God, but His essential unity remains intact. Different people perceive different colors even though there is only one sun. Imagine a theater in which spotlights are used. There may be a different spotlight for each color, or there may be a single spotlight, with various filters used to produce the desired colors. Alternatively, the colors may be produced not by the spotlights or filters but by different glasses worn by the viewers. The many variations do not emanate from the source, but from the glasses we are wearing. Similarly, God's numerous attributes do not call His unity into question. In fact, God has one attribute, one name, but this unity is perceived in many different ways.

Modern science, however, shows that the analogy as presented above is not perfect. We understand today that we perceive different shades of light because white light is actually a combination of all the colors. It is not itself a single color. The unity of white light is perceived because it is a combination of all the colors. But Halevi is really saying something else: the analogy would fit if the sun itself was imperceptible and only its rays shone in different colors. Then the true light could not be perceived at all, and only the colors, produced by the filters, would be visible.

This idea is upheld by a number of modern-day scientists. One common theory teaches that certain entities, such as electrons, cannot be perceived. Yet, we can and do discern their effects. In any case, we must learn from here to be cautious in using analogies; they may soon be outdated.

A Philosophical Walk About the Room

These ideas led Halevi to develop a unique philosophical theory—that what we experience through our senses is not exactly identical to what exists in reality. By way of analogy, assume we wear special glasses that distort reality. We know that we have a picture of reality but that it is not accurate. We perceive a reality, but the portrait is not faithful to the original. On the other hand, we must realize that filters do exist. We do not have the ability to see other wavelengths besides visible light, such as infrared or ultraviolet. If we could see infrared, we could perceive that when two people approach each other, one can slightly penetrate into the other. This is because the heat of infrared spreads a little beyond the boundaries of the body. Similarly, if we could "see" electricity, the whole world would look completely different. We would see that all of space is filled with waves, and a new colorful ocean would appear to us, blocking our view of anything beyond it. The opposite is also true, for we cannot perceive shorter waves either, such as X-rays. This means that the world we experience is not actually the real world. It is strained through filters and is processed by our senses. Our senses do this, apparently for our own good, so that we can function in the world. We perceive a small fraction of reality, but it is a useful fraction, which aids our ability to survive, support ourselves and function in the world.

Another analogy will highlight the difference between the two approaches. Various attempts have been made to create three-dimensional films. To see them successfully one must use special glasses. If we take off the glasses, we see strange things, which do not create the impression of three dimensions. If we put them on again, we feel or "see" the third dimension. So too, in reality, the sensory world that we experience is the result of a particular pair of glasses—the mechanism of our senses. The information we receive helps us in our daily lives, but it does not show us the true essence of the things around us. Still, it is possible that reality can be perceived in a totally different way, and that is Halevi's assumption. According to this approach, our sensory perceptions conceal something that lies beneath them but is not identical to them. That is the reality which is perceived by the prophets. To illustrate, we will use one of Halevi's analogies.

Imagine that we are drops of water in a river. Each of us knows of the existence of other drops, but none of us knows the river. The river, however, comprises not only its present, but also its past and its future. According to this approach, beneath the biography of the river lies a different reality. The reality which we perceive with our senses is merely one expression of that hidden reality. The same is true with man. We can perceive man from the outside and obtain a series of images that show us his traits at various times. But there is something concealed behind all these pictures. We will call the hidden reality the essence. Our senses are built to perceive the traits. If we could perceive the essence, not the traits, we would "see" the world entirely differently. We would see not people, things and events, but the essence that is harbored beneath the sensory perceptions. That is how a prophet perceives reality.

We can examine a human being minutely, even taking X-ray pictures of him, yet remain far from his essence. A doctor can give a complete physical description of his patient, and yet know nothing about him. The prophet views the same reality from a completely different perspective, a perspective beyond time and place.

According to Halevi's account, the prophet looks with an inner eye, which sees beyond the externals and penetrates the essence of reality. Halevi uses another model, also taken from our visual world. The relationship between our vision of reality and that of the prophet is comparable to the relationship between a person with impaired vision and a person whose vision is excellent. The vision impairment can cause the sufferer to be unable to focus his vision. Each of his eyes presents a different picture to his brain, and he cannot merge them to create the real picture of reality. Sensory perception is a type of vision impairment. In contrast, the prophet sees the true reality. He cannot directly demonstrate to us the correctness of his perception. Because of our impairment, only a prophet can bear witness for another prophet. But the Torah's signs of a true prophet can help us determine that he does indeed see the essential reality.

Imagination: The Mind's Tool

What exactly is the prophet's inner eye? I would suggest that it is a kind of sixth sense. Halevi suggests another possibility that brings us closer to Maimonides' approach. The prophet's inner eye is actually his imagination, which the intellect uses. Imagination is here held in high regard. Cooperation between intellect and imagination makes prophecy unique. But the nature of this partnership must be clarified.

The tremendous power of the imagination is expressed in dreams, where the imagination presents us visions that have characteristics of prophecy. We see things that do not exist in reality, yet we cannot deny their actuality. We were really there. In dreams, the imagination is autonomous. It is involved only with reconstructing materials that it finds ready-made in our daily lives. But if we could connect the imagination to some different source, it could show us worlds that the senses cannot perceive and, in a way, be more fertile than the intellect. In any case, the imagination could serve the intellect, improving its capabilities and scope. Indeed, in prophecy the imagination can capture the vision that comes from without, from above. It creates sensory images of a different reality. The intellect stands beside it and tries to decipher what the imagination sees. This is Maimonides' understanding.

Imagine that I have to pass on a message to Reuben. I could give him a verbal message, which would be very limited. But I could also present a much more complex message by drawing him a picture, worth the proverbial thousand words. If I am an artist, the message might be so replete that all I wanted to convey to him would be included. A picture has many more dimensions than language does. On the other hand, when Reuben receives the letter, he will generally understand its main message immediately, but the picture will need to be interpreted. This does not mean that the entire letter will be understood immediately or that various levels of verbal understanding are not possible. But the essence of the message in the picture will need to be deciphered and explained. This is true not only of Picasso's paintings, but also those of Rembrandt, which seem on the surface to be much more readily comprehensible. The message in the picture is not given to us explicitly. The information must be extracted from it. The greatest artist, greater even than Rembrandt or Picasso, is the imagination—the great artist that resides within each and every one of us. If the intellect, which is the philosopher, and the imagination, which is the artist, can work together, they can perceive realities that would otherwise have remained hidden. A hidden message reaches man from above. The artist can paint it. The intellect can understand it. If this cooperation exists, prophecy is possible—assuming, of course, that there is no blockage in the pipeline from above.

This necessary cooperation can teach us why prophecy is perceived in images and sensory visions, similar to the dream experience. The philosopher alone is helpless at times, while the artist alone is liable to lead man into idolatry. The intellect is needed to save us from the dangers of the imagination. But language has its dangers as well. We transform images into words, but language remains full of the creations of the imagination, which has left its imprints there. That is where the importance of deciphering comes to the fore.

The prophet perceives God in physical or human images: "And one sees in You [both] age and youth; in the hair of Your head [both] graying and black." Sometimes, he is an old man teaching Torah to the Jewish people, "aged on the Day of Judgment," and sometimes as a "youth on the day of battle" (An'im Zemirot). This is what the artist can do. But the prophet continually underscores the fact that what he sees is only a vision. Thus, for example, in Ezekiel's vision of the Chariot, the prophet repeatedly emphasizes that what he sees is an "image" and a "vision." We must understand that the vision is a picture in need of interpretation. Even if our attempts are not successful, we must accept that the vision hints at a hidden reality.

This reality allows for interpretation and questioning of biblical imagery. Thus, for example, one of the images we use for God is light. Perhaps this image expresses the divine immanence, in other words, the fact that God is with us in every place. On the other hand, the approach to the heavens which is discussed by Halevi, may be interpreted differently. The heavens describe divine transcendence, the fact that God is beyond all of reality.

The Picture within the Picture

Let me now illustrate another important principle in the theory of prophecy, using a technique employed by many artists. A simple example can be found in the classic picture of the laying of the cornerstone of the Hebrew University, an event attended by all the great leaders of the period. (The picture is on display at the University's Mount Scopus campus.) In one corner of the picture, we see a person painting. This is the artist himself, who put himself into his own picture. Although logically this is a paradox, we see that the small picture being painted is a copy of the big picture. Similarly, Maimonides teaches us that the prophetic picture contains a representation of the actual process of prophecy. In it, too, there appears a picture within a picture. In most prophecies, the prophet meets with darkness, and within it, light, and usually an angel. This angel in the vision is, according to Maimonides, an expression of the process through which we receive prophecy. The angel who speaks to the prophet is a messenger of God. He represents the mechanism that exists in our inner world. He is like a painter painting the picture that reaches him from above.

According to Maimonides, in our everyday lives we process the input of the personal senses and thus create an image of reality. This image exists inside us, where there is a kind of movie screen upon which reality projects itself. Sometimes, however, we project onto this screen things that are not real, such as when we dream. In prophecy, a similar process takes place. In order to explain it, we will try to continue the analogy of the movie screen. The first requirement for watching a movie in a theater is that it be dark. Only then do we lose our connection to daily reality and create the possibility of viewing another reality. Such is the case with the prophet as well. The first requirement is that it be dark. In other words, the prophet must be cut off from the outside world. He loses his regular consciousness, or he is already in a state lacking consciousness, like sleep. Then the outer world stops affecting him. When the outer world is turned off, so to speak, a different, deeper world can appear to the prophet. He sees a reality that is inside his inner world, but this reality reveals secrets to him that he would not otherwise reach.

Halevi teaches us that when we look with our eyes, we see reality, but not all of reality. In fact, we may see a distorted reality. The world appears before us as it does because we use our senses. If we could find a different mechanism, we would see the world differently. If we had a third eye, we would see a different, much truer reality. This third eye exists but it is not turned outward; it is turned inward. This is the "inner eye" (IV:3). Our psychological world is no less rich and important than the factual outer world. This "inner eye" shows the prophet the true reality hidden from the senses. The intellect can try to understand the true reality, but this is an indirect way of perceiving these realities. One having an "inner eye" can see them directly and palpably.

How does the prophet see with his inner eye? We can give two answers to this question, which do not contradict one another.

1. The inner eye shows us the reality as it is. This is comparable to a person who is sent for an X-ray. The X-rays penetrate and show us a different reality, one we cannot see with our ordinary senses. The prophet sees the reality that is before us but he sees it with such a penetrating perception that it looks totally different.

   However, the X-ray example is not exact. Halevi prefers the example of the short-sighted person, who is not wearing his glasses and sees a distorted reality. We perceive the world "without glasses." In contrast, the prophet sees a different reality with his complete vision.

2. We spoke about X-rays, but there are other ways—magnetic resonance imaging, for example—in which one can receive information about one's inner self. What both these possibilities have in common is that it is not enough to see. We must understand and interpret.

God displays a message for the prophet. The message is not physical, but it is real. The message describes facts, but it describes them in such a way that they need to be interpreted. This principle, which Halevi hints at, was developed by Maimonides. According to his approach, the vision of the prophet is formed by the paintbrush of the imagination, and the picture that is received needs interpretation. In order to understand the prophecy, we need the power of interpretation, the ability to explain. Now we can return to the parallel between prophecy and dreams. Dreams are one-sixtieth of prophecy. In dreams we see a "private" reality that we use to learn about our inner reality, our fears and hopes. In the prophetic dream and vision we also learn much, not about our own inner reality, but about the entire world.

Section 9:
God and the World

CHAPTER 39:
PAGANISM

The Kuzari's starting point is idolatry, or paganism. Although this it seems passé today, we must devote a few lines to the idea.

Idolatry Interpreted Non-Literally

In a certain sense, idol worship has not disappeared. Many modern thinkers look at it in a larger, more figurative sense. According to their approach, a polytheist is a person who has many foci in his life but has no one central ideal that directs his actions. Such a person can be compared to a weathervane, which changes direction with each gust of wind. A person who is lacking a center in his life is governed by each passing whim. He cannot give a general accounting to himself of his own life.

Idolatry Interpreted Allusively

The foregoing was, essentially, a non-literal portrayal of polytheism. It seems to me, however, that another current interpretation of idol worship is much closer to the mark. Modern-day idol worship may be seen as a position that transforms means into ends. It discards faith in God as an absolute standard, replacing it with other values that become absolute, such as money, sex, respect, sports, etc. In this way, money and wealth become idols. Hasidic and Musar teachers alike interpreted the verse "Gods of silver and gods of gold ye shall not make" to mean "do not make silver and gold into gods." Sports and entertainment also become idolatrous when they take over the center and meaning of life. While we must understand the importance of sports to a person who is actively involved in them, we must realize that sports and entertainment can become, or have already become, a form of idolatry, which continues to develop its own gods.

All these values are not negative in and of themselves, so long as they serve greater ideals. One of the most powerful examples of this is patriotism, which is a negative factor when it becomes the ultimate value, without relation to any other goal and without being subject to the criticism of any outside source. In Judaism, the concept of the nation is closely connected to the religious ideal. When this interdependence disappears, the nation becomes a religion—in effect, idolatry.

One of the best examples of this type of idol worship was the approach of Ahad Ha-Am, a Jewish author and thinker at the turn of the last century. He believed that we must turn our perceptions inside out and understand reality differently. He maintained that religion merely served the nation. We know that the nation is of great importance, but as Rav Kook teaches, this is also because God reveals Himself through the nation.

One of man's central problems is that sometimes he is so involved in achieving the means that he stops thinking about the end. Sometimes we stop asking why we need the means, and we get stuck at some intermediate point. The classic example of this is the man who works in order to support himself. Imperceptibly, however, his work becomes the central goal in his life. When this man retires, his life loses all meaning. One of the purposes of the Sabbath is to combat this type of idolatry.

Rav Kook maintains that the moment we place a single value as our goal, instead of making God, who contains all values and ideals, into our focus, we are worshipping idols. Monotheism means unity of ideals. Every pagan idol represented a particular ideal. If God is one, this means that we are expected to fulfill all the ideals. The belief in divine unity means not only that God is One, but that He is complete. The Jewish ideal must be a complete model, containing all the ideals. Therefore, as Isaiah and other prophets stressed, God will not accept the offerings of one who exploits his fellow man, for he is emphasizing one ideal and ignoring another.

The meaning of our belief in divine unity is expressed in the conflict between mythology and Torah. Let us look for example at Homer's account of the Trojan War. The war begins with the capture of Helen, wife of King Menelaus of Sparta, by Paris, the son of the Trojan king. But the war is actually sparked by the jealousy among the three goddesses of Olympus: Hera, the queen of the heavens, Athena, the queen of wisdom, and Aphrodite, the queen of beauty. Their differences arose over the question of which goddess was the most beautiful of all. This story foreshadows what will become clear later on: the existence of many gods means that there is no single moral standard. The gods on Olympus who must judge this act are of different opinions. The god of justice of course is against it; the goddess of love disagrees. The Jewish prophet, in contrast, demands that one change one's entire life. The Jewish alternative to the story of Troy is the story of David and Bathsheba, in which the prophet stands before the king representing the unequivocal quality of justice.

This is also what our Sages mean when they teach us that one who worships his evil inclination worships idols. "Let there be no foreign god within you" means, in its simple sense, that Jews should not worship any foreign gods. But our Sages interpret it to mean "let there be no foreign gods *inside* you," and the only foreign god that could possibly be inside you is the evil inclination.

Thus we see that even lofty ideals can be transformed into idolatry. Communism took the social ideal and made it into idol worship. It created a church with holy books, accepted readings and interpretations of the sacred texts as well as forbidden interpretations, canonized interpretations and heretical ideas. It also created an inquisition. Millions of human sacrifices were offered up on the altar of this idolatry.

Idolatry in its Plain Sense

Until now we have discussed allegorical interpretations of idol worship. In the modern world, however, we see the revival of literal idol worship.

The most outstanding expression of the revival of pagan mythology is found in Nazism. Wagner chose motifs from early German mythology for his compositions. In this way, he expressed his opposition to Christian culture, and indirectly to its Jewish origins. In his music, Wagner returned to German myth, which was a world of gods of war, and thus he heralded the revival of German mythology in Nazi philosophy.

Another, no less important example, is connected to the phenomenon of witchcraft and Satan worship, which often go hand in hand. In my opinion, these practices explain the strong opposition on the part of the Torah and the Sages to the phenomena of witchcraft. Some practices are forbidden because they are groundless superstitions. Others, however, are forbidden because they are dangerous, to individuals and to society as a whole. We know of the existence of groups all over the world that continue to worship Satan through cruelty and torture. Every so often we even hear that human sacrifices are still offered to Satan, even in our modern world.

The Fifth Principle of Faith

The fifth of Maimonides' thirteen principles of faith commands us to worship the Creator and not any of His creatures. This principle translates faith into action. Sometimes idolatry can be identified in faith. Sometimes it is apparent only in practice. The fifth principle ensures against this danger. The final barrier between idolatry and monotheism is found in one's form of worship. If man worships any other creature, he impairs the monotheistic faith. But idolatry's greatest offense is not only the creation of alternatives to God. Leafing through the Prophets we read of lechery and wine that "take" the heart. Here lies another deep source of our battle with idol worship. We are faced with an imperfect world that has suffering and injustice. The injustice may be combated. Yet, the priests of idol worship, instead of contributing to the battle against injustice, create an artificial paradise of emptiness. They use sex, drunkenness, and in many places, drugs as well, to attract people in the name of religion and remove them from the continuum of suffering. But this is done in a way which leads them to sink deeper into the very miseries they wished to escape. The classic example of this approach is those people who get drunk every weekend, and in this way find themselves an "artificial paradise" which allows them to forget their families and their poverty-stricken surroundings. Too often the drunkenness itself is the cause of the poverty.

Idol worship means replacing God. This is like betraying one's spouse. But idolatry has still other negatives. We sometimes create imaginary and artificial beings that keep us from seeing and solving the real problems that we face. Rav Kook teaches us in *Ikvei Ha-Tzon* that this idea was expressed in the *midrash*. As is well known, Ibn Ezra interpreted the phrase *elohim aheirim* (lit, "other gods") as what seem to others to be gods. This is a subjective claim. There are no other gods, but there are those who accept these imaginary beings as gods. Rav Kook, in contrast, cites a wonderful midrashic idea, based on a play on words: "Why are they called *elohim aheirim*? Because they delay [*me'aharim*] the entrance of good to the world." True, there are no other gods; these are only illusions. Still, they are dangerous illusions, because they obstruct the good. If a person takes a wrong but harmless medication, it can still be dangerous, not because of what it contains but because of what it is lacking. It stops the person from taking the real medicine. Idolatry is not competition for God. There is no foreign god who wants to sit on Gods throne. The Torah nevertheless combats idolatry, because it impedes the realization of ideals and it causes man to give up so much of his potential good.

That is the great danger of idolatry. Idolatry was an effort not to better the world but to escape from it. Unlike Christianity, however, idolatry escaped not to the beyond, but to physical excess. This approach is of course also found in the modern world. The most outstanding example is the carnival. We find a society filled with problems, guided by the idea that the central point of the year are those days on which we "let loose." This is a kind of idolatry that does not allow man to extract himself from his real difficulties—or, at least, does not help him do so. Sometimes it is even worse. The most outstanding example is again found in a monotheistic religion. We hear that in certain Islamic groups, drugs were used in order to create a group of fanatic murderers with no restraints, who were promised a "paradise" that the drugs created for them. They had experienced "paradise" and would do anything to return. The Torah wants man to achieve happiness, but not happiness that is artificial and destructive.

Idolatry Understood Mystically

The Torah teaches that God created man in His image. The atheist responds glibly: man created God in his image. This battle of slogans expresses two opposing philosophies. The truth, however, is more complicated, and I am convinced that both sides are factually correct. "Man created god in his image" is the very definition of idolatry. In contrast, prophecy attempts to offer a concept of God that is utterly divorced from our ideas about ourselves. "The image of God" is a kind of directional sign, pointing the way to a more exalted life.

Picturing God in one's own image is indeed a sort of idolatry. Man projects what is in him onto the image of God that he constructs. One of the messages of prophecy is the need to overcome this type of projection. We will cite the simplest example of the struggle of prophecy to free itself from this trap. Prophecy divested God of any concept of gender. God is neither male nor female; He is completely above sexuality. This is particularly noticeable when we compare this approach to the overpowering sexuality of pagan mythology. The Bible treats God as grammatically masculine, using for example masculine pronouns, but this grammatical gender has no significance. God has no gender at all. This distances God from human concepts. This is of course only the first stage, which would later develop into an attempt to construct religious concepts that are not a projection of our human lives. This would develop as we saw earlier, in the philosophical theory of attributes.

The desire to overcome anthropocentricity is expressed in the battle against polytheism. The gods constitute a kind of heavenly family characterized, like human families, by lust for power, sex and war. The conflicts among the gods describe the various aspects of human emotions, projecting what exists inside man. But the Torah teaches that God is beyond the vices and petty desires of man.

Judaism fought against perceptions like these, yet Christianity returned to them, reintroducing the idea of a heavenly family. The concept "son of God," treated allegorically in the Bible, now again becomes a realistic concept. Later in the history of Christianity the mother also appears, the Virgin Mary. The idea of the Virgin Mary is a projection, and we here see again the projection of the image of man onto God.

This is a human projection that fits into the psychological mechanism that Freud investigated. This means that indeed, the Freudian approach is applicable here. The gods of idolatry are a projection of human desires, weaknesses and limitations. Clearly, Freud's analysis was correct to a great extent even with regard to Christianity. In Christianity, for example, we find sacraments and holy rites that alter man's status. One of these sacraments is related to the Last Supper. Jesus, as we know, died around the time of the Paschal sacrifice. Jesus the Jew ate *matzah* and drank wine, as was the custom. However, this eating received a very different interpretation in later generations, when the *matzah* came to be regarded as Jesus' body and the wine as his blood. I will not go into the issue of the drinking of the wine, which is an issue of contention among the various churches. But in classic Christianity the person swallows the holy bread, which is the body of Jesus. This is clearly a custom with idolatrous origins, which can be traced to various ethnic tribes, whose rites include a holy meal. In the meal the group eats the god, which is identified with a certain holy animal, the Totem. The image of the god is a human projection.

Idolatry and Nature

Idolatry is based on a number of guiding principles. The first principle is the mythic image of the world, which means the projection of the human reality onto the world and onto God.

However, there is another central element in idolatry: the recognition of nature as a divine being. Rabbi Akiva fought against this principle in his debates with the pagan philosophers. One of Rabbi Akiva's counterparts claims that if God created poor people, we must not "disturb Him" by trying to alter their poverty. When we give charity we are opposing the divine decree. This type of view is in essence a recognition of nature as a power, and thus also a recognition of the rights of the powerful. The "right of the powerful" is an idolatrous principle. This leads us to the question of our attitude towards nature, which we will discuss in the next chapter.

Saving The Princess

The world of mythology found expression through two great media: art and tragic theater. Remnants of the connection between idolatry and these two worlds remain until today. This is the reason for the historical antagonism that exists between them and Judaism.

Here lies the significance of one of the teachings of Rabbi Nahman of Braslav, who speaks of the need to save the *hen* (beauty) in the world. Many of the great artistic expressions were vehicles for idolatry, but they are not idolatrous themselves. In Rabbi Nahman's writings we find a recurring motif, that of the princess who is captured by the *sitra ahra* (lit. "the other side," a kabbalistic term for the power of evil) and must be saved. On one interpretation, the princess represents art. In other words these are the means that idolatry used to express its mythology. One of the missions of redemption is, perhaps, to redeem this princess.

The debate over the status of the arts is part of a larger argument about our understanding of reality. To use a kabbalistic phrase, we could say that the great debate is whether the concept of *tzimtzum* is to be taken literally or not. In Hasidic terms, the question is whether the world is indeed "void" of God's presence, in which case God's word can be heard only through the study of Torah, or whether (as Hasidism insisted) the divine voice emanates from the world as well—albeit, in Rabbi Nahman words, not as a direct voice but as an echo of the original divine voice heard at the creation of the world.

One of Rabbi Kook's central ideas was that all the world's phenomena contained a divine spark that we must uncover. The human ideal, according to this idea, is not to confine oneself to the four cubits of *halakhah*, but to search for religious meaning in all the various levels of human existence. The prophets taught us to look to the heavens and ask who created all this. Nature is God's creation; culture is man's. The connection with nature exists even if its status is problematic. The attitude toward human creativity is even more problematic. Often man's baser and more primitive drives find expression in art. Here we must remember what we learned from Rav Kook, that human creativity must be respected. We must separate the baser drives from the artistic creation and search for the holy spark inside the latter.

CHAPTER 40:
JUDAISM AND NATURE

Shem and Japheth

Rational religious philosophy is the outcome of the fruitful union of two sources—the biblical perspective and the Greek conceptual language. (The sources are represented by Noah's sons Shem, ancestor of the Jews, and Japheth, ancestor of the Greeks.) The matchmakers lived in Alexandria, and the most prominent was Philo. In a sense, Maimonides was the *wunderkind* of the match, and the match seems to have pleased Maimonides, who saw his two sources as existing in harmony.

But this harmony was not complete, and every so often thinkers arose who wanted to bring about a divorce—none more so than Rabbi Nahman of Braslav, who wanted to free the Jewish spirit from the bonds of the synthesis with Greek thought. Without going into that issue, we will discuss the relationship between the two sources and the two foci of their union.

The Common Denominator: Philosophical Language

Philosophy helped Judaism in its fight against anthropomorphism. This was the continuation and development of the prohibition against making graven images and creating physical images meant to describe God. This common ground created the opportunity for Shem and Japheth to walk a long way together. The partnership is expressed in the theory of attributes, considered earlier.

The pagans created gods in the image of man. The most important example of which is the division into gods and goddesses. The gods have human strengths and frailties, but on a larger scale. The Scriptures negate any such image and present us with a different ideal. We must strive to become similar to God by ethical behavior and keeping the commandments. Following in God's ways is itself the image of God that we can reach.

137

In the world of idolatry the imagination rules with no limits or boundaries. The message of prophecy is the power to overcome this childish type of imagination. This spiritual maturity is directly parallel to our scientific maturation. In science we slowly abandon our childish perspective, the world of legend built upon the forays of imagination, and we begin to attain wisdom. This process is ongoing, and we succeed in it only with great difficulty. It is possible that we will never completely abandon the imagination. Consider the following simple example. Astronomy was one of the first sciences to develop. As we saw earlier, Aristotle's approach assumed that the planets, or to be more exact, the spheres, have souls and/or intellects. Aristotelian astronomy still contained much of the naive and childish outlook based on imagination. In this perception, there were dangerous remnants of idolatry. Aristotle could not overcome these remnants in his philosophy. Therefore, we had to wait for the new physics and particularly for Newton, who abandoned the Aristotelian concepts and spoke of the power of gravity. In our generation, Einstein appeared and demonstrated that Newton's perception was also imaginative and primitive. He spoke of powers, and the concept of power is itself an anthropomorphic term. There seem to be powers, but Einstein shows that they are actually an expression of geometrical changes.

Slowly but surely we refine our scientific language. In that sense, prophecy and Greek philosophy could have joined forces under the flag of "you have seen no image." The prohibition against the image is expected of us in science and philosophy as well. The sophisticated Greek astronomer, who observed the celestial cycles and epicycles, could not, for all his scientific sophistication, overcome the trap of the human image. His language has not yet been refined. The need for constant refinement of our language compels us to develop constantly. Rabbi Nahman of Braslav calls this process "repentance for the [earlier] repentance."

The Source of the Conflict: Nature

Both sides gained from this partnership, and many Jewish sages benefited, knowingly or unknowingly, from the advantages afforded by philosophical language. But Greece brought a very problematic dowry to the union: the worship of nature that is at the basis of Greek thought.

As we have already seen, the Bible teaches us a truth that contains an "anti-nature" element. This idea, part of Maimonides' theory of divine unity, was nicely explained by Hermann Cohen and further developed by Yechezkel Kaufman, who made it the basis of his system. The concept of divine unity is the focus of prophecy, indeed, of the Scriptural revolution. But what does the idea really mean?

The idea of divine unity is much more than a "numerical" argument. True, the pagans believed in many gods, and we believe there is but one Father in heaven. But the Scriptural revolution is much more than a change from oligarchy to monarchy. The idea of divine unity means a much more fundamental revolution: the common denominator of all idolatry is the idea that the gods exist within the world, and that they are governed by its laws, the laws of nature. If, for example, we were to draw the world as a circle, we would have to draw the gods inside the circle. It reminds me of those stories in which the protagonists are dogs. In some of these stories, the dogs refer to the people as the gods. If I were a dog, I would reach the conclusion that people were stronger than me, if not because of their muscles, then because they have guns! In any case, although they are stronger than I am, they are also limited by hindrances and weakness. They, too, are subject to forces and laws. I can bite the person or I can fawn on him. I can act against him, since although he is stronger he is not omnipotent.

This was also the view of idolatry. The gods are stronger than man, but they do not have absolute power. They are under the power of the laws of nature. There are many strings that move us about without asking our opinion, as though we were puppets in a theater. But if I am a puppet who thinks a little, I know that if I myself pull at the strings that move me, I can move the finger of the one who is manipulating me. Strings are a two-way street. If I knew how to move the right strings, I could manipulate the gods. This movement is magic. Magic means that the gods are not free. To some extent magic is the father of science, because it claims that there are laws that govern the world. But it is wrong when it believes that this system of laws controls God. In contrast, the Scriptures teach us that God is beyond nature and outside of it. The laws of nature do not place obligations on God.

Divine unity does not only mean that God is one, but that He is unique. God is totally different from everything that exists in the world. The Scriptures teach us that we must believe not in magic, but in miracles. Miracles are an expression of the idea that God is above nature. This is the case with regard to prayer as well. Rabbi Nahman writes: "Prayer is above nature because nature mandates and prayer changes nature."

On an ironic note, when we ask for miracles, we are asking for nature to change. But we should not let that bother us much, because when the miracle does occur, we will certainly find a way to explain it naturally.

In philosophical language, we could call this the principle of transcendence. This is Maimonides' philosophical position, but Hasidic thought teaches us that this is only a half-truth. God is beyond nature, but we must not conclude that God is distant. This idea is expressed in the Scriptures by the words "holiness" and "glory." We proclaim, "Holy, holy, holy is the Lord of hosts, the entire world is filled with His glory." Holiness implies the distance of the transcendent God, but on the other hand, His presence is near. That is the glory, the Divine Presence.

Nature and Beyond

Maimonides believed that nature creates necessity. He also believed that this view of nature is consistent with the Bible. We will illustrate this shortly and discuss his dispute with Halevi. First, though, we must situate ourselves, as moderns, with respect to this issue. It would seem that we are closer to the position which sees nature as the highest judge—a view against which Halevi and his successors protested. Despite it all, there exists some interaction between what is beyond nature and nature itself. We have not totally erased the importance of nature. But we believe this is not enough. Three examples will help clarify the matter.

The Messianic Age

The first example focuses on the question of how we are to understand the concept of the Messianic era. Maimonides, whose philosophy was the offspring of the union between Shem and Japheth, was a realist. In less positive terms, he was the captive of a particular conception of nature.

Nature is not merely a conglomeration of mathematical formulas. It also has a non-mathematical reality—the law of the jungle, continuous warfare. A prominent expression of this warfare is the wolf's devouring the lamb. In Isaiah's vision, however, we are told that "the wolf shall lie down with the lamb." How are we to understand this verse? Should it be taken literally or figuratively?

Maimonides believed this verse should not be understood literally and that fundamental changes in nature are impossible. Nature is a reality so basic that one cannot even conceive of the possibility of change within its realm. Therefore, the prophet could not possibly have been saying that in the messianic era the wolf will undergo a hormonal change and he will no longer attack the lamb. What, then, is the meaning of the verse? It is a parable. It does not speak of nature but of history, and it refers to the place where future changes will take place, in society. Civilization will no longer be based on warfare, and the lion of Russia and Germany will live peacefully with the lamb of Poland.

Viewing the messianic era through normal historical eyes was one of Maimonides' important contributions to our modern philosophy. Religious Zionism was nourished by this approach. But Rav Kook teaches us that hope for a normal historical redemption and social utopia ought not to make us forget the utopia in nature: that the wolf shall actually lie down with the lamb. The vision of the end of days judges nature according to divine criteria, which are beyond nature.

The "Ought" and the "Is"

Another example of subordination to nature is found in Spinoza's theory of ethics. A central distinction in ethical theory is that between what is and what ought to be, between the ideal and reality. Morality is built not on the power of dominion, nor on social norms, but on our perception of the ideal state of affairs. This is one of the important messages of the biblical revolution, and it means we must perform certain acts though nature does not require them. Sometimes we are in conflict with the nature that is outside of ourselves and sometimes we are in conflict with desires and psychological structures that are inside us.

When we defy the law of the jungle, and we do so not out of fear but out of conviction, we declare that we are guided by ideals that are not in nature.

Nature as an Idol

As a final example, consider how one should act in one's financial affairs. Should nature be allowed to take its course, or should one defy the natural course of the world's economy and give charity? "Economic man" will act only in accord with his own good. I, in contrast, am called upon to act in accord with a higher vision.

Maimonides and Spinoza

Spinoza was consistent in his approach to nature, adopting the pantheistic view according to which God is nature. This formulation has metaphysical significance, but it also has practical and moral importance. Maimonides, on the other hand, believed in the middle road between pantheism and Aristotelian philosophy. He claimed that miracles are within the bounds of possibility, and they are dependent on the idea that the world was created. In other words, since the world was created and has not always existed, miracles are possible. Maimonides explains that if the world had always existed and God had not created it, He would not even have the power to clip a fly's wing. In explaining this observation, we will come to see the basic difference between Maimonides and Spinoza.

One of the ways in which television programs entertain small children is to take two objects, such as an elephant and a fly, and switch their traits. They make the fly big and the elephant small, switch the ears, and so on. The final stage of that process poses the fascinating and paradoxical question of exactly what is left at that point. We will not pursue the matter that far but will pause at the first stage, where the size of the fly is changed. Maimonides explains that this is an example of something that the imagination enjoys playing with, but which the intellect rejects. Why? Because the person who changes the size of the fly's wings and thinks that the fly will continue to fly doesn't understand a thing about aerodynamics. We must understand the fly in the context of the relationships among its various parts. The possibility of flying is a function of size. Here, Maimonides asks whether a miracle can take place. Is another reality possible, in which the fly could fly using longer or shorter wings than the current fly has? It depends, says Maimonides, on our fundamental belief. If we believe that the world was created by God, then the world could have been different. The world is not necessary; it is contingent. That is the objection to Spinoza's view: the world is not God and therefore could have been different.

Imagine

Jewish folklore tells of a matchmaker instructing a young man before his date with a prospective bride. In light of the young man's questions, the matchmaker suggests a few topics to discuss. "Talk," he says, "about family and about food."

"And what if we exhaust those topics?" asks the young man anxiously.

"Then talk about philosophy."

The story preserved the transcript of the conversation:

"Do you have any brothers or sisters?"

"No."

The first topic was now at an end.

"Do you like noodles?"

"No."

The topic of food had failed as well. However, philosophy was still an untried source.

"If you had a brother, would he like noodles?"

The hero of our tale saw philosophy as dealing with imagined realities. To a large extent he was right.

Children very quickly learn to use the word "if" in order to imagine a realistic scenario. If you put your finger in the socket, you will get an electric shock. It is much harder to use "if only," that is, to imagine a radically counter-realistic scenario. The child undergoes an important stage in his development when he learns to do this. It is the ability to move outside the existing structure and think, or dream, of another one. It means that I see neither my reality nor the existing laws of nature as the only dimension. The deepest meaning of the concept of creation is that the world could have been different. Despite all the laws of nature, I can conceive of a completely different system of laws. Even if I cannot think of another system, I can conceive of the world not existing at all. Imagining the counterfactual constitutes a great revolution in human thought.

At this juncture we may ask the *haver* to relate to the ideas of the philosopher's spiritual grandson, Baruch Spinoza (and thus examine his view of the relationship between Judaism and nature). Any discussion of a philosophical theory is, above all, an attempt to discover the value of the truth in its claims, but we cannot do that here. I do not want to level accusations against Spinoza the man. Yet, we must take note of the implications of his ideas. In doing so, we must examine his explicitly stated conclusions. One may, of course, try to defend any thesis and link it to some other respected approach. But that sort of defense cannot prevail against explicit statements in his *Tractatus Theologico-Politicus*.

As far as I am concerned, these statements form the "*J'accuse*" against his approach, and against those who in certain areas, either knowingly or unknowingly, followed in his footsteps. It is an indictment encompassing eight counts:

1. The sin of immanence: ethics

This is the first sin, from which all others follow: "God is the world." This is not merely a philosophical claim. Nature is the world of facts. Above nature spreads the world of values, which are not facts. But no distinction is made here between nature and norm. One who draws his values from nature accepts the decree of nature: the law of the jungle and the conviction that might is right. In this regard I see Kant as the polar opposite of Spinoza. The contrast between the law born of logic and the law of nature, including human nature, is none other than a restatement of classical Jewish ethics.

2. The political sin: the state as omnipotent Leviathan

In the sphere of politics, the identification of nature with a norm means that the law is laid down by those in power. The person who has no power to enforce his rights has no rights. Power and rights are synonymous! The final conclusion from these ideas was developed in the philosophy of Nietzsche. He tried to teach us to extract all the implications of various philosophies, however paradoxical and appalling. A new concept must arise in place of the Judeo-Christian ethic. Nietzsche was willing to take this theory to its ultimate conclusion, which would have meant detention and extermination camps. Nietzsche's Jewish admirers can comfort themselves with the fact that the victims of his approach were not supposed to be Jews. But this does not change the moral and political implications of his approach.

3. Power Politics

Spinoza's moral positions imply a Machiavellian approach to government. Following Isaac Pollegar, Spinoza teaches us that the destruction of the Temple was the result of a "feminine" politics that does not rely heavily enough upon force.

4. Economic Implications

As Rabbi Nahman's student Rabbi Natan taught, money and nature are intertwined. Marxism in part represents the application to economics of the conclusions stemming from the idea of divine immanence in nature. Marx believed it impossible to base the improvement of society on the human ideals. Prophetic visions and other such philosophies constitute a mere "Utopian Socialism" in the Marxist view. In the face of social visions, the Marxists created scientific socialism, which is not in the hands of man's will, but rather constitutes a process that functions and develops on its own.

5. Nature and Freedom

Man is part of nature. One implication of this idea is the denial of human freedom. This seems like a way of overcoming Dualism. The implications of this principle were voiced by Darwin and in the Darwinian philosophy in general. I do not intend to discuss the evolutionary process here, but it should be noted that Darwinian social philosophy follows logically from Spinoza's philosophy. According to this position, it is the struggle with and triumph over moral restraints that will ultimately bring about the progress of humanity.

6. Elitist Freedom

Spinoza's view implies that freedom is significant only in the world of thought. Everything is in the hands of the government, except philosophy. Everything is permitted for the government, except to forbid an elitist group to develop and believe in its own philosophies. This is an elitism that we find in the *Kuzari*'s philosopher.

This idea has far-reaching implications for Jewish survival. It suggests that the government has the right to impose religious obligations on the citizens of the country without exception. Here we are witness to the debate between Spinoza and Mendelssohn, who fought for the religious freedom of the Jewish minority.

7. Spinoza and Judaism

Some people try to present Spinoza as the first secular Jew. Out of his complex attitude to Judaism I will note only one aspect that seems to me to be especially significant. Spinoza was a victim of the great temptation that lies in wait for every philosopher. The involvement in philosophy is abstract. He sees in his mind a fascinating war of ideas, but whoever is outside cannot perceive the tension and the attraction it holds for him. The philosopher is tempted to give a tangible representation of the abstract. Spinoza did this. The representation he gave to his philosophy in a theological-political manifesto transformed the conflict of ideas into a kind of philosophical Western movie. The good philosophy was represented by Jesus, the bad by Judaism. This had significant and disastrous results, giving rise to philosophical anti-Semitism, which affected various philosophers in Spinoza's wake.

8. Spinoza and Jewish National Rebirth

Religious rights are merely a function of political power. The Torah is none other than the constitution of the Jewish state. This means that only the birth of a Jewish state could usher in the binding power of the Torah. Until then, it can have no power, and the state has the absolute right to pass religious laws that bind its Jewish citizens, without any limitations. There are those who try to see Spinoza in a positive light based on his comment about the possibility of a rebuilt Jewish state. This is an interesting theory. But the context teaches us the real meaning of this statement. Wagner also made a statement which could imply recognition of a Jewish state, but this did not make him any less of an anti-Semite.

CHAPTER 41:
MIRACLES

The miracle is a concept, like many others, that cannot be defined at the outset. Its definition and meaning are under debate. In other words, the definition will be not the starting point but the concluding point of our discussion.

Looked at simply, miracles may be termed a completely extraordinary phenomenon, which cannot be explained within the natural system. On further consideration, however, as both believers and philosophers have stated, the greatest miracle is the very existence of the laws of nature. The order, the fact that the world functions according to unvarying laws, constitutes the greatest miracle of all. But man must reach a high level of development to understand how extraordinary the order of nature is: the miracle of planetary behavior, which "adheres" to the laws of mathematics and physics, or the movements of subatomic particles. Macrocosm and microcosm alike sing the praises of the Creator. Certainly, it is a wonder! But we have grown used to this wonder and are like a child who thinks that amazing inventions, the result of thousands of years of scientific and technological development, are to be taken for granted. We are not amazed at the works of creation that surround us. As a result of this lack of amazement, we transform nature into an independent being. Nature, the conglomerate of principles that control the world, becomes all powerful and a ruler of the world. This was, phrased differently, the view held by idolaters, and it has not disappeared from the world. It is returning in a modern form, either in pantheism on the one hand or, on the other hand, in the beliefs of those who treat nature as an explanation for everything. We will only recognize a power that is beyond nature after our tendency to see in nature the final and undisputed law and principle encounters a crisis. This power is the divine element. When it penetrates into nature, inexplicable events occur.

Humanity has often witnessed wondrous and amazing phenomena. The *haver* teaches, however, that although these experiences can bear witness to the existence of a level above nature, we must not base our religion upon them. This surprising claim is found explicitly in the biblical verses that warn us of the possible appearance of a false prophet who can perform miracles. We must not blindly follow a mistaken mathematical proof, which might teach that 0=1, nor should we follow a miracle that is purported to prove the truth of idolatry, or of religions that are, in essence, its modern versions. We must distinguish between miracles and phenomena that are the results of hallucination, illusion or extraordinary sensory perception. We must further distinguish between miracles and legitimate phenomena that are not miracles and perhaps belong to the field of parapsychology. It is possible that some people not only possess the powers to bend spoons or forks through a mental exercise but also have the psychic power to change things in reality. It is possible that some people have the power to set a compass using only their thoughts, or to light a fire without using their hands. These things merely teach us that there are other natural powers that we must study, if they do exist. This is clearly a breakthrough to spiritual powers that materialism has tried blot out, but this is not a breakthrough into the world of divinity. The breakthrough into the divine is expressed in commands that only the Creator of the world can give and carry out. The connection with the divine is expressed mainly through revelation, in the encounter that contains in its essence something that will one day dispel all doubts. The existence of collective revelation is based on the principle that we must neutralize personal error, subjectivity and the fact that we could be faced with an illusion or a hallucination. There are miracles that are tied to individuals, such as healing the sick and resurrection of the dead. In the exodus from Egypt, we are faced with changes in the powers of nature. We are witness to truly cosmic phenomena. The miracles refer to powers that are beyond human existence and even beyond the universe itself.

The Natural Explanation of Miracles

There is a tendency to try to explain miracles naturally, and such explanations can often be provided. Surprisingly, they do not detract at all from Halevi's proof. To understand this, we will discuss the ideas of Rabbi Isaac Breuer, one of the greatest of Halevi's modern successors and author of a book whose title may be translated (from the original German) as

The New Kuzari. Although R. Breuer does not argue with the Aristotelians or the Karaites, there is a basic similarity between Halevi's *Kuzari* and the *New Kuzari*. The philosophical basis of Breuer's approach is found in the writings of the modern philosophers, particularly Immanuel Kant and Arthur Schopenhauer. We cannot plumb the depths of this work, but we will try to present his approach in general terms.

Breuer's theory is based on the idea that we must distinguish between reality itself and the way we perceive it. Nature, the cause-and-effect reality that we perceive, is not the true reality. Rather it is the product of our perception. To illustrate, think of a person wearing sunglasses. The color of his vision is determined by the color of his glasses. This is also true of optical glasses that distort one's vision. We can also think of night-vision equipment, which processes data and provides us images that imitate the originals.

In our perception and consciousness there are two elements: the thing-in-itself, and the way we process it. We do not understand how very important this processing is. It is like a person sitting in a theater innocently watching a play, who does not notice that this sophisticated theater is built in such a way that the observer is also the director of the play. Part of the action on the stage takes place in accordance with the actions and reactions of the observer. He is not an objective, uninvolved observer. The very fact of his presence involves him in the play. We know today that the fact that the observer interferes in reality, and that the "play" changes in accordance with the presence or absence of observers, is one of the most amazing elements of quantum physics. It is important here to point out that according to this approach, as Rabbi Breuer says, the very fact of our encounter with reality creates a framework of cause and effect. Human perception places reality in a natural framework, which will later create the illusion that miracles can be explained. Rabbi Breuer uses a number of models to express this duality. One of the best models is the relation between the Tetragrammaton and the other names of God. We do not pronounce the Tetragrammaton because it is the "real thing," while the other names are our perceptions of the Tetragrammaton. In this way, wonder of wonders, there is a Tetragrammaton, which expresses the true reality, while the laws of nature stand at the opposite pole, expressing the other divine names, our perceptions of reality.

Rabbi Breuer points to the possibility that certain miracles may be explained naturally and still retain their miraculous character. Prophecy is in essence a breakthrough to the true reality. If we return to the example of the theater, we are familiar with the curtain that rises to reveal the play, but we are not aware of the fact that behind this curtain there is another curtain. This is the entrance to backstage, where the illusion of reality that we see behind the first curtain is created. Neither in the theater nor in a magic show do we sense the other side of things—the players without their costumes or the tricks of sound and light that create the magician's illusion. Rabbi Breuer claims that God created the world such that we will always construct this framework and never be able to see behind the scenes. Prophecy is the breakthrough to backstage. If a regular person sees a miracle, even if the miracle is clearly significant, he can try to explain it. But only the prophet can identify the meaning that is beyond the miracle.

Let me offer a "trivial" example: Was the salvation of the Six-Day War a miracle? Whoever lived through it with open eyes will say it was miraculous. Yes, in hindsight, explanations can be given, proving that all the events were completely natural and inevitable. Nevertheless, anyone who lived through that experience knows that it was miraculous. If we return to the example of the theater, it is similar to the story of the actor who shouts "Fire, fire!" and the audience applauds in appreciation of his extraordinarily realistic acting, without understanding that a fire has really broken out. The audience remains stubbornly convinced that this is a part of the play, although really what is going on is outside the framework of the play. Similarly, we sometimes find a person persisting in explaining the miracle, without sensing that something outside the framework of the play is taking place. Seeing is no guarantee that people will understand that what they are seeing is extraordinary. Man—in reality, his perceptual ability—insists on putting events into the framework of a known system. Yet, a miracle can be seen. Sometimes things are just too coincidental to be a coincidence.

The Sages distinguished between a hidden miracle and a revealed miracle. Halevi teaches us that a miracle is a one-time historical event, and its role is to shake man out of the closed scientific play he is watching. The Torah wants to explain to him that what appears to be nature is really a costume and a disguise. As the Hasidim say, the world is an act of concealment, and the role of miracles is to remove us from this concealment. The first obligation is to prevent the concealment of the concealment—in other words, to understand that the concealment exists.

Nature and the Divine Elements (II:2)

Halevi begins by discussing those divine elements that relate to God's actions in the world, and he later relates this to an additional area, the attributes associated with God's true name, the Tetragrammaton. In other words, he distinguishes between attributes that express God's intervention in our world through the forces of nature and attributes that express His behavior as a creator of realities that transcend the laws of nature.

Halevi relates: "The active divine elements are derived from the actions that come from God through the medium of natural causes." In other words, we use these descriptions to attribute the events in our lives to divine causes. For example, when we speak of God as the One who makes us rich or poor, or as a jealous and avenging God, we are describing the effects of a normal life, with its social, financial and other aspects, except that we attribute these powers to God, their original source.

The second category of divine elements appears at first to be very similar to the former group. On closer examination, however, we find that the difference between them is substantive, not merely linguistic. This second group consists of the attributes "associated with the Tetragrammaton." Attributes such as "Creator" and "Maker of Great Wonders" fall into this category. These titles suggest God's absolute freedom and His ability to transcend the laws of nature.

The difference between these two categories is expressed well at the beginning of the Book of Exodus. God appears to Moses and says, "I appeared to Abraham, Isaac, and Jacob [using the name] E-l Sha-ddai, but using the name [Tetragrammaton], I did not appear to them." Halevi explains that the lives of the forefathers were guided by God through the forces of nature. This type of guidance is described by the name Sha-ddai. Sha-ddai refers to the divine power that acts through the laws of nature, in contrast to the Tetragrammaton, which represents a complete departure from all natural laws. A miracle is a departure from the laws of nature. How much more miraculous is the creation of those very laws of nature.

In his commentary on this verse, Nahmanides quotes the opinion of Ibn Ezra, which is similar to Halevi's: "Using the name E-l Sha-ddai refers back to the first part of the verse and it means "I have shown Myself to Abraham . . . using the name E-l Sha-ddai, and through my name [Tetragrammaton] I did not make Myself known to them." Until this point, we have a precise parallel. But Nahmanides continues in Ibn Ezra's name:

The verse that says that [God] appeared to the Patriarchs with this name implies that He orchestrates the celestial systems and performs great miracles with them in which the natural order of the world is not nullified. During a famine He saved them from death. In war [He saved them] from the sword. He also gave them wealth and honor and all manner of good things. These are all mentioned in the promises in the Torah, both the blessings and the curses. For man receives good as a reward for a good deed and bad as a punishment for a bad deed only through miracles. If man were to be left to his nature and luck, his actions would not add nor detract. However, the rewards and punishments of the Torah in this world are all miracles and they are hidden [such that] the observers will think that this is the way of the world and man does not really receive reward and punishment. Therefore, the Torah expounds upon the warnings in this world but not on the promises for the soul in the world of souls, for these are miracles and are against the natural progression. While given the existence of the soul and its devotion to God, it is fitting that it would return to the God who gave it.

Nahmanides teaches that it does seem as though nature is following its own set of laws. The world follows its natural course, and everything is left to chance. Nature's random behavior cannot contain any concept of reward and punishment. Yet, the behavior of the righteous person constitutes a natural cause that affects the behavior of nature. The germs and the white blood cells that fight them do not recognize this behavior, according to the laws of nature. When ethical realities are expressed despite everything, this is a hidden miracle, a hidden system that fits itself onto nature. Divine providence can be discovered in cosmic and human history. We detect consideration of and relation to the actions of man, to justice and evil. This fact, that hidden miracles exist as an additional system of laws beyond the laws of nature, is what is described by the name, "E-l Sha-ddai." This is an additional force that enters into the natural system, and it has a name: divine providence.

Thus, Nahmanides suggests that we have three systems. First, there is the normal, natural system. Although God is hidden behind it as well, this system is expressed (for instance) in the rains falling as a result of climatic changes. At the opposite extreme, we have the revealed miracle, which is the absolute departure from the laws of nature. The classic examples are the great miracles and creation itself. Creation founded the laws of nature but did not act according to them itself. Between these two systems stands a third system—divine providence, working within the recesses of nature. This element does not express itself through a dramatic breakaway from the natural framework. It functions within the system of apparently random events. In the encounter between various causes, it becomes evident that God directs nature. The biblical descriptions of the lives of the Patriarchs are an example of the providential presence in nature. This is a hidden miracle, of which the Purim story is the classic example.

Thus, we are faced with three possible regimes: the regime of nature, the regime of hidden miracles and the regime of revealed miracles. Maimonides generally stresses the first and third of these regimes, though in his "Epistle Regarding Resurrection of the Dead," he speaks explicitly about hidden miracles. Nahmanides coined the term "hidden miracle" (*neis nistar*) and thus succinctly expressed Halevi's distinction between the attributes which are "borrowed from the actions that come from God through the medium of natural causes" and the "attributes which are attached to the Tetragrammaton," in other words, the action that takes place as a result of the principle of the Tetragrammaton, the absolute departure from the boundaries of nature and its laws.

Halevi teaches us something paradoxical at the end of this section. Because the Patriarchs were on so high a level, God did not need to use revealed miracles and could guide and direct their lives through hidden miracles alone.

The Existential Miracle

The topic of miracles would not be complete without a final point from the teachings of Rabbi Nahman of Braslav. In R. Nahman's thought, the Land of Israel symbolizes faith, while Egypt symbolizes nature. In existential translation, Egypt (*mitzrayim*) symbolizes the narrow pass (*meitzar*) that reality shows us. We are sometimes locked into a situation of distress and pain, in narrow straits. Yet even then, the Exodus can occur.

We are shut into our particular situation, like Noah shut in the ark. But even if everything is shut and locked, there is always a window. There is a way out. Our burden is the rule of nature, but we can escape it. Health is a miracle, and we must believe that miracles can happen.

CHAPTER 42:
THE DIVINE IMAGE

The *Kuzari* and Maimonides

At the end of the section discussing the divine attributes (II:2), Halevi mentions two specific attributes: "wise of heart" and "courageous in power" (Job 9:4). "Courageous in power" is clearly an attribute of action. "Wise of heart," Halevi claims, demonstrates that "intellect is His essence."

Maimonides appears to take a similar position, and he devotes the first chapter of Part I of the *Guide* to clarifying the concept of "divine image." As we shall see below, however, there is a fundamental difference between Halevi and Maimonides. Devoted to his theory of divine attributes, Maimonides denies even this imagery and accepts the definition only after interpretation and qualification.

Maimonides begins by clarifying a point that to us is self-evident: the term "divine image" refers not to man's physical form but to his essence, the intellect. Man is in the image of God because he has an intellect. This idea would seem consistent with Halevi's view. But Maimonides continues:

> Now man possesses as his proprium something in him that is very strange as it is not found in anything else that exists under the sphere of the moon, namely, intellectual apprehension. In the exercise of this, no sense, no part of the body, none of the extremities are used; and therefore this apprehension was likened unto the apprehension of the deity, which does not require an instrument, although in reality it is not like the latter apprehension, but only appears so to the first stirrings of opinion. (*Guide* I:1; Pines trans. p. 23)

Maimonides here means to help us avoid a mistake. It would seem that the concept of the "divine image" means that there is a similarity between man and God, but Maimonides puts up a warning sign. God's perception is not like man's perception, and there is a tremendous gulf between the two. The philosophers tended to compare the two essences and speak of God in the image of man's reason. Although they of course assumed a distance between them, they understood God's mind to be merely a more complete form of man's mind, in quantity or quality. That is the rationalist philosophy. Maimonides, however, argued for an essential, fundamental difference between man and God, objecting to any comparison between them. The resemblance between them can be described only by means of the negative attributes. What characterizes the human mind? It is unique in the world. The human mind is something completely different from all other things that exist "under the moon." It is strange and foreign in this world. Man and God share this strangeness. They are similar in their very uniqueness and difference from everything else. There is but a weak analogy between man and God, which allows us to compare them only through their shared lack of resemblance to anything else. This negative similarity defines the limit of what we are permitted to say. According to the first chapter of the *Guide*, then, Maimonides did not accept Halevi's opinion that the "intellect is the essence" of God. We may have here one of the side streets of Halevi's thought, perhaps even the remnants of a philosophical first draft.

The Uniqueness of the Intellect

What is unique about the human mind, which makes it so very different from everything else that exists in the world? Many people simply deny this uniqueness. Their immediate reaction is to claim that the intellect is merely a conglomeration of processes that take place in the human brain. Maimonides, for his part, can easily attack this claim and prove that the actions of the intellect cannot be explained through the actions of the brain. In our times, we can describe this through a simple analogy: we cannot explain the telephone operator by explaining the central operating station, or the engineer by explaining the computer, even though they use them. The reality of the intellect is a totally different reality. It is an abstract reality. The human intellect is self-contained and creates a reality inside itself. It constitutes, according to Maimonides, a kind of wondrous camera that does not need film to record images.

The uniqueness of man expresses itself also in the immortality of the soul. Someone could destroy the telephone switchboard, or cut the wires and leave the operator unhurt but with no connection to the outside. Before us is a totally independent reality that does not rely on physical, chemical or biological implements, one that uses "no sense, no part of the body, none of the extremities." This abstract quality, not an attribute in its own right, but in essence a common lack of a particular attribute, is what man and God share.

The Garden of Eden

Maimonides' foregoing interpretation leads him to a discussion of the "Garden Of Eden" episode. His interpretation is important not only because of the subject's importance but also because it is an example of philosophical exegesis of the Bible.

Our starting point will be a legend from the world of Greek mythology, the story of the discovery of fire. Prometheus is a Titan, a cross between a man and a god. He feels sorry for the humans, and steals fire from the gods to give it to them. The world of the humans is cold, hard and dark until Prometheus brings the redeeming fire from the heavens. The idea of this legend is that in giving fire to mankind, Prometheus acts against the will of the gods and is therefore punished. The gods are "jealous." They don't "give the people a break." They keep the fire for themselves because they don't want the people to enjoy it as they do. Fire is the basic tool and classic symbol of human technology, and the gods may have been motivated not by jealousy but by fear that people might be able to use their technology to enter the world of the gods and demote them from their status. According to this legend, science and technology are a challenge to the gods.

As we have seen before, there is a system that has made Prometheus its symbol: Marxism. Prometheus appears there as a symbol of the man who reaches his goal through struggle and rebellion against the gods and against religion. From their perspective, the challenge was positive, the symbol of man conquering nature. This is the same Prometheus who made himself felt in the catastrophe in the atomic reactor at Chernobyl.

In light of this approach, we can understand the symbolic significance of fire in Jewish law and lore. The Friday night candle is the symbol of holiness, joy and spirituality. At the same time, fire is the symbol of human technology. The prohibition against kindling a fire ends on Saturday night in a blessing over a kind of torch, over fire and technology.

The blessing of Saturday night means that man does not steal the fire. He makes a blessing over it every Saturday night because God gave it to man in His benevolence.

While the Garden of Eden story cannot be explained as a manifestation of divine jealousy, it has been widely interpreted as alluding to the danger and pain that originate from wisdom. This interpretation is evident in contemporary discussions of whether science is a dangerous treasure. We live in a period of genetic discoveries, but is that activity positive or will it create a new danger like that of nuclear weapons? Genetic engineering can be dangerous not only because of its biological results but also because—and here we enter the realm of science fiction—it can create a way for despots to transform humanity into a flock of slaves. Is the alternative to live in a paradise of fools, where the central condition is really not to know? Or perhaps we must understand the account of the Garden of Eden differently. The judgment one passes on science and technology depends on how one understands the story.

Maimonides suggests a different approach. He believed in the basic alliance between Torah and intellect. Man was created in the divine image, and this means that his intellect did not come into being as a result of sin. In interpreting the Garden of Eden episode, Maimonides writes as follows:

> Years ago a learned man propounded as a challenge to me a curious objection. It behooves us now to consider this objection and our reply invalidating it. . . . This is what the objector said: It is manifest from the clear sense of the biblical text that the primary purpose with regard to man was that he should be, as the other animals are, devoid of intellect, of thought, and of the capability to distinguish between good and evil. However, when he disobeyed, his disobedience procured him as its necessary consequence the great perfection peculiar to man. . . . (*Guide* I:2; Pines trans, pp. 23–24)

This questioner thus assumed that the gift of the intellect was a result of the sin.

Maimonides rejected the questioner's premise. He explained the "divine image" as referring to the intellect. Man is the only creature who has a dialogue with God, and that dialogue is based on the assumption that man is free and has an intellect. Man faces the conflict and choice between the divine command and the serpent. The fact that man faces a test means that the possibility of sin exists, and, therefore, so do reason and freedom. Man can and must decide.

Maimonides is teaching us a basic principle in biblical exegesis. We must not read the Scriptures in the same way that we read a story or a poem. We must look more deeply into it. The tree of knowledge of good and evil did not grant man his intellect. In order to understand this, we must distinguish between two types of evil. We must distinguish between the "knowledge of good and evil" and the "knowledge of truth and false-hood." What is the difference between them? We must search for a solution in the Scriptures. Truth and falsehood were realities in man's consciousness even before the sin. But what is the good and evil that they discover? This we must learn from the rest of the story. Man discovers the meaning of shame.

Maimonides teaches us well that the knowledge of truth and falsehood refers to objective knowledge, such as mathematical knowledge. In contrast, in other areas, such as aesthetics, there is no such objective reality. The first knowledge, that of the Garden of Eden, was in the area of objective knowledge. After the sin, man fell to the area of subjectivity. This is the meaning of his eating the fruit. The consumption of the forbidden fruit taints our worldview with subjectivity, and our vision becomes distorted. The Musar teachers explain this taint of subjectivity with a pithy example. If one places a small coin over his eye, it can completely conceal any other person. Our interests are represented by the Tree of Knowledge.

We must realize that wisdom and science are constantly in danger of falling under the serpent's influence, that is, of being guided by personal desires and selfish interests. Only when man overcomes these and reaches an objective viewpoint can he discover the truth and free himself. Knowledge is freedom, but there is a different kind of knowledge, a subjective knowledge that endangers both man and the world.

Freedom and the Divine Image

As we have seen, one characterization of man's divine image associates it with his intellect. Other philosophers and commentators, however, saw the divine image as manifested in other human attributes. Maimonides and Rabbi Judah Loew of Prague (the Maharal) emphasized the importance of freedom in defining the essence of man. This was beautifully expressed in the writings of Rabbi Me'ir Simhah ha-Kohen of Dvinsk, author of *Meshekh Hokhmah*. The divine image in man is his freedom.

Oedipus and Rabbi Akiva

The Jewish concept of freedom will be better understood through a comparison of two stories—the Greek myth of Oedipus and the legend of Rabbi Akiva's daughter.

In the Oedipus myth, representative of Greek thought in general, man is ruled by powers he cannot escape. Even advance knowledge of the danger man faces cannot help him escape it. Oedipus is prophetically informed that he will murder his father and marry his mother. Both Oedipus and his father fight against this prophecy, but to no avail. In the end, Oedipus brings his fate upon himself.

The Sages relate that Rabbi Akiva had a daughter. The astrologers told him, "On the day of her wedding she will be bitten by a snake and will die." Rabbi Akiva grieved over this news.

On her wedding night, his daughter took her golden pin and thrust it into the wall for safekeeping. The pin pierced the eye of a snake and remained there. In the morning, the pin slid out and the dead snake with it.

Her father asked her, "What did you do?"

She answered: "On the eve of my wedding, a beggar came to the door, and everyone was so preoccupied with the wedding feast that no one noticed him. I took the portion that you gave me and I gave it to him."

He said to her, "You did a good deed."

Rabbi Akiva went forth and explained, "Charity saves from death"—not merely from an abnormal death, but from death itself.

This story is a powerful statement against the belief that everything is predetermined. The contrast between these two worlds is evident. The astrologers ascertained man's predetermined fate. It would seem that they were right. Yet their prophecy is not absolute; escape is possible.

Astrology

We are not concerned here with the question of astrology. Rather we will focus on the claim, clothed sometimes in the language of astrology but often in the scientific language of biology or psychology, that a man's fate is set in advance. The Sages' overall perspective on the matter appears in their statement that one born under the planet Mars is destined to be a murderer, unless he becomes a butcher or a surgeon. This may give us a new perspective on Rabbi Akiva's statement "Everything is preordained, yet freedom of choice is granted." The accepted interpretation, which appears, for example, in Maimonides' commentary on tractate *Avot*, is to explain this statement as a response to the question of divine foreknowledge and free choice. In light of the story about Rabbi Akiva's daughter, however, it can teach us that although there are constraints that affect the future, man is given the opportunity to overcome them. Freedom thus means the possibility of escaping one's fate.

Jewish philosophers have held differing opinions with regard to the merit and significance of astrology. Maimonides saw astrology as a pseudo-scientific superstition, and was therefore totally opposed to it. Others, such as Rabbi Abraham Ibn Ezra, believed in the truth of astrology. Still, most of those who believed in it were convinced that "Israel has no sign." In other words, he who behaves like a Jew is not controlled by the stars.

The theoretical question, however, is only one aspect of the problem. The central question, even for those who grant astrology some merit, is our attitude towards it. Are our fates in fact sealed by the movements of the stars? Ought we to make the critical decisions of our lives based upon those movements, or ought we to follow the logical path and make decisions based on the reality before us and the values that guide our lives? In the long term, we will certainly reach the conclusion that this type of "science" is totally destructive and will cause humanity terrible misfortunes. It is well-known that Hitler had an astrologer and that he followed his advice in planning his battle strategies. Apparently, the English also used an astrologer, but his job was to decipher what the suggestion of the enemy's astrologer would be.

An important expression of these ideas was given to us by Nahmanides. On the one hand, Nahmanides believed there might be some truth in astrology. We must approach it, however, within the very general framework of the commandment, "You shall be whole-hearted with your God." According to Nahmanides, this is a positive commandment, and it teaches man to act according to the Torah and not according to this type of "supernatural" guidance. Nahmanides believed that the future is predetermined, but in a very relative manner. Our fate exists in the form of "letters," and through our actions we combine them into words. For example, imagine that the heavenly decree consisted of the letters *gimel*, *ayin*, and *nun*. They can be read in two different ways: *nega* (plague) or *oneg* (pleasure). The formation of the letters into words is not determined by the stars. The future is preordained to some extent, but the practical ramifications are not decided by the constellations.

Astrology is an interesting, often pleasant, amusement. Yet, we must be wary of it. As mentioned earlier, Maimonides completely rejected what he regarded as superstitions. A society that adheres to such futile and empty ideas is in some way self-destructive. In his epistle to the sages of Marseilles, for example, Maimonides suggests the hair-raising idea that part of the terrible events of the destruction of the second Temple occurred because, instead of studying war, our ancestors were preoccupied with astrology and the like. Man must search for realistic solutions, in this case a military solution, and not look to irrational illusions. They are forbidden because they are false, and lies are dangerous when they take the place of truths that can offer salvation. People stop thinking when they depend upon such phenomena. In addition, for every real phenomenon, we will meet a thousand phenomena of falsehood and deception. Maimonides' consistent denial of any form of dependence upon magic and soothsaying reflects a rich rabbinic tradition, but there were others who were more open to these esoteric phenomena. In this regard, it is important to stress the essential difference between astrology and phenomena that stem from parapsychology. This brings us once again to what can be termed "practical Kabbalah." In these cases, the person giving the guidance receives his information not from any science but from what is revealed to him in his own soul, sometimes through all kinds of facts that serve merely to give him inspiration. Parapsychology is much closer to Kabbalah, and it is possible that the soul can grant us glimpses of the future. The Kabbalists don't use the facts in the way they would be used in solving a mathematical problem. Rather the facts that they know serve as a kind of inspiration to find the solution. There are difficult situations in which fateful decisions are made and there is no way to know what will happen. Turning to a source which transcends the rational is understandable then. However, even in such cases one must be very careful. In particular one must ensure that realistic solutions are not overlooked as a result.

Halevi discusses astrology in a number of places and explains to us unequivocally that the stars have an effect on the earth, but as part of the natural order. In other words, their effect is part of the general order of things, while the astrologers want to learn details from the stars. "The astrologer claims that he knows the details, but we contradict him in this and bear witness that this thing cannot be perceived by flesh and blood" (IV:9). The statements about astrology in the writings of our Sages are to be understood in a totally different way. Astrology is merely "conjecture and casting of lots in the heavens, which has no more truth in it than in casting lots on the earth."

Freedom and Its Ideological Antagonists

Recall the two philosophical triangles, discussed in volume one, that make up the Star of David. The first triangle presents the premise, shared by many philosophers, that man is constrained either by his ties to God (Fatalism) or by his ties to the world (Determinism).

Fatalism is an essential component of Islamic thought, which maintains that all is preordained and consequently man is not free. Interestingly enough, one can act on this belief in two diametrically opposed ways. On the one hand, Fatalism can bring man to total despair and indifference. On the other hand, it can lead people to extreme fanaticism including the suicidal terrorist acts we have witnessed in recent years. If all is set in advance, one can perform the most daring acts without risk.

Judaism, in contrast, believes that man is an architect who participates in the construction of his own world and in the building of the world in general. Thus, Maimonides writes in the Laws of Repentance (6:3; Twersky, *A Maimonides Reader*, p. 78): "This doctrine is an important principle . . . as it is said, 'See, I set before you this day life and good, and death and evil' "—in other words, life and goodness are indeed in the hands of man. "And again it is written, 'Behold I set before you this day a blessing and a curse.' This means that the power is in your hands, and whatever a man desires to do among the things that human beings do, he can do, whether they are good or evil; and because of this facility, it is said"—this is Maimonides' proof—" 'O that they had such a heart as this always.' " This is the ultimate proof of human freedom: God says, "O that they had . . . ," a paradoxical statement meaning that this choice is not in His hands. Here the rabbinical adage "All is in the hands of Heaven, except the fear of Heaven" has its strangest, most paradoxical application.

We will discuss the question of predetermination and free will later on. For now, we consider only Maimonides' statement. Maimonides teaches us (ibid., 5:1; Twersky, p. 77) that "Free will is bestowed on every human being. If one desires to turn toward the good way and be righteous, he has the power to do so. If one wishes to turn toward the evil way and be wicked, he is at liberty to do so." That is Judaism's approach. We must accept this truth and not be misled by "the notion, expressed by foolish Gentiles and most of the senseless folk among Israelites" (ibid., 5:2, p. 77), who believe in Fatalism, that is, that all is preordained.

Maimonides uses two interesting terms here: *tippesh* (foolish) and *golem*. In Jewish law, a *golem* is an uncompleted implement. We may refer to the fatalist as a *tippesh*. He has reached the limit of his religious development and believes completely in the tenets of his religion. Thus, for example, most of the versions of orthodox Islam are fatalistic. Everything is in the hands of God, and one's actions will not make any difference. Such a person cannot be accused of being a bad Muslim. One can only claim that his opinion and position are false. But when a Jew is a determinist, he does not make this claim as a Jew. In taking this position he proves that he has not reached the end of his Jewish development. Therefore he is essentially a *golem*. His religious development is not yet over. He is incomplete, and he is mistaken in his understanding of Judaism.

The Pinocchio Ideal

The *golem*'s mission—to become a person—is the great mission of mankind. Man is not a being so much as a becoming. Two Jewish psychologists spoke of this idea, each in his own way. Erich Fromm wrote about the difference between two ideals, those of "being" and of "having." In the first, the goal is "to be," in the second, it is "to own." Silvano Arieti, an Italian Jewish psychologist, stressed a third ideal, which he formulated not as "to be" but as "to become." Man is not born a whole and perfect entity. He must continue to form himself. When he came to America after the Holocaust, Arieti understood that this is the inner meaning that made the story of Pinocchio a universal children's story. For him, Pinocchio expressed the idea that we are not born perfect, but that we evolve and become. We are like wooden puppets who have to become people. The story of Pinocchio is a kind of symbolic archetype of this evolution.

This idea is expressed in various ways by classical Jewish philosophy.

Maimonides conveyed it in citing a *midrash* telling that the store of souls before birth is not identical to that after death. The divine image is not something we are born with. It is something we must reach by walking in God's ways. That which is truly human in a person must undergo development.

One of man's big problems is his tendency to look at the here and now, which essentially expresses the desire to be, without effort and evolution. To become means that one must occasionally forgo the now for the sake of the future. One must sacrifice current desires for the goal that one has set, for an ideal, or even for oneself, for something one will need tomorrow.

It seems to me that the difference between having and being is easy to understand, but the transition between being and becoming is difficult. In this context, Arieti mentions the great danger portrayed in the book *The Lord of the Flies*. The book tells of a cruel world created by children left to their own devices. Cruelty is a danger that lurks on our path, indeed on the path of all those who cannot educate themselves.

CHAPTER 43:
FOREKNOWLEDGE AND FREE WILL

Our belief in the principle of freedom raises the age-old paradox of divine foreknowledge and human free will. Assume, for example, that a brutal murder is to take place on April 1, 2009. Does God know beforehand—on, say, March 1, 2009 that the murder will take place? We cannot say that He does not know, for that would limit our conception of God. If, on the other hand, He does know, then it would seem that the murderer was not free to choose his actions.

Three Options

Three philosophical responses to the paradox are possible:

1. The first option chooses foreknowledge over free will. The classic example is found in Islam and in various Protestant groups, who claim that human freedom impairs God's greatness and omnipotence. Maimonides sharply objected to these views, stating his position in the *Laws of Repentance*, as discussed in the preceding chapter, and in his *Shemonah Perakim*.

Despite Maimonides' disagreement, several Jewish philosophers believed that Judaism could admit the negation of human freedom. The most outstanding of these were Rabbi Hasdai Crescas and Rabbi Tzadok ha-Kohen of Lublin. The true meaning of their position is a matter of debate. It seems to me that though they limited human freedom, they left a small area of life in which it could be exercised.

2. The second possibility is to limit the scope of God's knowledge. This was the widely attacked position of Gersonides, whose book, *Milhamot Ha-Shem (The Wars of the Lord)*, was said to describe Gersonides' war against God rather than on His behalf.

The Theory of the Continuous Present

3. The third possibility is essentially a search for theories that can resolve the paradox. The classic response to the paradox, and one of the most interesting, is the theory of the continuous present, which we will describe here briefly.

Returning to the example with which we began, the theory suggests that I erred in formulating the question. I asked if God knows in March about a murder that will take place in April. But the expression "God knows in March" is based on a mistaken idea. Because God's existence is not within the framework of time, I cannot say that He "knows in March." As a rough analogy, imagine that we are traveling on a winding, mountainous road. Although we do not know what awaits us beyond the next turn, a person situated at the top of the mountain and looking down can see the road in its entirety. God has a different temporal perspective, one above and beyond all of time.

Applying these ideas to foreseeing the future can be instructive. If I were to accurately predict which hand Mr. Jones will lift in five minutes time, the event could be understood in one of two ways. Either Jones is not free, or I guessed luckily. To claim that I knew which hand he would lift but that he was still free to choose would be paradoxical. But assume now that I am looking at Mr. Jones in what we call today "real time," that is, while he is doing the act. If I look not at the future but at the present, then both his raising of the hand and my knowledge of it are two things that happen simultaneously and do not contradict one another. God exists in a continuous present, in which knowledge of the future is the same as knowledge of the present. This is the philosophical meaning of the description of God as He Who "was, is and will be."

Maimonides' Position

Maimonides did not construct the entire theory of the continuous present. In his opinion we are faced with two different concepts of knowledge. The paradox stems from our attempts to make an analogy between God's knowledge to our own. Since this is an invalid analogy, we cannot solve the paradox. We cannot even formulate it.

Rabbi Meir Simhah of Dvinsk, author of the *Meshekh Hokhmah* and the *Or Sameiah*, believed that the theory of eternal truth in fact represented

Maimonides' position. But R. Meir Simhah added another important layer. The theory of the continuous present resolved the paradox. However, the real solution is that only God truly knows. Were this knowledge given to a prophet, the paradox would reemerge. This has an important and surprising implication: Scripture has dimensions that cannot be understood by prophets or by previous generations. They are revealed to us over time. These revelations constitute *hiddushei Torah*, novel interpretations of the Torah.

To past generations, this approach to the paradox seemed peculiar. In our day, the relativity of time and the fictional possibility of time travel, popularized in movies like *Back to the Future*, have become so common-place that these flights of the imagination no longer surprise us. Perhaps the reader will not even be frightened by another model and by the wild possibility that R. Sa'adiah Ga'on seems to refer to: God receives information from the future, information which flows in the opposite direction of time. One of the speculations of modern physics speaks about tachyons, particles that travel in the opposite direction to the arrow of time. In these particles the movement towards the past becomes a reality!

The theory of the continuous present denies the existence of the paradox. Other thinkers, such as Rabbi Nahman of Braslav, saw no prospect of the human mind having the power to resolve the paradox. Rabbi Nahman taught that there are two types of paradoxes, and that the difference between them can be described in kabbalistic terms. One is the type of paradox that originates in the "breaking of the vessels." These paradoxes can be solved, though the process is on-going. Another type is connected to the empty space that was created through the *tzimtzum*. These questions go back to creation, and no human intellectual effort can answer them.

Determinism

We will not here go into the second part of the problem, the question of determinism. Man has had to deal with this problem constantly, and here, too, contemporary science has opened new vistas in our understanding.

Classical science believed that the world is characterized by absolute determinism and that the future is absolutely set. This belief, which reached its height in the nineteenth century, was well formulated by the French mathematician Laplace, who said that if one knew the placement of all the molecules at the initial state of the world and had a complete description of all the laws of physics, one could have written all of universal history in advance. This is mechanism.

In the twentieth century, the discovery of quantum physics showed that determinism was not absolute. In various submicroscopic phenomena, nature is faced with two alternatives and chooses one of them at random. Take, for example a block of radioactive material. If we ask whether a particular atom in this block will break up within a certain time or not, there is a certain probability that it will break up, and that is all. We cannot formulate any absolute law. We have not denied the existence of a set of laws, but we know that this system of laws is not absolute. Completely random events do occur.

This opens a new gate to understanding the question of free will. It does not solve all of the riddles. Still, it is clear to us today that determinism is neither absolute nor universal. Today this is a definite truth.

Section 10:
Reward and Punishment

CHAPTER 44:
REDEMPTION AND THE SPHERES
OF EXISTENCE

Redemption

We now introduce a new and multifaceted topic, that of redemption. Redemption is the triumph of good over evil. This means that if we could catalogue the tragedies, we could also catalogue the redemptions, or to be more exact, the various dimensions of redemption. We will allow ourselves to do just that. But how does one make a catalogue of troubles? What principle ought we to use in constructing this catalogue? We will first define the principal domains in which we live our lives, and then identify the elements of suffering and evil within each domain.

The Four Circles and Ideals

To illustrate, picture a square representing the cosmos, and inside it three concentric circles: humanity is the largest circle, within it is the circle representing the Jewish people, and, within that, the circle representing the individual. These are the four worlds in which we live and act. Granted, we have ignored secondary circles within the big circles, sub-systems such as the family. Nevertheless, we will simplify the problem and speak of four domains: cosmos, humanity, nation and individual.

This division will help us understand the principles of Judaism. In the tractate *Avot*, Rabban Simeon ben Gamaliel teaches us that "the world rests on three things: on justice, on truth and on peace." This seems to me to mean that Judaism has three ideals. As an individual, my ideal is truth. As a nation, the ideal is justice. As humanity, the ideal is peace. But this is true not only of humanity. Peace is also an ideal of the cosmos. We speak of "He Who makes peace on high."

These are three values that must guide us in the various circles of our existence, but I believe a fourth must be added in each of the domains—

freedom. Freedom, in turn, also has three aspects: freedom for the individual, for the nation and for all of humanity:

1. Individual, personal freedom consists of free choice.

2. Freedom for society is the freedom experienced by slaves emerging from slavery.

3. Freedom for the nation among nations is liberty.

Our lives are guided by many values, which come into conflict with each other. Conflicts can be divided into two types: horizontal and vertical. How does the individual live within society? How do the nation and nationalism find their place within humanity? What is the relationship between all of humanity and the cosmos? How do we simultaneously fulfill the three ideals of truth, justice and peace? These are the vertical relationships. But there are also horizontal conflicts between ideals. For example, every Israeli knows that the great dream that we share is peace. This is an oversimplification, because what we truly want is freedom and peace. We are looking for freedom for society, which will not, God forbid, become a house of slavery. But we are also looking for justice, and justice means that each individual is granted the right to satisfy his minimal needs.

Our century has been torn between two ideologies in the shadow of a threatening conflict, a conflict that was symbolized by the iron curtain. This was the conflict between the ideology, to the left of the curtain, that believed it was necessary to forgo freedom to attain justice, and the ideology to the right of the curtain, that believed freedom so important as to warrant giving up social justice. The first group created a human bee-hive, with a secret police to maintain order. The others pronounced freedom to be so great and holy that man was free to die of hunger in the street.

History has proven that when ideologies are put into practice, they lose much of their content. Still, this introduction illustrates the need for synthesis, this time between justice and freedom. This need exists on all levels. The Torah teaches that we must strive towards the ultimate synthesis. On the one hand, the Torah emphasizes that man is free. As Nahmanides, Maharal and Rav Kook taught, each of them in his own way, that the image of God is freedom. They reiterated the idea that freedom is our divine trait in various ways. Every one of us has this divine spark within him. Judaism champions freedom. On the other hand, it is clear that it does not agree with that freedom is limitless and unbounded. This is because we also believe in truth. Here we reach the great conflict that we all sense: the conflict between freedom and truth. Judaism teaches us to strive towards a synthesis between freedom and truth. That is the most difficult task.

Let me illustrate this from Hayyim Potok's book, *My Name Is Asher Lev*. In this work, we read of a young boy growing up in a family with many problems. The child, who is very talented artistically, is encouraged both by his family and his family's Rebbe. The young man develops his talent and eventually exhibits his art work in a show. His parents come to the exhibit and are astonished to see that the central painting is of a crucifixion, a fundamental component of the Christian faith. However, in the painting the protagonists have been changed and in it, his father is crucifying his mother. The content is clear: the artist wished to express his feelings. Whether those feelings are justified is not at issue here. What is important is that he chose an exclusively Christian medium to express it.

My first thought when I read the story was bitter disappointment because the hero and the artist had another option: he could have painted his father *sacrificing* his mother in the manner of Isaac's *Akeda*. Or he could have used a different form of martyrdom, in which Jewish history is wellversed. But the author wanted to express the problem of the artist who refuses to be bound by any limitations. The artist speaks in the name of absolute freedom of expression, which becomes his ultimate value. We could accept this if we believed that freedom was the only value. But we are convinced that at least one value stands on par with freedom: truth. We therefore allow ourselves to approach the artist in the name of this truth and say: Do not use this image. Use an image of your own, not only because the image you have used has difficult historical associations, but also because this image is connected to something we have fought against in the name of truth, and to which we are justifiably opposed. We have given the artist a difficult task, but he may not ignore the dilemma. A person who creates a synthesis and is finding his way between freedom and truth does not betray freedom.

This dilemma is not limited to religious content alone. We are faced with similar dilemmas in all areas. In the name of freedom and artistic expression, anything can be sanctioned. I have heard someone describe an imaginary Roman play, in which the director used a slave as one of the actors in order to express the suffering of slavery. But to make the drama more thrilling, the director cut off the slave's hand, not as a theatrical action, but in reality. This artist was not satisfied with art as an imitation of life. He wanted his art to occur in reality. Similarly, we find artists who think that art expresses itself in tattoos or various types of body mutilations, including castration. It is no secret that there exist underground films that document immoral acts culminating in actual murder. What would be the opinion of the artist about this freedom and this art? Clearly, there is a practical question about the limits of artistic expression. This is a much-debated issue. But we cannot help but cry out in protest against those who speak in the name of freedom and neglect the call of truth.

What Is Freedom?

Each of us is the captain of a ship but is also the ship itself. The ship is tossed on a stormy sea, the sea of life, and we must bring it safely to shore. We use maps to aid us in this purpose. The captain's status is one of freedom; the map is truth. We can sink our ship in the sea or bring it to shore. We can hit a snag by accident or on purpose, by force or by choice. That is freedom. But we believe that there are maps. We are free and we can alter reality, by building a new port, for example. The maps, however, exist. This is the truth. To find our way we need maps. Our relationship to the maps is described by the concept of autonomy.

Those of us who are not intimately familiar with the problems of the captain, like me, can translate the parable to a better-known model, that of driving. Driving is a good allegory for life, for driving requires three things: knowledge regarding the car and the roads, skill and morality. Knowledge and experience are not enough. We also need rules of behavior, so that we know which moral principles to apply when we find ourselves in difficult situations. In other words, in addition to the technical skills we also need facts and values. I use the example of driving because it can help us clarify the different levels of autonomy.

On the first level, autonomy gives expression to the fact that the driver must learn to drive on his own, without an instructor present. The instructor should sit in the car with the student for a period of time, but the goal is that the student will eventually drive alone. This is the most basic, primary level of autonomy. Of course there are various stages within this level, but this is its essence. Translated to our reality, the first skill is a cognitive skill. In other words the child should be able to recognize and distinguish between good and evil on his own, without his mother or some other guide making decisions for him.

Beyond the first level there exists a different type of autonomy, which has ethical significance. We expect the driver to stop at a stop sign, not because he sees a policeman, but because he knows that this rule is important, not only because it is an obligation, but because disobeying this law could have disastrous results.

But we have not yet finished teaching our student freedom and autonomy. We can teach him to use the car technically and to adhere to the rules of traffic. However we must still teach him to make choices within the framework of these laws. Autonomy in Judaism follows the same pattern. A person must choose his own paths from among the available options. There are lanes that man must open for himself. This is in essence the Hasidic idea expressed by Rabbi Zusha, that he will not be judged because he failed to be Moses, but because he failed to be Zusha. This wise saying can be interpreted in numerous ways. But the simple and basic interpretation is that every person in the world has his own path, his own vocation, which he must find. Self-actualization is not collective. It is not the same for everyone. Every person has his own purpose, and God expects him to fulfill it. The third level of autonomy means that each person has individuality.

Beyond all this, there is a fourth level of autonomy, a different level of freedom. This is the freedom of sages and righteous people. This is the autonomy of the person who can make halakhic decisions, who can decide with regard to very serious dilemmas, or even of the person who can, in a moment of danger, go against the stream, against traffic, transgressing the laws of traffic in cases that warrant special measures. But while this type of autonomy exists, the sages have taught us that it is absurd to think that a person who has not yet passed through all the prior stages of his development could achieve this type of autonomy. This autonomy requires knowledge, self-control and self-criticism. It means that God makes man into a partner. This is the great autonomy of the sage who renders an innovative halakhic ruling.

Jonah and Freedom

Of course, there are levels and forms of freedom other than those we have discussed. But just as we must lament the person who has not attained freedom, so must we lament the person who has exaggerated his freedom and failed to recognize his responsibilities. Such a person has not attained self-actualization. An insight into such a person appears in psychologist Erich Fromm's wonderful interpretation of the book of Jonah. Fromm drew largely on Jewish sources. Though he altered and interpreted his sources, his writings are rich with Jewish tradition.

We read in the scriptures of Jonah the runaway, a symbol of the person who flees his calling, his vocation. Some commentators defend him, perhaps justifiably. Ultimately, however, there is no denying that he runs away from his mission and from his responsibility toward others. If we read the book correctly, we find that Jonah was sent to others, and that the term "mission" connotes anti-freedom. Jonah refuses the mission and flees, entering a ship, hiding and falling asleep below deck. He thinks he has found safety. His adventures end when he is thrown into the sea and finds refuge in the belly of the fish. Here Jonah finds his reward and his punishment, which turn out to be one and the same. Inside the fish Jonah is alone. There is no longer anyone to disturb his peace.

Jonah thus symbolizes the person who refuses a call to responsibility, to a relationship with others. Usually—though not in Jonah's case—the refusal is motivated by the desire to avoid limiting one's freedom, just as some young people refuse to enter into a marriage or assume the responsibility of parenthood. Jonah teaches that the true punishment for refusal to accept responsibility is loneliness. A person lives in a city populated by millions, but he lives in a closed and locked apartment. The man can watch television and open the door to the delivery boys who deliver the goods he has ordered. He is protected, but he is lonely. There is a feeling that modern man has become free because he has freed himself from the pressure of the tribe, of the small town, of the family. In the big city, in the megalopolis, he is apparently free. He can be an individual, not part of any group which determines his life. But the truth is different. Man may have freed himself and achieved individuality, but at its height he has also achieved complete isolation. The person who flees responsibility ends up in the belly of the fish, protected but lonely.

Blending Values

The use of these two words together teaches us that a single value does not govern our lives. Rather there are many values that we try to incorporate, and we must try to blend them. The young person growing up discovers the call to freedom and also experiences the trauma of not being able to fulfill his desires. Time will pass until he feels something else, the problematic nature of freedom.

Many people see birds or other animals as symbols of freedom. They are unaware, however, of the saddening fact that, no matter how free they seem, birds and animals are bound by many invisible strings. They are similar, within certain limits, to fish in an aquarium. They have a certain level of freedom of movement, but even birds have very strict territorial boundaries. Man too, though he thinks he is free, is sometimes bound as tightly as a prisoner. Actions that seem to us to be the result of our free and spontaneous decisions are merely the result of external pressures we internalize, an invasion from the surrounding world. Advertising functions according to the same principle. It repeats and emphasizes the name and qualities of a particular product, to the point where when we need to buy, it will be the first name that rises to our lips and we will therefore buy it. We often find ourselves singing a line from some commercial that has invaded our thoughts. Sometimes the voice that seemingly comes from within actually comes from without. Regarding the Ten Commandments inscribed on the tablets the Sages say, "do not read *harut* [inscribed] but *heirut* [freedom]." This implies that man is perhaps free to do what he wishes, but sometimes he is not free in those very desires. His desire is the result of the influence of the surroundings. *Harut* that becomes *herut* means that only education, effort in personal development, and sometimes the adherence to the inscribed rule can grants us *herut*.

Consider the example of two people. One is lying on his couch, watching a soccer game on television and drinking can after can of beer. The second is exercising or playing basketball in order to improve his health. The first seems relaxed, while the second is perspiring profusely. But who is the free man? Our first reaction will be that the free man is the one lying on his couch. But he cannot even raise himself up. In contrast, all the work of exercising—if not done for commercial reasons—gives the person control over his body and maximal development of his talents and abilities. In other words, it affords freedom. The person who exercises in order to give his body the necessary freedom fulfills the injunction, "do not read *harut* but *heirut*." He shows that, paradoxically and strangely enough, we attain freedom through self-subjugation and self-discipline. The second way sometimes promises much, but actually enslaves one. It is freedom that leads to enslavement.

The meeting of these two paths recalls the beautiful way that Rabbi

Samson Raphael Hirsch explains the two goats used in the service on Yom Kippur. One goat is sent to be a sacrifice in the Holy Temple, the other is seemingly released to freedom, but it actually falls down the cliff of Azazel. Both goats had to be as nearly similar as possible, according to Hirsch, in order to show that they are really one. They are the two options each person faces. One option is the option of bringing the sacrifice. It does contain an element of self-sacrifice, but it is a self-sacrifice that brings one into the holy of holies. The second option creates an illusion of freedom, but actually ends in a fall and deterioration, as we see in many areas of life, particularly in the use of drugs.

Freedom and the Inner Self

The highest level a person can reach in Judaism, as expressed in Hasidism (and elsewhere), is that he will act and fulfill his obligations not by struggling with and overcoming his inner-self, but by an inner drive motivated by his inner-self. This idea is expressed in the Hasidic idea that each of us has an inner world that is essentially good.

To help clarify this idea, let me sketch three models of prayer. The first is free-form prayer, as though I were to ask a person to take up a flute and play whatever comes out of his heart. The flute is an expression of spontaneous prayer, and Hasidism places great emphasis on prayer that comes from the heart.

This type of prayer would appear to be the greatest and most important, but there is another type in which all is reversed. The *siddur* plays its music through us, and we become its instrument. As we see in a choir, no single person can sing the entire song, or whatever comes out of his heart at the moment. Each person must sing within the framework of an arranged group.

The music produced in the second model is beautiful, but not spontaneous. Rav Kook describes these two states in kabbalistic language as inner light and surrounding light. The inner light comes from within the person, while the surrounding light is received from the outside, just as the conductor of a choir or an orchestra stands before me and sets the pace. But Rav Kook defines the essential quality of prayer, as was expressed by A.J. Heschel, through the idea of resonance. Sometimes a certain musical instrument will strike a note, and then another instrument which is in tune with the first will begin to play on its own. The trick is for there to be agreement between the surrounding light and the inner light. One day, at a certain stage of our development, we will come to the recognition that the obligations imposed upon us from without comport with our inner dictate, and that there is harmony between them. We have melodies within us that ought to be aroused by the music from without. This is true prayer.

What is hidden within man's inner world? This has been a topic of debate for generations. Freud's claim means that the inner world is similar to what we find when we lift up the carpet—dust and dirt. There were also ethicists of the school of Rabbi Israel Salanter who felt the same. However, other ethicists, particularly in Hasidism, and Rav Kook among them, had another position. A carpet may indeed conceal dirt. But if we dig into the deepest parts of the human soul we will reach a spring of fresh water. There are various levels in the "inner world." Many things that happen within us are actually "dirt" that comes from outside. The great Hasidic thesis, expressed in the writings of the *Sefat Emet*, among others, and the approach of Rav Kook, is that behind this first inner world there is a deeper inner world. There is a kind of spiritual umbilical cord that unconsciously connects us to a different world. The Torah is not merely a commandment coming from the outside. It grants man the opportunity to uncover inner levels of his personality. This is what is termed by many thinkers, "achieving authenticity."

Education as a Tool

The analogy of the melody, used to illustrate the meaning of prayer, is particularly apt for a third reason. Sometimes we take a child, put a violin in his hands and force him to do tedious exercises. What will be his response? He will be angry, will have difficulty working and, with some justification, will see my actions not only as coercive and constraining but also as cruelly limiting the other activities he wants to do. We only hope that the day will come when the child will realize he has been given a new instrument for the expression of his inner world. The violin, which had been a symbol of external coercion, will become an expression of the inner self, enabling him to express the music that is inside him. He now has an instrument to express his inner self. If he is successful, it can also gain him fame and fortune.

Of course these things should be done gently and pleasantly, without coercion. Nevertheless, it is clear that any human advancement is connected first of all with self-discipline. One must be honest with oneself and clarify whether this self-discipline causes one to give up, or if it allows one to gain new ways to discover one's inner world. We can also fall into the opposite trap. To borrow an allegory from the Hanukkah story, all the oils have been defiled, except for the one small flask. Many times we use holy things for unholy purposes. A great idea such as the idea of education has often been used for evil. In various countries and cultures education has been used to make people into animals or robots. These dangers exist, but they cannot make us forget the true educational ideal. Coercion is not a goal. It is sometimes the only means to try to give a person freedom, to help him to create channels that will give expression to his true freedom, to his inner world and to the truth. People have always used beautiful and ethical ideas to defend evil actions. This is the reason for the great commandment to distinguish between the holy and the profane, between the pure and impure. With regard to our issue, we must differentiate between different types of education and freedom.

We have learned from Hasidism and from the writings of Rav Kook that freedom is one of the basic ideals of Judaism: political freedom, social freedom and also individual freedom.

Political freedom means the liberation of the nation. The month of Nisan is called *Hodesh Ha-Aviv*, "the month of spring." Rav Kook sees it as the month of the "Spring of Nations." This name refers to 1848 when many revolutions broke out in Europe. This was the Spring of Nations, but like the Prague Spring more than one hundred years later, this Spring, which seemed to promise change in the world, ended in utter failure. Rav Kook teaches us that the true Spring of Nations is Passover, the holiday of spring. It is the national symbol of a nation's liberation and a social symbol of freed slaves, a successful slave revolution. Individual freedom is an ideal as well. Sometimes we have to give it up for the sake of the other freedoms, but we must aim for integration. Just as we must be aware that martyrdom is sometimes necessary, we must know also that life is a value, and we must strive to live, for we were commanded "and you shall choose life." Similarly, we must understand that in every act of self-discipline there is a type of martyrdom for the sake of Heaven. However, the final goal of these acts is integration and the melding of truth and freedom.

CHAPTER 45:
FOUR EXPRESSIONS OF REDEMPTION

To understand the idea of redemption, we must first discuss its multi-dimensional character. We will then try to isolate its dimensions, analyzing them one by one. This structure may seem artificial, but it is productive and necessary.

From the outset, the Torah hints at the meaning of redemption. The Torah opens with the divine statement that everything that is created in the world is good, and in the final summary of the story of creation, the world in its entirety is termed "very good." This sets the background for understanding the second story, the story of the Garden of Eden, in which evil makes its appearance. In the Garden of Eden we find a tree: the tree of knowledge of good and evil, a tree that contains the potential for the existence of evil. When we look at the world today, we do not see it as "very good" but as "good and evil." Both good and evil function in it, and the shadows sometimes are more apparent than the light. Evil appears in two guises: natural evil, which man suffers, and moral evil, which man causes.

The contrast between the two biblical stories demonstrates the premise that there is a divine plan for a world that is all good. But once this plan is put into effect and man appears, evil appears as well. That account has been the basis for all thought about the subject in the Bible and in Judaism generally. The Torah depicts an ideal situation, in which there is only good, and a real situation, in which there are good and evil. But it will also teach as well that repentance and redemption are born together with sin. The return to the Garden of Eden, the redemption and the End of Days are present in potential from the start. This potential reality gives us hope for the day that is all good, the day on which good will triumph over evil. The existence of good and evil is a fact. But the Scriptures refuse to accept and agree to this fact. They give us hope for an ideal world, a world that is all good. This is essentially the definition of redemption. The world of evil is merely a stage in the process. Evil will be wiped out, "and God will wipe the tear from every face."

We can now present the central model, which will help us understand the multi-dimensional character of redemption. The key to building this model is what I would call the principle of spheres: the spheres of the nation, humanity, the individual and the cosmos. Exile represents evil and our national suffering. War represents the evil in humanity, the sin of the nations. To represent the suffering of the individual, we have chosen Job's question, the question of evil that besets a righteous man. The evil of the entire cosmos is without a doubt death, which rules over humans and galaxies.

Redemption in Judaism means correcting the evil in the world. This is the source for the four principles, or four expressions, of redemption. Personal ills can be corrected through the idea of immortality. In this world, the reward for keeping the commandments is not always apparent and sometimes does not exist at all, but there is a "tomorrow" when reward will be received. The national ill is resolved in the messianic idea, and the international ill is resolved through the vision of the End of Days, in which "nation shall not lift a sword against nation, neither shall they study war any more." Beyond these, there is a final utopian vision of the correction of the entire world, of triumph even over death, of the return to the Garden of Eden. The lion and the lamb living in peace is a parable for peace among the nations, but it also reflects the fact that there is violence in the non-human cosmos. The ultimate vision of the prophets means triumph over this violence as well.

There are in fact parallels between the dimensions of redemption and the sphere of human life in general. The various components can be arranged in a diagram that might clarify their relationships, as follows:

Sphere	Ill	Redemption
Individual	The righteous who suffer	Immorality of the soul
National	Exile	Messianism
Humanity	War	The end of days
The cosmos	Death	The World to Come

Classical Jewish tradition, that of the Scriptures and the Talmud, present these four ideas without clearly defining the relationships among them. Various Jewish philosophers have attempted to structure the ideas into an integrated system. The classic example is in the work of Rabbi

Sa'adiah Ga'on, who tried to unify the ideas and create a consistent historical continuum of the events of the future. The positions of the philosophers are essentially theories. We are free to find our place among them. But we must retain the four basic ideas. These can be seen as the building blocks used by the philosophers to construct various theories.

These ideas can be presented in a different way, with the four expressions of redemption arranged along historical and meta-historical axes. The historical axis runs between the end of days (the historical destiny of all of humanity) and the messianic era (the historical destiny of the Jewish people). The meta-historical axis runs between the World to Come (the utopia of a cosmos that is "all good") and the immortality of the soul (personal immortality).

These two axes constitute two possible answers to one basic question: Where and how will the redemption occur? Does redemption means fixing this world or does it mean a transition to another world? In other words, does the redemption occur in historical, realistic time, or in another world (the immortality of the soul) or through a basic and general change in the cosmos (the resurrection of the dead)?

With a slight change we can speak of three different ideas of redemption:

1. Individual redemption

2. Historical redemption

3. Cosmic redemption

This schema allows us to understand the great debates in the history of the idea of redemption. Maimonides' ideas can be summarized as an attempt to focus the idea of redemption on two perspectives: the individual perspective (the immortality of the soul) and the historical perspective (the messianic idea and the End of Days). In contrast, Nahmanides saw these two perspectives as an introduction to the true meaning of redemption, the alteration of the entire cosmos.

The Jewish concept of redemption has had a definitive influence upon world culture. The model I am suggesting here allows us to observe and investigate these developments. Christianity generally applied the redemption idea outside the realm of history, negating any tangible historical foundations. The idea of redemption beyond history became a reality in Christianity, in a world where history followed its natural course. In other words, in an unredeemed world, oppression, slavery, poverty and suffering reign.

In the modern world, in contrast, cosmopolitan and national movements have arisen that revolve around ideas of historical redemption. These ideas can be paralleled to the two poles of the historical axis. It is important to recognize that these two poles—one nationalist, the other universalist—were in conflict.

Judaism unites all these dimensions. It presents us with a vision of national liberation and of a social utopia that encompasses all of humanity. In this sense it is similar to all the modern movements that dream about changing the world. But Judaism also believes in personal immortality, alongside the vision of a utopic world.

The model we have used is not complete. It omits some perspectives, such as the mystical. It also does not discuss the changing of history, or cosmic change, or even a spiritual world after death. The mystical experience was perceived as redemptive, as a revelation in which man perceives the true reality. This mystical approach is similar to the existential approach that sees redemption in the encounter between man and God. Rabbi Soloveitchik uses a similar concept in his book *The Lonely Man of Faith*.

It is particularly surprising that even Professor Yeshayahu Leibowitz, who objected to the historical use of the term redemption, used the term in a sense not far removed from the one suggested here:

> Religion, defined as Torah and *mitzvot*, redeems man from the bonds of nature. This is not redemption in the Christian sense, in which man is redeemed because of his sense that he is redeemed. It is actual redemption, liberation from the chains of nature's meaningless cause and effect. This man who lives in the world of *halakhah* . . . does not act solely in accord with natural realities, and his life is not the product solely of natural factors, which operate through his body and his instincts just as they do in the life of an animal. Instead, he shapes his life, meaning that he is autonomous in the precise sense of the word . . . and only an autonomous creature is worthy of the title "Man." . . . This is the power and greatness of *halakhic* religion, which transports Man from the natural world of necessity to a world of choice, intention and purpose. (Y. Leibowitz, *Yahadut, Am Yehudi U-Medinat Yisra'el* [Jerusalem and Tel-Aviv, 1975], p. 60).

This position has parallels in the thought of Rabbi Soloveitchik and in early Hasidic thought.

Denying Redemption

Although the concept of redemption has made its mark on all of humanity, it stands at odds not only with those who would see it one dimensionally but also with those who would deny it absolutely. This denial stems largely from the failure of modern utopian visions and from the corruption of ideologies that we have witnessed in the last century. Believing that history has a goal, the faith in redemption conflicts with nihilist ideas. But some thinkers deny any such historical goal and therefore believe the concept of redemption to be meaningless. In some works of literature and theater, we are exposed to the idea that it is the longing for utopia itself that is the source of the problems and troubles. In these works the here and now become the preferred contenders and take precedence over tomorrow, the redemption and the promised land.

Certainly we must distinguish between the messianic ideal and the attempts to make it a historical and political reality, which can lead to the rise of false messiahs. The messianic ideal is a measure against which reality is to be judged. It thus forces us to confront the defects in reality and arouses us to combat them. This is what distinguishes us from one who believes in the here and now. However, many times the messianic idea and political utopias are profaned when they are realized. But still we can and must believe in redemption.

CHAPTER 46:
IMMORTALITY OF THE SOUL
(I:104–117)

Personal Redemption and the Paradox

Redemption has many facets, but one central idea lies at the core of the concept: the redemption of the individual and the immortality of the soul. Halevi considers this issue at the end of Part I and in other passages, particularly in Part III (III:21).

The discussion of the soul's immortality must begin with the concept's place in the Bible. First, however, it is important to note the historical paradox surrounding this issue. Halevi writes, "Regarding the destiny [promised by] the other religions that impressed you, our Rabbis preceded these religions in this regard; they were the ones who described both Heaven and Hell." (I:115). This is a historical truth that many people tend to forget. The nations of the world have labeled the Torah as materialistic, for it speaks of reward and punishment in this world but seemingly says nothing of the spiritual reward in non-material world of the spirit. Halevi points out the absurdity in this: those very monotheistic religions that make this claim in fact owe their own spirituality to Judaism. All their doctrines are based on those of our ancestors in the Mishnaic and Talmudic periods—in other words, the doctrines of our Sages. This is but one example of the absurd charges that have been leveled against us throughout our long history.

Our Sages stated that belief in the World to Come is one of the principles of Judaism. But what place does this belief hold in the Scriptures? Why is it never mentioned explicitly? The answer, I believe, is provided by Rav Kook in his great essay, *Le-Mahalakh Ha-Ide'ot Be-Yisra'el*. Rav Kook's answer will help us understand how faith in the soul's immortality fits within the larger framework of Jewish thought.

Rav Kook speaks about the scriptural idea of immortality of the soul as a "candle in the afternoon." This Aramaic phrase describes a lamp burning during the day, whose light is not seen because of the greater effect of the sunlight. If we allow ourselves to translate it into more modern terms, we can consider a car emerging from an underground parking lot. Once he is out, he cannot see that his lights are on. Imagine his car driving for many hours with the lights on, until the sun sets—or, to be more dramatic, until the onset of a solar eclipse. Suddenly, he becomes aware of the headlights. People might even think that the driver had just turned on the lights at that moment. In truth, however, the lights were on all the time. We were just not aware of them until the sunlight vanished. If we are careful to note the differences—and we will discuss the most important of these soon—we can say that that belief in the immortality of the soul appears in the Scriptures as well. There, however, it is like a lamp burning in the middle of the day, which cannot be seen because a greater light is shining. This great light, the sun, is none other than the general, collective redemption, the redemption of the nation. The fate of the nation, its future and its redemption, are such central elements and shine so brightly that the inattentive or casual reader may not notice the many other lights shining along the way.

Sometimes we see a procession of cars with their lights on, usually following a coffin to the cemetery, the lights signifying a state of mourning. At other times, lights are a symbol of protest against a particular phenomenon. The belief in the immortality of the soul has all of these elements because it teaches us that the cosmic accounting is far more complicated than many people would like us to believe. There are at least two types of account books: the collective, public account book, which calculates and determines the fate of the nation, and the personal account book, which involves not history but the personal biography of each and every one of us. In the latter book there is either a light that accompanies man on his final journey to the cemetery—the faith in the immortality of the soul—or a light that constitutes a protest and a refusal to accept the world as it appears to us through the lens of our physical existence.

The Religious Confrontation

Methodologically, we ought now to follow in Halevi's footsteps and look more closely at these lights that shine in the daytime. Before that, however, let me discuss certain problems that arise from this belief. Although the immortality of the soul serves as a significant building block of personal belief, it can also become the source of many dangers. In order to understand this, we must look back to pre-Christian times, to our classic adversary, idolatry.

The belief in the immortality of the soul belongs to the general heritage of humanity. The expression of this belief is the grave, which has accompanied civilization from the beginning. The existence of the grave is the most outstanding expression of the idea that man is not like all the animals. His body is not all there is, and death is not the end for him. Idolatry related to this belief in terms of its own categories and frames of reference. One of the central concepts of idolatry is the compartmentalization of the world, the belief in different gods ruling over different aspects of existence. According to this theology, in the underworld, the world of the dead, a god rules who imprisons the souls. This belief is expressed in many myths, among them the well known myth of Orpheus and Eurydice. Pagan philosophy perceived death as the person's entrance into the kingdom of a different god, with no way out for either the person or the god. This belief directly clashes with the basic Jewish principle of divine unity and the belief in God's absolute dominion, which extends beyond death and the abyss. As such, the possibility of resurrecting the dead constitutes one of the basic components of our belief in God.

The Pitfall: Forsaking This World

The greatest danger posed by the belief in the immortality of the soul is manifest in our confrontation with Christianity. This belief can form the basis for a society that despises this world and searches for a safe haven in the World to Come. Judaism teaches that we must not build the World to Come at the cost of destroying this world. If put into practice, this ramification of believing in the soul's immortality would be catastrophic. The Church, particularly during the period of its reign in the Middle Ages, preached faith in the world after death, where one can find solace from all the misery of this world. It therefore abandoned this world to the hands of flesh and blood rulers, who used it for the satisfaction of their evil desires. What emerged was an unholy pact, in which the state and the Church divided up the world, a pact whose drawbacks far outweighed its benefits. Redemption, meaning the perfecting of this world under God's rule, clashed with a faith that spoke only of the World to Come and abandoned this world. In addition, belief in the immortality of the soul at times became a tool of deception in the hands of dishonest connivers. Judaism refused to pay this high price for belief in immortality. It insisted that the belief should complement, rather than displace, the effort to perfect this world.

The image we described earlier, of lights shining in the daytime, is instructive. Rav Kook tells us that in the time of the Second Temple, with the decline of prophecy, the loss of political independence and the consequent decline of the hope of altering society and the world, the belief in the immortality of the soul became more prominent. This was precisely the time when Christianity was drawing its sources from Judaism. Christianity saw itself as drawing from the world of the Bible, while differing with Judaism regarding the Oral Law. Herein, explains Rav Kook, lies one of Christianity's fundamental errors. Judaism draws from both sources, the vision of the prophets and the teachings of the Sages. Christianity's great failure stemmed from having developed in a situation in which the comprehensiveness of religious life had been impaired. It seized on the personal, heavenly component, thereby losing the biblical vision of the perfection of the world. This was a tragic step that impaired all human development. Only a comprehensive religiosity can ensure man's welfare and perfect the world under God's rule.

Mysticism and Its Dangers

There is another pitfall, one that has existed from the period of idolatry to this very day. This danger is expressed most prominently in the belief among certain nations that the souls of the dead can be gods. This belief was common, for example, among the Romans, and it is also present in many Far Eastern cultures. In less extreme manifestations of this phenomenon, the souls of the dead became a focus of sorcery. The Torah strongly objects to such beliefs, as the story of Saul at Endor exemplifies. Although times have changed, these phenomena have not disappeared and they continue to express themselves in various forms of Spiritualism. The Torah objected to any communion with spirits and forbade these practices under the general rubric of consulting the dead. The belief in the immortality of the soul often became a source of superstitions, a focus that detracts from man's intelligence, freedom and spirit. Feeling insecure in this world, people sought the spirits of the dead, thereby putting prophecy—the seeking out of God—in jeopardy.

The story in the book of Samuel about the medium at Endor is a classic example of the dangers of the occult. The medium is said to have been frightened when she saw Samuel, apparently surprised at her own success in raising the spirit of the dead prophet. However we may understand the episode, the medium was clearly surprised when she succeeded is raising Samuel's spirit: "And when the woman saw Samuel, she cried with a loud voice; and the woman spoke to Saul, saying: 'Why have you deceived me? For you are Saul'" (1 Samuel 28:12). Only then did she realize that it was Saul who had been standing with her this whole time. The Talmud in tractate *Sanhedrin* attributes the medium's fright to Samuel's having arisen in an upright position, in contrast to other deceased, who would rise upside-down. It seems to me that the Talmud's statement reflects a common practice among conjurers, who likely made use of the *camera obscura*, a principle of physics that underlies the way in which the camera and the eye function and that was discovered and explained by Gersonides. Imagine a hole in the wall of a dark room, connecting it to another room, which is brightly lit. When a person moves about in the lighted room, his image will be projected into the dark room. By very simple optical principles, however, the pictures will be upside down, just as our eyes actually see reality as an upside-down image. Most of the cases of conjuring of the dead were frauds. They used this method in order to fool people. Therefore, the souls that they "conjured" always appeared upside-down. When the medium saw Samuel appear upright, she realized that this one time it was real. Samuel appeared in a vision, but the interactions continued without a medium. Samuel did not appear for the medium; he appeared for Saul.

This hypothetical analysis of the Talmud's comments is an example of an important principle regarding occult phenomena. Although they contain an overwhelming percentage of lies, tricks and illusions, they also contain some truth, truth that is couched in dangerous trickery.

The Kuzari king's dream is a phenomenon that transcends normal human limits. This requires us to consider that subject overall. The Torah absolutely forbade looking to diviners and soothsayers for guidance—a prohibition that, like many others, lends itself to two possible interpretations. A rationalist interpretation, like that of Maimonides, explains the prohibition on the grounds that the practices are dangerous superstitions, analogous to medical quackery that can put a person at risk by keeping him from obtaining genuine medical help. The alternative interpretation sees some validity in the practices, but regards them as involving powers that are dangerous and forbidden to invoke.

Regardless of how we interpret the Torah's prohibition, we must distinguish clearly between two phenomena. First, there is "Spiritism"—in essence, a religion grounded on ties to the dead. A powerfully influential force in ancient times, Spiritism later waned but never disappeared entirely. It reemerged in the nineteenth century, becoming a sort of alternative religion. A very different approach is that taken by parapsychology, the product of scientific work on the part of many investigators who have sought to show—in their view, successfully—that there exist all manner of psychic phenomena that differ fundamentally form normal psychological phenomena. Examples include telepathy, divination, clairvoyance and telekinesis.

These phenomena must be distinguished from psychological phenomena, like hypnosis, that, though borderline, are normal. One may say that the hypnotic state does not differ in principle from that of a dream, in which one believes certain things to be true. A person may see himself, for example, as struggling though a hot day, sweaty and thirsty, even though he is in a room at normal temperature. In some strange way, the mind can exercise almost absolute dominion over the body. Although this says much about the connections between mind and body, we remain within the sphere of the normal and need not adjust our usual perspectives. When we go further, however, we find an entire realm of phenomena that cannot be explained through materialistic analysis. Yet, those who recoil from gross materialism must confront the opposite temptation and avoid being excessively drawn after these phenomena.

Maimonides considers these prohibitions in *Hilkhot Avodat Kokhavim*, and states: "One must not follow the ways of the idolaters . . . not seeking the guidance of soothsayers or diviners, nor engaging in sorcery" (Introduction). We see here that Maimonides' central idea is that these practices are forbidden because they lead to idolatry. The classic instance for him is that of sorcery, concerning which he says (11:16; Twersky, *A Maimonides Reader*, pp. 75–76):

> These practices are all false and deceptive and were means employed by the ancient idolaters to deceive the peoples of various countries and induce them to become their followers. It is not

proper for Israelites who are highly intelligent to suffer themselves
to be deluded by such inanities or imagine that there is anything
in them, as it is said, "For there is no enchantment with Jacob, neither is there any divination with Israel" (Num. 23:23); and further,
"For these nations that you are to dispossess hearken to soothsayers and diviners, but as for you, the Lord your God has suffered
you so to do" (Deut. 18:14). Whoever believes in these and similar things and, in his heart, holds them to be true and scientific and
only forbidden by the Torah, is nothing but a fool, deficient in
understanding. . . . Sensible people, however, who possess sound
mental faculties, know . . . that all these practices which the Torah
prohibited have no scientific basis but are chimerical and inane,
and that only those deficient in knowledge are attracted by these
follies and, for their sake, leave the ways of truth. The Torah,
therefore, in forbidding all these follies, exhorts us, "You shall be
wholehearted with the Lord your God" (ibid. 18:13).

Sorcery is a special case, for it easily recognized to be based on simple idolatry, on a sort of covenant with Satan. But there is a difference
between idolatry on the one hand and folly and superstition on the other.
Sadistic satanic cults, involving murder and abuse, have always existed—
and have been renewed in our times. Many women who were burned as
witches were, without doubt, victims and scapegoats, but sorcery has
always included menacing phenomena and dangerous, sadistic rituals.

As we have already seen, Maimonides reiterates the rationalist premise in his Letter to the Sages of Marseille. He offers the interesting suggestion that the Second Temple was destroyed because the Jews had
pursued spells and sorcery rather than rational military preparations. He
thereby once again teaches the importance of on-going rational activity.

Parapsychology poses an obvious and significant challenge to any
materialist picture of the world. It likewise calls into question the very
concepts of space and time. The possibility of leaping mentally beyond
space and time paints a different picture of spirituality. Many of these
phenomena are linked to what might be called mysticism. They are also
tied to practical Kabbalah, though are not necessarily a part of it.
Gersonides, a philosopher normally considered highly rationalistic, even
speaks of parapsychological phenomena. R. Moses Narboni similarly
speaks of parapsychological phenomena that he observed. Yet, even

within the realm of the normal, a wondrous phenomenon can be found—the dream, which offers the prospect of bursting forth to what lies beyond. This shows, importantly, that the soul is more than merely an expression of what transpires within the body. Materialism's limitations are shown not only by parapsychological phenomena but also by something more fundamental but no less wondrous—the existence of our inner world.

Cleaving to God (*Deveikut*)

Judaism believes in the immortality of the soul. But what sort of recompense does the soul receive? In describing the view of the Muslim sage, Halevi writes: "The believer's reward [is] his soul's return to his body in the Garden of Eden, where he is sated with pleasures and lacks none of the food, drink and fleshly delights he may want." Halevi teaches us, however, that the true reward is the one derived from drawing close to the Holy One, blessed be He:

> For what does he seek in this world other than that the human soul become divine, be separated from its senses, gaze on the supernal world and draw pleasure from seeing the glow of the angels and hearing the divine voice (I:103).

That Torah that can bring us close to God is the Torah that can ensure immortality of the soul. God's dominion over the world means that there are no limitations on Him. He can descend to *she'ol* with us and bring us up from there. The entire Torah, as Halevi said, is a Torah helping us to cleave to God, a Torah from which we learn to walk together with the Master of the Universe. The conclusion that necessarily follows from that belief is that we walk together with God not only in this world but even after death. With perfect faith, we look forward to closeness to Him, in this world and in the World to Come.

CHAPTER 47:
THE WORLD TO COME
AS A BIBLICAL CONCEPT

We have briefly discussed the immortality of the soul from three perspectives:

1. Content: what does the Torah teach us about this issue?

2. Philosophical and scientific attitude toward this principle of faith.

3. Sources of this belief in the Torah.

We will not attempt here to present the arguments, interesting in and of themselves, through which Jewish philosophy has attempted to prove the immortality of the soul. Most of them are built on medieval psychological principles and are of purely historical interest, at least with respect to their details. While they remain important for general philosophical discussions of the absolute divide between the physical and the spiritual, the body and the soul, we must recall Halevi's observation (V:14) denying the significance of these proofs. Everything came into being through the will of God and there is no necessary rational order. Accordingly, there is no point to drawing conclusions on the basis of what appears to us to be such. Had God so decreed, the soul would be immortal, even if it was physical.

In what follows, we discuss the third of the perspectives noted above. At first glance, it seems that the "World to Come" is mentioned nowhere in the Scriptures. A closer look at the text, however, discloses that at least three aspects of the theory of redemption appear in the Scriptures: the immortality of the soul, the resurrection of the dead and the redemption of the cosmos. Regarding the first, we follow Halevi, who considered Elijah's ascent to the heavens as a model for the scriptural faith in the soul's immortality. There are other examples, such as scriptural heroes who are "gathered to their people" and Samuel's soul, which returns to earth to prophesy once more even after his death. We know also of the Psalmist, who hopes and waits for God to redeem him from She'ol. As for the second dimension, the Scriptures also describe the World to Come. Finally, the prophets speak of the redemption of the world. Before we begin, I should add that a full understanding of this issue requires acceptance of a fundamental assumption: the existence of the Oral Law, which completes the written Torah and helps us understand it properly. It must be made clear that these are not two separate entities, an Oral Law completely detached from the Scriptures. The Oral Law helps us read the Scriptures and understand them, and it is alluded to within the Scriptures themselves. We will illustrate this later on.

"There is dominion over the day of death"

We find many Scriptural references to She'ol, where souls go after death. She'ol exists. It is an actual place, figuratively described as a lower world, an image which connotes the grave. We cannot describe the exact essence of She'ol, but we will not be mistaken if we view it as a place of static existence. This is existence without life, with no action, anger or injustice. If our world is the world of action, She'ol is the world of rest for the weary.

But to appreciate the meaning of She'ol in the Scriptures, we must first understand its meaning in pagan mythology. With certain limitations, the pagan gods were regarded as immortal and therefore free of the dominion of She'ol. But they did not rule over She'ol, which was under the rule of a specific god. Even if at times the gods could grant immortality to humans whom they favored, they could not revive the dead. They did not posses that ability. In the pagan view, oddly enough, man in She'ol was free of the rule of the gods.

In the scriptural view, this approach meant a corruption of monotheism, of God's absolute control as the Creator. Just as the borders of the land of Israel do not confine the power of God, neither are the dead "free" of the divine rule. The Scriptures emphasize that God's hand reaches She'ol: "If they dig their way to She'ol, from there My hand will take them, and if they ascend to the heavens, from there I will bring them down" (Amos, 9:2). God's dominion is not only in heaven, but also in She'ol, for "If I search the heavens You are there, and if I descend to She'ol, You are there" (Ps. 139:8). Using a play on words, Isaiah (7:11) suggests asking (*she'al*) God for a sign, whether from She'ol or from on high. Essentially, "She'ol is exposed before Him and there is no shelter for ruin" (Job 26:6; Prov. 15:11). She'ol offers no protection or asylum from the divine presence.

The stories of Elijah and Elisha teach us this idea through the concept of miracles. Their lives feature many achievements that demonstrate their control over nature. They have been given all the keys: bringing down rain, granting fertility to the barren, and resurrecting the dead—three symbols of God's control over nature and its laws (*Bereishit Rabbah* 77). Their control over leprosy also may be seen as a type of control over death, as it is essentially the ability to revive dead flesh. This triumph over nature finds its ultimate expression on the day of Elijah's departure from this world. "There is dominion over the day of death."

The centrality of Elijah's ascension was emphasized by Nahmanides:

> And those who leave behind all the interests of this world and disregard it as if they are not bodily creatures, and all their concentration and thought focus on their Creator alone, as was the case with Elijah, when their souls cleave to [God] . . . , they live forever in their bodies and souls, as it appears from the Scriptures regarding Elijah.

The passage appears in Nahmanides' comment on the phrase "And live by them" (Lev. 18:5). He notes that "The wording includes all sorts of life, as is appropriate for each and every person.

Reward and Punishment in She'ol

The existence of She'ol teaches us that the naive approach, which views the Scriptures as a book devoid of faith in the immortality of the soul, is fundamentally wrong. One critical question, though, remains. Are reward and punishment parts of the experience of immortality? At first glance it would seem that the answer is no. I intend to prove that this answer is entirely incorrect. In order to prove this we must examine the existence of She'ol, but from a different perspective.

The dead occupants of She'ol maintain, even after death, certain characteristics of their lives even after death. The classic example is Samuel's dress: "An old man rose up and he was clothed in a cloak (1 Sam. 28:14). Moreover, death reflects and reinforces the state of the person during life.

Jacob laments, "For I will go down to my son in mourning to She'ol" (Gen. 37:35). This does not merely refer to anguish unto the point of death. It refers to anguish that the person continues to experience after death. This fact itself carries with it a particular view of reward and punishment—the dead in She'ol remain in the same state which typified their lives.

Scriptural Sources for the World to Come

The story of Jezebel will illustrate the concept. Jezebel hears that Jehu the rebel is on his way to Jezr'a'el, "And she placed powder on her eyes and arranged her hair" (2 Kings 9:30). Why did she do this? Not to find favor in the eyes of Jehu, whom she receives with scorn. Nor does she do it only to appear beautiful in her own eyes at the final moment. She adorns herself before her death, I believe, in order that she remain beautiful in She'ol, forever. The Scriptures, however, emphasize her punishment. When she is to be buried, only her head, feet and hands are found. Jezebel will remain in this distorted form forever.

We find various sources for the idea that punishments meted out on earth will continue in She'ol. David commands his son Saul to punish Joab ben Zeruyah: "See that his white hair does not go down to She'ol in peace" (1 Kings 2:6). It is no exaggeration, therefore, to assume that according to the original perspective of the Scriptures, the dead sages sit and study Torah, and when a law is mentioned in their names in the world of the living, "their lips move in the grave." The Judge who administers justice does so in She'ol, as well. The punishment and reward in She'ol is thus a continuation of existence in this world.

There are, however, reward and punishment that are not a continuation of this world. They serve as a reparation. God punishes there in order to rectify what happened here. We learn this from the lamentation over Egypt in Ezekiel chapter 32. Egypt believes that she will live on in She'ol as a valorous warrior, yet the prophet mandates that the appropriate location for her is "among the dead by the sword" (32:21). This serves as punishment for their "placing fear in the land of the living" (32:23). The prophet teaches us that there is no correspondence between a person's fate in She'ol and the circumstances of his death. A person's fate in She'ol is determined by his behavior throughout his life. Thus the prophet writes, "and warriors . . . who have gone down to She'ol will not lie wearing their implements of war." Instead, "their sins will be [inscribed] upon their bones." The sins of the evildoers will be inscribed upon their bones and remain with them forever.

This leads us to the concept of various "chambers" in She'ol. This belief is found explicitly in the apocryphal and midrashic literature, whose descriptions are consistent with the Scriptural account. For example, the book of Enoch (1:22) states that springs of water shine for the righteous, since She'ol is made of chambers. As we shall see, the righteous will be redeemed and returned to the Garden of Eden from this same She'ol, if they triumph on the day of judgment. Returning to the prophecy of Ezekiel, the prophet repeats, in various forms, the call to Pharaoh: "Than whom are you more beautiful? . . . Go and lie among the uncircumcised" (Ezek. 32:19). Pharaoh hopes to dwell in a special chamber, yet the prophet sends him to the chamber of the uncircumcised! This recalls the idea of *karet*, the penalty of being "cut off," which contrasts to the blessing for the righteous of being "gathered to his people."

The arrangement of the graves symbolizes existence in She'ol. This also accounts for the Patriarchs' desire to be buried in the Holy Land (cf. also Amos 2:1). The burial of Elisha and the resurrection of the dead that he performs after his own demise further demonstrate this concept. No other person can dwell with Elisha in the same grave, since no one is as holy as Elisha. Therefore the dead person arose immediately upon his contact with Elisha's corpse (2 Kings, 13:21). The fate of the deceased's children and their recollection of him also affect the soul after death. This is clear from many verses in the Scriptures, such as when God "visits the sins of the fathers upon the sons," or "remembers loving-kindness for thousands of generations." He causes the parents to actually suffer through suffering of their children. Rachel cries over her children (Jer. 31:14), and God comforts her by saying that "There is hope for your final end" (ibid., 15). These two words—*tikvah* (hope) and *aharit* (end) may very well refer to existence after life.

With respect to the living, hope expresses itself in the anticipation of eternal life. For the dead, hope means the yearning for resurrection: there is hope for the final end of man. Indeed, this belief arises in a number of places in the Scriptures and its most direct formulation is, "God puts to death and resurrects, brings [souls] down to She'ol and raises them up" (2 Sam. 2:6 and elsewhere). Even if we understand these expressions only as literary imagery to express healing of illness or the protection from the danger of death and travail, a comparison to another figurative phrase, such as "all those who enter shall never return" (Prov. 2:19) suggests that our expression must also refer to a description of reality. If not, what significance is there to the imagery employed?

Escape from She'ol

Let me turn now to another idea: the release from She'ol. As we see at various points in the book of Psalms, God will redeem the righteous person from She'ol and bring him close to the Almighty Himself. There he will bind his soul in the bonds of life, and it will live forever. Man will not die, or if he does, God will then bring him up, and he will live a new life, an immortal life.

Other verses in Psalms suggest this possibility, as well. "Therefore my heart will rejoice . . . even my flesh will dwell in security, for You will not abandon my soul in She'ol" (Ps. 16:9–11). The soul's existence in She'ol prevents the deceased person from seeing the vision of God. Therefore, the psalmist prays that he may enjoy the divine presence forever. This is a vision of personal redemption, part of the ancient Oral Torah.

The most obvious Scriptural symbol of the soul in She'ol is Jonah in the belly of the fish, which symbolizes the misery of the bowels of She'ol, far from the world of the living and from God. Indeed, just as the whale discharged Jonah, God will redeem the worthy soul from She'ol. "But God will redeem my soul from hand of She'ol, for He will take me, Selah" (Ps. 49:16). An earlier verse (49:8) states, "A brother will not redeem another person, nor will he pay God his bail." Though I cannot expect to be redeemed by my fellow man, God will redeem the soul from She'ol, "For He will take me, Selah." God's "taking of a man" refers to the level of spirituality found regarding Enoch and Elijah.

The Garden of Eden

To understand the meaning of the release from She'ol, we must first look at the story of the Garden of Eden and its place in the Scriptures. As we have seen frequently, this story deals with the emergence of evil in the universe. Our situation in the world is represented by the expulsion from Eden. As we shall see later, the experience of She'ol constitutes a similar type of expulsion. The release from evil is redemption, and redemption is in essence a return to the Garden of Eden, the lost perfect world. The concept of the Garden of Eden and the End of Days comes to explain the phenomenon of evil itself, and not merely the suffering of the righteous. Evil originated in sin, and sin did not exist in God's original creation. It will therefore disappear when all the sins and sinners vanish. This marks the annihilation of cosmic evil and also the end of human suffering, which, as part of cosmic evil, originated from sin. During the period of Jewish sovereignty, the experience of evil within the nation and the associated suffering brought about the formulation of the belief in national redemption and peace among the nations. Similarly, cosmic evil, which is also personal evil, brought about a belief in cosmic redemption, the return to Eden, and the good that is in store for the righteous—a belief that has existed since the beginning of the Jewish religion.

The prophets emphasized mainly national redemption, but many elements of the national vision of redemption point to another matter raised in the oral Torah—the return to the Garden of Eden as a vision of the individual's redemption. Jewish faith teaches that each individual will return to the Garden of Eden and achieve immortality. It is no coincidence that the traditional name for the World to Come is "Garden of Eden." It annihilates death, and eternal life is thereby achieved. As the prophet says, "Awake and rejoice, dwellers of dust . . . (Isa. 26:19); "Death will be destroyed forever and God will wipe the tear from every face" (id. 25:8).

Without going into a full discussion, let me note a few points regarding the view of redemption as a return to Eden. First, consider the actual nature and location of the Garden of Eden. The biblical description of the primeval Garden is not of this world: it identifies four rivers that merge, apparently at some central point between Egypt (*Gihon* and *Pishon*) and Mesopotamia (*Perat* [Euphrates] and *Hidekel* [Tigris]). From this description it is reasonable to suggest that this place is a kind of ideal Land of Israel, before the sin. This means that the new Garden of Eden will be located in Israel. At present, the Land of Israel lies somewhere in between sin and redemption and therefore its general state and conditions deviate from this ideal. This imperfect reality will change at the End of Days.

The expulsion from the Garden of Eden means death. This expulsion has a dual meaning, as manifest in another type of expulsion from God's Presence—the movement to She'ol. The souls in She'ol exist in a kind of prison, which frees and shelters them from the outside and from others (Job 3:17,18). On the other hand, it locks them in, and they have no ability to act on their own. Even if the entire world and all its secrets were revealed to them, even if the future was revealed to them without boundaries of time and space, and even though it is forbidden for the living to ask them about what they know, their knowledge and wisdom cannot save them from the oppressive imprisonment, an imprisonment that is also religious in nature. The creation of She'ol, or the world of the dead, resulted from the expulsion from the Garden of Eden.

"God Is Israel's Source of Purification"

The meaning of ritual impurity and its laws are also connected to the expulsion from the Garden of Eden. The Temple is a kind of Garden of Eden disconnected from death, and we create this reality by observing the relevant laws. We relate to ritual impurity in the same manner. The outcome of ritual impurity is a kind of exile and distancing from the divine Presence. The ritually impure individual, as well as anyone who has been involved in or connected with the results of ritual impurity, is distanced from the Temple, and sometimes also from the Israelite camp, itself a dwelling place of the divine Presence. The place designated for the *metzora* (leper) is a "prison" of sorts, similar to She'ol itself. He has been distanced from the divine Presence. The sources of ritual impurity in its technical sense—death, certain illnesses that also cause distancing, and menstruation and birth, which are also accompanied by bleeding—are the direct results of the first sin. Ritual impurity is indeed a result of sin, and it means distancing from God, expulsion from the holy nation.

It is interesting that certain immersions must be performed specifically in "living waters" (natural water sources). In a certain sense, the immersion affords new life, or re-creation, certainly at least in part because of the return to the presence of God and to holiness. Here again the ideas implicit in the Scriptures are made explicit in the writings of the Sages. The purity of the world in the End of Days involves the idea of the resurrection of the dead. When Rabbi Akiva identifies God as Israel's *mikveh* [ritual bath], he expressed the final stage of total purity in the age of redemption, for it is God who ultimately purifies Israel. Rabbi Akiva is alluding to a verse in which the word *mikveh* means "hope" (Jer. 17:13). But the word is ambiguous and can also mean the pool used for ritual immersion, and Rabbi Akiva thus understands man's final hope as implying man's ultimate, absolute purity.

Ascent to Heaven

In light of the foregoing, we may suggest another level of interpretation. Sometimes an interpretation is far from literal, yet this very reading is suggested by the Torah itself. We find the concept of the ascent to heaven in a number of places. It clearly underlies the entire incident of the Tower of Babel. Why the ascent to heaven? Perhaps because the goal is to achieve immortality. With the path to the Garden of Eden closed, the ascent to heaven is an attempt to break through. Scriptural history is full of the tension surrounding the concept of human ascent to heaven. Enoch merited this ascent. He did not die. God took him, and like Elijah after him, he lives on in heaven. The builders of the Tower of Babel tried to make this ascent on their own. Our Sages interpreted the text in Genesis to mean actual ascent, and even if the literal meaning of the text is different, the conclusions remain the same. The text makes use of a satiric play on the word Babel. The Babylonian etymology of the place name, "gateway of the gods" (Akkadian *bab ili*), is transformed into "the place where God confused (*balal*) all the languages." Both this original meaning of the word *babel* and the description of Jacob's ladder of angels as reaching to the heavens point to this attempt to ascend to the heavens, as mentioned in the books of the prophets. Jacob's ladder serves as the biblical antithesis of the Tower of Babel. As distinct from the Tower, its top truly does reach the heavens (Gen. 28:12) and Jacob indeed proclaims that this spot is "the gate of heaven."

What is the meaning of Jacob's dream? Before he leaves the Land of Israel, Jacob has a dream informing him that the Land is holy. Although the vision took place in Bethel, it declares the holiness of the entire Land, and the Land of Israel is described as the House of God. What is the house of God if not the Garden of Eden, the place where God walks, as it were, "the Land which God observes from the beginning of the year to its end?"

The Scriptures themselves suggest a somewhat midrashic interpretation of the Garden of Eden, identifying it as the Land of Israel. But this identification is not spelled out directly, but rather through an intermediary stage: the Mountain of God. In the primal Oral Torah, Gan Eden is identified as the Mountain of God. From the high mountain of Eden flowed a river that watered the Garden (Ezek. 25:14–15). In the End of Days, as well, a river will flow from the Mountain of God (Zech.14:8). As Abravanel, among the early commentators, and Cassutto, among the later ones, demonstrated, the Torah describes the Garden of Eden as existing in our world. Our reality is, however, drastically different, for we live in the world after the sin. Does the Mountain of God not exist in this world after the sin? It does. It is the House of God, the gateway to the heavens, the Mountain that God Himself chose. It is the place to which God took Abraham from Aram Naharayim, whose holiness was proclaimed at the binding of Isaac, on that same "Mountain that God shall choose."

Jacob sees the holiness of the Land in his dream. The Land emerges as the House of God. The heavens belong to God and the Earth to man, yet there are still the proverbial "four cubits" on this earth that belong to God: the Gateway to heaven that God chooses. For a brief period, Mount Sinai served as the mountain of God, as it possessed several of the characteristics of the Garden of Eden. It was prohibited to ascend and to touch both places. Just as the path to the Garden Of Eden—which is the way up to the Mountain of God—is closed, so too is the path to Mount Sinai: "And the people shall not attempt to go up, lest God burst out among them" (Ex. 19:24). But Mount Sinai was a temporary Mountain of God. The Land of Israel and specifically the home of the Shekhinah—the Mountain of God in Jerusalem—were chosen as permanent, while the Tabernacle was a kind of traveling version of Mount Sinai that accompanied the Jews until their arrival in the Land of Israel.

Do these concepts appear in the Scriptures? Yes. The book of Psalms retained these two principles. It speaks of the Temple as the Mountain of God, as God's holy sanctuary in heaven: "God is in his holy sanctuary," "God's throne is in the heavens" (Ps. 11:4 and 2:4). Presumably, this gateway can be used in the opposite direction as well: "Who will go up to the Mountain of God, and who will stand in His place of holiness?" (Ps. 24:3). What is the Mountain of God and His holy place? The Psalms that ask, "Who is the man who desires life" (Ps. 34:13) and "Who will dwell in Your tents and who will live on Your holy mountain?" (Ps. 15:2) speak of traits that a person must posses to prevail in judgment: "Who will stand before You?" (Ps. 76:8). Of the man who fears God it is written, "His soul will rest in goodness" (Ps. 25:12). Although the verses may refer to an ascent to the physical mountain, they undoubtedly involve as well an ascent to the real Mountain of God, that is, immortality.

From this discussion, we may conclude that the Temple and the Tabernacle also contain something of the image and symbolism of the

Garden of Eden. Although this conclusion requires further research, of particular interest is the fact that the gems in the Garden of Eden (Ezek. 28:13) appear on the breastplate of the High Priest. Even if this should be purely coincidental, the Temple was the place of life and ritual purity, and ritual purity means triumph over ritual impurity, which represents death. Another interesting parallel is that in both the Temple and the Garden of Eden the *keruvim* ("cherubs") protect the treasure. In the Garden of Eden they protect the Tree of Life, while in the Tabernacle they protect the stone tablets, the Torah itself. According to this parallel, the Torah is indeed the Tree of Life.

The Tree Of Life

The Hebrew verb to live (*lichyot*, from the root *ch-y-h*) denotes the continuation of life more than the state of being alive. On that basis, the verb came to connote as well the recovery from illness. We have difficulty understanding the verb accurately because we are accustomed to more static European verb forms. That is the case with respect to many other verbs as well. A good example is the verb "to be" (*h-y-h*). In Hebrew, it means "to become" or "to evolve" rather than "to exist." The verb *h-y-h* in the sense of continuing to exist appears in 2 Sam. 2:12: "May God grant me my desire that the child live" and in Ex. 33:20: "For no man shall see Me and live." (See also Num. 21:8,9; Deut. 4:42, 5:21, 19:4,5; Jer. 21:9, 38:2.) This sense of the verb also takes the form of a commandment: "And your brother shall live [*chai*] with you" (Lev. 25:36). Adam and Eve were banished from the Garden of Eden lest they eat from the Tree of Life "and live forever" (Gen. 3:22). The Tree of Life was inside the Garden, and it had the power to grant immortality. When Adam and Eve ate of the Tree of Knowledge, they were banished from the Garden of Eden, thus ensuring that they will not begin or continue to eat from the Tree of Life and live forever.

With entry to the Garden barred, is there any way to achieve eternal life? The Scriptures teach us that there is. The phrase "eternal life" appears several times in the Scriptures, most strikingly in Daniel's prophecy regarding the resurrection of the dead: "Many of the sleepers in the earth of dust will awaken, some to eternal life and some to shame and degradation" (Dan. 12:2). In quite a few places, however, this phrase refers to the Torah and its wisdom. According to King Solomon, wisdom is the way of life and the source of life (Prov. 2:19, 6:13, 13:14). Does the word "life" here refer to eternal life?

It is certain that at some point this interpretation was accepted, for it is found in the Apocrypha and in the writings of the Sages. Do the Scriptures themselves imply this connotation? It seems so, and at least one verse from the Psalms demonstrates it: "For there God commanded the blessing of eternal life" (Ps. 133:3). The psalm interprets the blessing of life in the Torah as referring to eternal life. This type of explanation permits a different understanding of many verses. The wisdom of the Torah is "a tree of life for those who cling to it" (Prov. 3:18). The Torah has become the path to life, and it is the lost Tree of Life. Perhaps this is the meaning of other phrases in the Scriptures, such as "the fruit of the righteous is the tree of life" (Prov. 11:30). The phrase "way of life" (*orah hayyim*) also appears once in an unequivocal reference to eternal life (Ps. 16:9–11):

> Therefore my heart shall rejoice and my honor be glad
> my flesh will also dwell in safety . . .
> for You will not forsake my soul to She'ol
> You will not permit your disciple to see destruction
> You will teach me the way of life . . .
> pleasantness is forever at Your right [side].

Prov. (15:24) likewise states "[Adopt] a way of life above to avoid She'ol below." More explicitly, "Through the way of charity is life, and a charted path [leads to] immortality" (id. 12:28).

These explanations shed light on the final verses of the Torah. The ending of the Torah uses imagery grounded in the beginning: "See I have placed before you life and goodness and death and evil" (Deut. 30:16). The two trees appear before us once again. The preceding verses hint at a search for the elixir of life: "It is not in the heavens . . . nor is it across the sea" (id. 12,13). Particularly interesting is the phrase, "It is not in the heavens." The Torah did, in fact, come down from the heavens, from the mountain of God, which Moses ascended, and that very Torah holds within it the key to immortality.

Originally, in the Garden of Eden evil was unknown to man. This is the obvious meaning of Adam and Eve's partaking of the Tree of Knowledge and its aftermath. After eating from the tree man became aware of evil, and the need to choose between good and evil arose. As one of the great leaders of the Musar movement, the Sabba of Novardok, said, one might say that in the Garden of Eden man was faced with the choice of having a choice. With the banishment from the Garden of Eden, good and evil became intertwined. It was as though the fruit of the tree suddenly mixed together, and man must now choose his fruit with care. Indeed, the fruit of the Tree of Life became intermixed as well. From now on there is no more Tree of Life. There is a tree of Life and Death together: "If [one] merits, it becomes his potion of life, and if [one] does not merit, it becomes his potion of death" (*Megillah* 18, *Shabbat* 88, and elsewhere). The Torah teaches man the commandments, the way of life, the way of the Tree of Life. The Torah is actually the Tree of Life itself, and the symbol of the covenant is the Tablets, which are guarded by the Cherubim—as is the Tree of Life in the Garden of Eden. In the Temple we construct a halakhic Garden of Eden. The commandments connected to holiness, ritual purity and impurity transform the Temple into the symbol of the Garden of Eden, and thus into the place where the Divine Presence dwells among the Jewish people. The Temple is the place of life and of holiness, within which there can be no death.

The Fate of the Individual

Complete redemption must include redemption from the results of the three primeval sins: the sin of the Tower of Babel, the sin of the generation of the flood and the sin of Adam. In the end of days, death will be annihilated as the people will repent and consequently return to the Garden of Eden, where they will eat of the tree of life and live forever.

These ideas can help us understand a traditional interpretation of the punishment of *karet* (lit, "being cut off"). The traditional interpretation is "If one cuts himself off in this world [by choosing to sin], he will be cut off from the World to Come." The Torah writes that the sinning soul will be "cut off from its people," the opposite of the term commonly used in the Scriptures in reference to death, "gathered unto his people." Beyond the national and universal hope of redemption, the additional dimension of personal redemption emerges in the book of Malachi, where the prophet promises us that all the righteous will be rewarded on the Day of Judgment. God's "book of remembrance" is inscribed with the names of the righteous, a "list" of righteous people who will rise again at the resurrection of the dead, thus vividly illustrating this idea. Malachi's description of Elijah relates to this idea as well. What is Elijah's role? Among his acts during his lifetime, the resurrection of the dead is paramount, and it is only fitting that he return just before the righteous are brought back to life. Needless to say, Elijah's return is connected to the fact that he did not die. He is the scribe who records people's good deeds. He is the first citizen of the new world.

What will people be like after the resurrection? Will they be the same as they were—flesh and blood—or will this image be altered? In most places our Sages emphasize their own lack of knowledge regarding the Messianic era. But our sources do speak of an altered appearance, a sort of "raiment of light [or]" as opposed to our worldly "garment of leather ['or]." "In the World to Come there is no eating, drinking, copulation, jealousy, hatred or competition. Rather, the righteous sit with crowns upon their heads and enjoy the radiance of the Divine Presence, as it is written, 'And they saw God and they ate and they drank'" (*Berakhot* 16b). The use of this verse, which refers to the princes of Israel, according to this unique interpretation, implies that mystical experiences are an example of another life. The mystical experience is viewed as a brief experience of the World to Come. Moses' sojourn on Mount Sinai and Elijah's ascent to the heavens also must have been examples of spiritual life in a "purified body." This idea is reiterated in the *midrash* and *Zohar*, and a similar concept appears in the Scriptures themselves, in that only Elisha witnesses Elijah's ascent. This is a prophetic vision, upon which the fulfillment of Elijah's promise depends.

She'ol was created as a result of man's sin. It signifies banishment and distancing from the Divine Presence. Therefore death, like other outcomes of sin, is the source of impurity, and it distances man from what is holy and Godly. Man's soul, however, will be redeemed. Just as exile is followed by redemption, so the soul of the dead will be redeemed from She'ol. If the soul is deserving, it will live again in the next world. In fact, the Scriptures indicate that even prior to the resurrection, the soul is not completely abandoned in She'ol, for the souls of the righteous will not even see She'ol. Even in She'ol, a distinction is drawn between the righteous and the sinners. The fate of each person after death is determined by the actions he and his family performed in their lifetimes (see, for example, 2 Hasmoneans 12:46). His fate will be a just one. Justice follows man even after death, and Ezekiel formulated the final statement of this belief when he declared that neither sorcery nor rites of worship can alter the ultimate fate of the sinner.

Nevertheless, She'ol is always a prison, a place of punishment. The soul in She'ol awaits redemption. Can man achieve immortality? Indeed, this is a central question in biblical history. Although there have been unsuccessful attempts to reach the heavens, a path does exist. What can man do to live forever? Where is the Tree of Life? The commandments are the way because the Torah is the Tree for those who cling to it. God will create the Garden of Eden on the Mountain of God as in days of old. That Mountain is "the place which God chose." It is the place of holiness, the land of the living, the place of purity where death will vanish forever. Death exists. It is the end of each human life. But the Scriptures speak also of hope, hope for both the living and dead. It is the hope that was never lost, of the recovery of the Garden of Eden during the final redemption. Man will live once again, on the great and awesome day of God.

CHAPTER 48:
THE PROBLEM OF EVIL
AND DIVINE PROVIDENCE

As we have seen, the first portion of Genesis—the story of creation—concludes with God's assessment of the world: "And behold, it was very good." Only in the second portion, in the story of the Garden of Eden, are we introduced to the presence of both good and evil. Evil makes its appearance in the world as a result of Adam's sin. This moment in history created both the presence of evil in our world and the source of ultimate redemption. It engendered the hope of return to the "very good" and to the ultimate "day that is all good." Today good and evil are intermixed. Mankind, therefore, must conquer and alter reality. This has an important impact on our attitude towards the world. We are not judged by the world; we judge the world. We do not see nature as a yardstick by which to assess ourselves. We look at nature and proclaim that it contains both good and evil. Thus the idea of redemption is born—God expects us to correct the evil in our world.

The concept of evil can be explored from various perspectives. At the very outset, Genesis poses the question of how evil can exist if God is completely good? The prophets command us to destroy evil, but they also ask the classic question: Why do the righteous suffer? This is the question of divine providence. Any attempt to deal with this question must begin with the Scriptural source of this issue—the book of Job. The debate regarding Job, in essence the discussion of the question of good and evil, is an existential one. Whoever expresses a position enters the fray, for this is no abstract discussion. It touches on our most sensitive and basic existential problems.

The great surprise in Job is that we may not simply assume that suffering is a function of sin. The book teaches us that the righteous suffer and that the suffering is a test, not a punishment. As we will see, the book

presents an answer to the basic question, but this answer in no way elim-
inates the concept of God testing the righteous. The different answers
exist on different levels, and they do not contradict one another. In fact,
they may even complement one another.

There are different types of tests. A basic one is to place money before
a person to see whether he will take it, whether he is trustworthy. In Job's
case, however, there is no need to check whether the man is righteous. We
are actually evaluating something completely different. Job is an instrument for a purpose much greater than himself. God expects Job to succeed
at an impossible task. God has entered into a wager with Satan and, for
cosmic reasons, "needs" Job to respond correctly. Job must prove that man
can worship and love God even under these terrible conditions. Is this possible? Or perhaps love of God is ultimately judged according to principles
of success and utility. As we shall see, this was one of the central questions of inter-religious polemics throughout history. The story of Job
teaches us not to be tempted to judge truth according to success. A child
instinctively calls out to someone who was hurt, "You deserved it!" But
life is more complicated than simplistic scorekeeping, and we must not
judge people on the basis of their suffering or what we may see as their
"punishment." The book of Job also teaches that the final accounting must
end with redemption. But before we reach chapter forty-seven of Job, we
must first face the test.

Suffering, Not Sufferance

There is a vast difference between acceptance of suffering, and apathy or
passivity. Passivity means giving up on the attempt to change the situation.
As Rabbi Soloveitchik has commented, it entails the free subject becoming an object of manipulation by forces greater than himself, over which
he has no control and no ability to respond effectively. Judaism's response
is different, for Jewish law sanctifies the war against suffering, sickness
and death. The prophets command us to fight the war against suffering,
particularly when caused by moral or social injustice. We cannot remain
indifferent in the presence of others' suffering. We are forbidden to "stand
idly by our brother's blood," and we may not refrain from extending a
hand to the poor and the miserable. When a person faces suffering he must
attempt to correct it. At the same time, however, we must recognize that
beyond what can be corrected is suffering, particularly personal suffering,

that we cannot mend. Then we ask for a miracle. We ask for God's help with those problems whose solutions lie beyond our abilities.

The Answer of the Book of Job

The book of Job inquires into the meaning of suffering. Although the commentators disagree as to the essence of the answer, I believe we can seek it in four places:

1. Chapter 28, the chapter of wisdom: "Wisdom from whence shall be produced, and what is the place of understanding?"

2. Elihu's response (32–37).

3. The most important text, namely, God's answer "from within the whirlwind" (38–39).

4. Job's redemption (42).

In each of the three first places, we are faced with the limitations on human knowledge. Despite its presumption, human wisdom disappoints. It solves the mysteries of science and technology. It investigates the origins of silver and copper, and helps us overcome darkness and want. Yet we still cannot find the true wisdom, the answer to the question of why good people suffer. According to our Sages, this is the question Moses asked of God when he pleaded, "Show me Your ways" (Ex. 33:13). To this question Moses received the mysterious answer, "I will grant the grace that I will grant and show the compassion I will show." The answer ultimately remains hidden from human understanding. This is conveyed as well in God's response to Job, which the Talmud formulates through a play upon a different verse in the book. If we were to translate God's answer to Job into contemporary language, we could say: "Can the One who can distinguish between quarks of different types, between an electron and a positron, not distinguish between Job [in Hebrew, Iyyov], and an enemy [in Hebrew, *oyev*]?" We are in a state of suffering with no rational explanation, but we must nevertheless realize that God accompanies us in these situations and participates in our suffering. Even in suffering, Iyyov is no *oyev*.

But God's answer is not complete unless He returns Job to his former state. In an as yet unredeemed world, we are faced with a test. God wishes that we not only emerge from it successfully, but also that we feel that He is with us. This is a difficult demand when directed to the Job who stood facing the gas chambers at Auschwitz. However this is essentially the imperative that emerges from the book: to know and understand that God has not abandoned Job.

Rabbi Soloveitchik's Viewpoint

Rabbi Soloveitchik discusses the question of evil and suffering in his work *Kol Dodi Dofek*. His interpretation echoes the book of Job in rejecting the answer given by philosophy. There is an answer, he argues, but are we capable of understanding it? In a wonderful analogy, he compares the divine cosmic plan to a gorgeous wall hanging, similar to the Chagall wall hangings in the Knesset. Each thread has significance as part of the complex tapestry. But we view the tapestry from its reverse side. All we see are thread ends, and the beautiful picture is meaningless to us. Any attempt to solve the riddle will fail. This is our state, the state of faith. Even though I am on the wrong side, I must believe that there is a picture, and that my suffering has meaning.

We cannot attempt here to summarize the history of the search for the meaning of suffering in Jewish thought. Rabbi Soloveitchik tries to direct our gaze in a different direction, so that we may rediscover the halakhic meaning of suffering. Our Sages state that one ought to repent as a result of suffering. Here Rabbi Soloveitchik presents us with a halakhic-philosophical approach to the issue. There are two types of repentance. The first type is the repentance that must follow a sin. The second type of repentance is a response to suffering, rather than to any specific sin. One must repent after suffering not because he understands which sin brought about that suffering but because suffering is a terrible "gift" given to mankind, to be used in creating a different, better life.

Despite the difference between their approaches, we can tie Rabbi Soloveitchik's idea to a beautiful parable of Rabbi Nahman of Breslov. Ever sensitive to the danger of sadness and emotional suffering, Rabbi Nahman imagines a wedding at which a circle of people are dancing but one person stays outside and refuses to join the circle. Sometimes we coerce him into joining the dance. Who is it who stays outside the circle of dancers? Sadness. We must force sadness into the dance of joy. In the same way, Rabbi Soloveitchik teaches us that although we do not know the explanation of suffering, we must use it in a positive way. That is why we must repent. The person who does not repent "wastes" his suffering! Our sages daringly described this concept as "suffering that comes from love." But they set a limit to this type of suffering: when one can no longer study Torah because of the intensity of one's suffering, the suffering is no longer from love.

This perspective must not lead us to a masochistic outlook. As we have seen, faith in our ability to overcome suffering is a central Jewish idea. Pleasure is not a crime. Still, we must see suffering as a constructive opportunity. When someone we know is sick, we must try to cure him. If that is impossible, we must at least try to relieve his pain. We know that we are not to prolong life artificially. We believe that historical developments are a step toward redemption, that is, toward triumph over suffering. While there are situations that go beyond the line, Jewish law still forbids a person to end his suffering by taking his own life. Why not commit suicide? Adherence to this law must not be viewed as a masochistic course. The suffering is heaven-sent, and man must take advantage of it, so to speak. Suffering helps build humanity. Suffering, more than riches and pleasure, gives man the ability to understand and forward the development of humanity. In this context, suffering also becomes a pedagogic punishment, like labor after the sin in the Garden of Eden and nationalism after the sin of the Tower of Babel. Man cannot know why he suffers. But he must construct an answer to a second question: for what purpose is he suffering?

We will not give up our belief in divine justice. Therefore, we must say that a complete understanding of what happens in this world is not possible unless we take the World to Come into consideration as well. We do not receive this belief in divine justice as philosophers, but as believers receiving their legacy of faith. The Kabbalah understands divine providence differently. The sages of the Kabbalah connected divine providence to the concept of reincarnation. That, according to Nahmanides, is the essence of Elihu's response in the book of Job.

Halevi and Suffering

The study of a great book is similar to an attempt to scale a mountain peak. On first reading, we are not yet familiar with the path we must take, that is, with the content of the book. Yet we climb under the pressure of the attempt to find the right path. Once we are already familiar with the path and we ascend a second time, we are capable of noticing the scenery, blossoming with flowers, which we did not notice the first time around. We can write a general schema of Halevi's book, comprising theories about the divine element and the uniqueness of the Jewish people. But there is scenery everywhere, blossoming with stunning flowers. One of these flowers touches on the question of suffering. What does the *Kuzari* say regarding this question?

We have seen that one of the central principles of Judaism is the belief that God accompanies us on our life's journey. Biographical events are not mere coincidence. Divine providence exists. But we cannot construct the complete human biography because we do not have a comprehensive picture.

Redemption is the plan for the nation and the world as a whole, but there is also justice for the individual, through the immortality of the soul. The story does not end in this world. Halevi discusses this question in Part III:

> Afterwards he accepted the concept of divine justice, so that it might protect him against the dangers and troubles that occur in this world. And he also came to accept the justice of the Creator towards all animals. (III:11)

The *haver* here discusses the question of divine justice and suffering, but he takes as a model the matter of justice toward animals. This brings us, indirectly, to the question of evolution. As generally understood, evolution constitutes an attempt to deny divine providence over the world in general. In other words, it is an attempt to deny that the order in the world, in nature and in each living organism, proves the wondrous involvement of God or His agents. God, not chaos, is responsible for biology. But we, as children of prophets rather than of philosophers, find general providence to be insufficient. We seek a higher stage: God is interested not only in biology but also in biography and in history. That is individual divine providence.

Let us use general divine providence as a model. We look at the animal kingdom and see wonders that only a blindly stubborn, evil or hypocritical person could deny or ascribe to coincidence. Halevi presents us with a creature. It is perfect on its level, and this perfection is made possible by the harmony between its various parts. But this harmony is not merely internal. It exists in relation to other animals as well. It is even more amazing than that, for we find that a certain type of flower needs a certain type of insect for its fertilization, and that this insect needs this same flower for its food. In the context of the history of species, we find ourselves faced with a paradox, for we find that two species need each other to exist. Neither could have existed at any time without the other. Yet both exist! Halevi also draws our attention to the fascinating fact that the psychology of each animal is fitting and appropriate to its anatomy and physiology.

Now we begin to discuss the question of justice in the animal kingdom. Immediately, the devil of the intellect tries to seduce us by mentioning, "the injustice done to the hare when it is eaten by the hyena, like the fly eaten by the spider" (III:11). The *haver* does not believe that this reality is the result of mere chance. It is impossible to see this wonderful order in nature and at the same time claim that "The hunting of the hare by the hyena and the hunting of the fly by the spider are [the results of] chance." The *haver* sees that a wise planner has given "the lion courage and ability, and given him hunting weapons, teeth and nails, and has given the spider the talent to make his web like a garment without having learned this, so that he may weave snares for the fly, and [the planner has] given him appropriate tools for this task, and presented him with the fly for his sustenance . . . and presented many of the fish of the sea with other fish for their food." In other words, everything has been planned intelligently, and "What can I say other than that this is all from an intelligence that I cannot comprehend? I have no alternative but to accept the judgment of the One called 'the Rock (divine Source) Whose work is perfect.'"

Halevi did not accept the position mentioned by Nahmanides, which claims that divine providence controls the fates of the spider and the fly as well. Maimonides as well as Halevi disagreed with this position. They did not see nature in such a human-like way. Halevi's discussion is of general divine providence, and it constitutes a model for human problems.

Halevi: Two Interpretations

Let us now return to a section of the *Kuzari* we mentioned earlier. In this section, Halevi explains that evil is not a chance occurrence but rather part of the divine plan, even if the plan is inexplicable to us. This section can be understood in two different ways. We will begin with Maimonides' thesis.

According to Maimonides' approach, evil is an absence of something, just as darkness is simply the absence of light. To use a banal example, we could call this the doughnut-hole approach. One cannot make a doughnut without making a hole. It is impossible to create a reality without the existence of an imperfect reality as well. This imperfection is what Maimonides calls evil. Before creation, God had two options:

1. To create a perfect world, without people.

2. To create people, with the world therefore being an imperfect one.

Our conception of reality is one of imperfection. We could not exist in a perfect world, and we have no entrance into a perfect world until we have perfected ourselves. God, the benevolent, created all possible worlds, and thus He also created the imperfect world in which we live.

Sadly, the time comes to pay the dues of imperfection. We must accept evil as well, because evil is also part of reality. In and of itself, it is really the absence of goodness. Imperfection is an absence. Evil has no meaning. It is a kind of doughnut hole that is necessary for existence.

This approach seems on its face to be optimistic, but Rav Kook criticized it as expressing despair. He chose to identify with the Kabbalistic approach, in which evil is not an absence but a reality, a structure built of *sefirot*, the same spiritual building blocks God uses to manifest Himself in His world. What does this mean? If evil were the necessary result of reality, it could never be uprooted and destroyed. But if evil is not a mere absence but a reality that God created so that we would have to pit ourselves against it and prevail, the possibility of obliterating evil begins to develop.

Halevi's words can be interpreted from each of these perspectives. In Maimonides' view, we must accept suffering as an unavoidable reality. This is stoic acceptance. We can turn for help, perhaps, only to psychologists. In contrast, Rav Kook teaches us that evil exists not merely as a natural phenomenon but in some way as part of the divine plan. Even Satan is God's agent, not merely a remnant of evil in a world which can never hope to attain perfection.

The Transformation of Evil

We can read the rest of Halevi's explanation in light of these two approaches. He writes:

One who has accepted all this will reach the level ascribed to Nahum of Gimzo, who would say about every difficulty he underwent, "This also is for good." He will then live a life of continual quietude, for troubles will seem trivial to him.

What did Nahum of Gimzo do? He turned suffering into a jumping-off point. He transformed the status of suffering.

He may rejoice in them, when he feels that the sin that was upon him is thus forgiven, just as when a man pays his debts, he feels relieved and happy.

How are we to understand Halevi's point? Does this mean that suffering is really the result of sin? Or perhaps we should understand it differently. Without presuming to understand the balance between sin and punishment, Nahum of Gimzo transformed suffering into a vehicle for the correction of sin. As Rabbi Soloveitchik taught us, the *halakhah* has given us the ability to transform suffering into repentance.

He will be happy in the reward and recompense awaiting him. His joy will give others the guidance to withstand suffering and believe in divine justice. (III:11)

This comment gives us an insight into human psychology, and is another of the flowers Halevi planted in the *Kuzari*'s scenery. When a believer senses the meaning of suffering, then to a certain degree that suffering is diminished, and he can view his situation differently. The person's perception of reality affects his experience of suffering as well as the place of suffering in general

Halevi thus teaches us that when we experience suffering, we must pass through several stages. First, we must accept the approach of Nahum of Gimzo. We do this when we believe that there is meaning to our suffering, even before we understand that meaning. Second, we must make personal biographical calculations of our own sins and suffering. We cannot do this for others—unless we are prophets—but each person can and must do it for himself. This second stage of awareness is the one emphasized by Rabbi Soloveitchik. He does not believe it is possible for man to reach an understanding of the larger theory of evil. Instead, Soloveitchik stresses the personal calculation that one must construct.

I cannot conclude without mentioning the unique Hasidic perspective on this question. This is not a popular approach, and it takes a tremendous effort to experience it, but I will describe it nonetheless. It forms the basis of early Hasidic thought and draws on the philosophy of Rabbi Moses Hayyim Luzzato. The reality we think we are seeing and experiencing is in truth a play. We are so deeply involved in the theater experience that we cannot see it for what it is, and we perceive it as reality. We are like children or simpleminded people who watch a play and get angry at the behavior of one of the actors. For them, this is reality and they are a part of the play. Our reality, the reality of exile and suffering, is merely a nightmare. When we reach redemption, we will understand that we were "in a dream" (Ps. 126:1). This does not mean that we will not be able to believe that the redemption has really come. In fact, we will then realize that the exile was just a bad dream from which we are awakening. We will awaken from our earlier perception of reality, and then we will be able to truly understand our history and the suffering we underwent. This is a mystical approach. At the height of a spiritually uplifting moment, there is no evil. We suffer, of course, because we are inside that reality, as though we are in a dream from which we cannot awaken. The ascension of the *tzaddik*'s soul is the possibility to see reality as it really is. The Exodus from Egypt was a revelation of this type, witnessed by the entire nation. It was the moment when night turned into day, and it presaged the day "which is neither day nor night." In the light of that day we will see world history differently. We will have the possibility of retroactive redemption, and the evil of the past will be erased.

Section 11:
Exile and Redemption

CHAPTER 49:
CINDERELLA

Rabbi Nahman of Breslov was well known for composing remarkable stories, full of Kabbalistic and philosophical allusions. He also taught us to pay careful attention to ancient tales, which contain deep secrets as well, even though those who relate them have lost not only the keys to understanding them but the very awareness that there is a lock—a hidden meaning—to be opened.

I will attempt to return the lost keys to three familiar childhood stories. I will do this because I believe in them.

Cinderella

I believe in Cinderella.

Once upon a time there were three sisters who lived together. One dressed in silk, the second in satin, and the third in torn rags. The two older sisters made their little sister's life miserable, treating her as their servant. The third sister had no friends except the mice in the kitchen. Since she spent most of her time washing the floors and removing ashes from the stove, she was called Cinderella.

One day, the royal heralds announced a great ball in honor of the prince, heir to the throne. The elder sisters, gorgeously arrayed, prepared to attend the ball . . .

The rest of the story is well known. The prince searches for the owner of the glass slipper. Cinderella wishes to try it on. Her sisters laugh at her:

"Do you consider yourself a princess? You are the queen of filth. The prince will marry me."

"The prince will not marry rags and tatters. The prince will marry me."

The prince places the slipper on Cinderella's foot, and discovers that she is the mysterious princess.

Cinderella's Sisters

Cinderella is the Jewish faith. Many chapters of the spiritual history of humanity have been written by Cinderella's two sisters. The sisters have said harsh things to Cinderella. Tertullian, the Church Father, was quite clear that Jews are suffering and in exile as punishment for rejecting the Christian messiah. For him, and writers who agree with him, Jewish suffering is proof of the truth of Christianity.

> It is a wonderful thing, and worthy of particular attention, to see this Jewish people existing so many years in perpetual misery, it being necessary as a proof of Jesus Christ both that they should exist to prove Him and that they should be miserable because they crucified Him; and though to be miserable and to exist are contradictory, they nevertheless still exist in spite of their misery. The carnal Jews and the heathen have their calamities, and Christians also. There is no Redeemer for the heathen, for they do not so much as hope for one. There is no Redeemer for the Jews; they hope for Him in vain. (Blaise Pascal, *Pensées*, 640, 747)
>
> The existence of the Jews, as is generally recognised, is an adequate proof of the existence of God. It is an adequate demonstration of the depths of human guilt and need and therefore of the inconceivable greatness of God's love in the event in which God was in Christ reconciling the world to Himself. The Jews of the ghetto give this demonstration involuntarily, joylessly and ingloriously, but they do give it. They have nothing to attest to the world but the shadow of the cross of Jesus Christ that falls upon them. But they, too, do actually and necessarily attest Jesus Christ Himself. (Karl Barth, Church Dogmatics [Edinburgh: T. & T. Clark Publishers, 1958], vol. 2, p. 209)
>
> The Christian message says in this context: God desired all this, Jesus the Messiah was rejected by his nation, prophesied the destruction of Jerusalem, Jerusalem was destroyed and it will never again return to Jewish sovereignty. (Carl Ludwig Schmidt, in a debate with Martin Buber, 14 January 1933)

The debate continues. Whom will the prince marry? Is it possible that the prince might consider the queen of filth, whose only friends are mice, and will abandon her more successful sisters? The encounter with the prince is the redemption, and as for the slipper—it is mentioned in a book that hints at the final redemption: "Now this was formerly done in Israel in cases of redemption or exchange. To validate any transaction, one man would take off his sandal and hand it to the other" (Ruth 4:7). This is the slipper which heralds the footsteps of the true Messiah.

Exile and Trial (I:112–115)

Cinderella's fate returns us to what Halevi has written about exile [I:115], and to the more general issue of suffering, and thus again to the book of Job. As we have seen, the book of Job describes the suffering of a righteous man. His friends respond to the catastrophes that befall him, and accuse him of being a sinner, deserving of God's punishment. The beginning and the end of the book are familiar. They describe two concurrent realities, as though they are taking place on two stages. On the higher stage, God is testing Job to prove to Satan that there is one righteous person on earth, that there is one person capable of worshipping God without ulterior motive. There, everything is clear. On the lower stage, however, from Job's perspective, we see the person suffering, and his feeling is that he suffers without cause. The book of Job is the story of man's trial as man perceives it.

This holds true for the individual, but the *midrash* and later commentaries offer another interpretation of the story of Job. Job is the symbol of the suffering of the Jewish people. Along come the friends, representing the theologians and sages of various nations, who use suffering as immutable proof that the Jewish people have sinned, and are not beloved to God. According to them, the history of the Jewish people proves that the Jewish faith is false, and the nation suffers because it did not accept the Christian Messiah or the Muslim prophet. Thus the exile was not merely an experience of physical suffering, but also a spiritual, psychological and intellectual trial of the first order. The gentiles used the exile, the alienation, the dispersion and the degradation of the Jewish nation to prove that this is a punishment from heaven for the Jews' refusal to accept the Messiah or the Prophet.

Job

Over the centuries, Jewish thought has looked at Job from various perspectives. There were those who saw him as the symbol of man, and others, such as Franz Rosenzweig, who saw in him a symbol of the world. Martin Buber, in contrast, felt that the questioning "I" is not the "I" of the individual, but the collective "I" of the Jewish people. Job's question "Why do You hide Your face and consider me Your enemy?" (Job 13:24) is the question of the Jewish people, which echoes and resounds in times of darkness.

The identification of Job with the Jewish people originates in *Pesikta Rabbati* (chap. 26): "Your affliction is similar to the affliction of Job. Job's sons and daughters were taken from him and your sons and daughters were taken from you . . . for Job I doubled his sons and daughters and for you I will double your sons and daughters."

The idea was developed, however, by the martyr Shlomo Molkho in his book *Sefer Mefo'ar*. The starting point for Molkho's discussion is the two-verse passage in Numbers bracketed by inverted letter *nun*s at its beginning and end. The passage, Num. 10:35–36, sets out Moses' declarations when the Ark was to begin moving and when it was halted. The Sages (*Shabbat* 116a) explained that this section "is considered a separate book," citing an otherwise cryptic statement in Prov. 9:1 to prove that there are actually seven books of the Torah. The inverted *nun*s divide the book of Numbers into three separate books, added to the remaining four. Shlomo Molkho disagreed, however, finding the explanation in a statement at *Bava Batra* 14b: "Moses wrote his book and the episodes of Bilam and Job." This teaches us that just as the story of Bilam is included in the Torah, so, too, is the book of Job. For even though the book of Job is outside of the Torah, it is actually included in the story of Bilam. The stories of Bilam and Job record the sufferings and trials that the Jewish people will undergo throughout history. The *nun*s in chapter 10 of Numbers thus allude to a book that remains outside the Torah even though it belongs within. "Even though it is outside, it is as if it were between the two *nun*s. The Book of Job speaks of two matters—his fall and his restoration—and both are alluded to in these verses: the fall in the first, which says 'Arise, O Lord,' and the restoration in the second, which says, 'When it rested he would say, return O Lord.'"

The stories of Bilam and Job encompass the meaning of Jewish history, and the messianic interpretation of the story of Bilam is familiar from early and late sources. But Shlomo Molkho understood the book of Job in that light as well. This interpretation is implied by the Talmudic statement, "Job never existed. He was a parable" (*Bava Batra* 15a). According to Molkho, this statement is not a discussion of Job's historical existence but rather an attempt to emphasize that the book of Job does not discuss the suffering of the individual but the fate of the Jewish people. This is the key to a new vision of the book of Job. Job is the Jewish people, and the three friends are the nations, as is hinted by their origins. The friends' indictment of Job as responsible for his plight is mere foolishness. Thus, God responds: "And God said to Eliphaz the Yemenite, my anger is aroused at you and your two friends for you have not spoken to me correctly as has my servant Job" (Job 42:7).

Molkho offers a related explanation for the passage between the inverted *nun*s. He writes: "Their [i.e., the *nun*s'] heads are bowed, to demonstrate that the goodness and divine benevolence that Israel received at first will turn around, and the holy ark will travel from its place, and Israel will be lowered from their former height and be stricken with suffering, and their lands will be settled by their enemies . . . and afterwards it says, 'Rise up, God' . . . and we do not say rise up except to one who has fallen, to hint at the toppling of Israel's enemies; and when God rises up to help Israel, their enemies will disperse and flee."

What is the book's answer to Job's question?

A cursory reading immediately shows that the end of the book of Job opens up various options for locating the solution or the conclusion. Where are the answers? Are they in Elihu's words, in God's response from the whirlwind or at the end of the book, in Job's redemption? Or perhaps in the words of Job himself, when he asks the place of wisdom? There are indeed various answers that complement each other.

Herman Cohen read the book of Job through the perspective of Maimonides' interpretation. He saw the suffering as "a kind of prophecy." Job "suffers for the sins of others," and so do the Jews. This is essentially "vicarious suffering," as suggested by Isaiah. This "representation" is not punishment but martyrdom, a sanctification of God's name.

The high point of the book of Job may be Chapter 28. Wisdom is not within man's reach, but Job finds justification for his life in the acceptance of the commandment, "Wisdom lies in fear of God" (28:28).

God's words from the whirlwind—"Where were you when I established the earth?" (38:4)—do not uncover the justice hidden in creation. Rather, they prove man's insignificance. Man cannot answer the question, but the main thing is that man receives an answer. Evil has not disappeared, and the mystery has not been solved. However, God is close to man and participates in his sorrow. "As for me, the closeness of God is good for me" (Ps. 73:28) is a continuation of the book of Job. Here too, the "I" is the collective "I" of the Jewish people, and it is inconceivable for the book to end without redemption.

According to this reading, the book of Job represents the inter-religious confrontation. Throughout the ages, Christianity and Islam alike have argued against Judaism on the basis of the "proof from exile." The success of Judaism's rivals is taken as apparent proof that God is on their side. I think the truth is with the opposite theory, that it is the suffering anti-hero who is God's ally.

Our ancestors recognized that the exile was a trial to be overcome. Job-Israel refuses to accept his friends' arguments and insists upon the jus-tice of his path. This insistence has a sublimity to it, which is expressed in the Jewish existence in exile. The members of the Great Assembly recog-nized this when they coined the phrase we use in our prayers, "the great, mighty and awesome God." When the prophets saw the destruction, they omitted parts of the formula one by one and questioned His might and greatness. These omissions are done to appeal to the popular view, but the truth is revealed on the battlefield or through political or financial success. The members of the Great Assembly reinstituted the authentic phrase "the great, mighty and awesome God" and argued that, paradoxically, it is through Jewish existence in exile that God's greatness and might are expressed. On the one hand, the continued existence of the Jews in exile is the miraculous existence of one lamb among seventy wolves, a continu-ity that cannot be explained rationally. On the other hand, the exile expresses the fact that the Jewish people submitted to the yoke of Heaven not in the context of the comfort of abundance bestowed by God, but despite their poverty and suffering, and without the hope that that would change in the near future.

Cinderella's sisters found proof of their preferred status in their suc-cess. But their success, of course, was advanced by the sword. Christianity and Islam used the sword to take over the world. Job, who worships God within his suffering, reaches the highest level of divine worship. Whenever Jews chose to suffer rather than utter the one traitorous word that could have altered their fate, it was a constant sanctification of God's name. Putting the Jewish people (and Job) through suffering was God's great gamble against Satan, and, cosmically, their continued accept-ance of God was a greater proof of the truth of Judaism than a triumph on the battlefield. This may sound surprising. But were we aware of the truth, we would be able to understand the profound value of our exile and our suffering. It is because we lack this awareness of the truth and the meaning of their own existence that the Kuzari king is justified in his criticism of the Jews. As the *haver* says, "You have identified our shame, King of Khazar" (I:115).

We sometimes lack an awareness of the significance of the life that we live and an understanding of what is really taking place in our lives. The Jew always knew that he could escape his fate by uttering one word, yet he refused to do it. We must be aware of this heroism, that we accepted our suffering out of love and longing for God. The Jew knows this, yet sometimes he does not know that he knows it.

Halevi teaches us that the suffering of the Jews in exile was a sacrifice for the sake of the Torah. It was a life of martyrdom, the highest level exalted by the Christians and Moslems. Halevi reiterates the principle (I:34, IV:22) that many of the values extolled in Christian and Moslem theology are Jewish values that were fulfilled by the Jewish people. The most obvious example is Isaiah's account (52:13–53:12) of the suffering servant of God. God's suffering servant is actually the Jewish people. The Christians applied this section to their Messiah. Halevi restores the section to its authentic meaning.

Halevi fought against a phenomenon that can be termed identity theft, manifested in several ways. Christianity claimed to be the true Israel. Islam claimed that the Koran is the authentic holy writ. Our return to the land of Israel has been accompanied by something analogous: the Palestinian national covenant is a reworking of the principles of Zionism.

Despite this re-evaluation of suffering, there is no doubt that it is impossible to discuss history without also speaking from the perspective of chapter 42 of Job. Judaism believes that redemption is assured. It is not possible that God will tolerate evil forever. But we are discussing reality from the perspective of an earlier stage, without the perspective of the ending. Our generation must view itself as fortunate because we can read the first few verses of the final chapter, the first glimmerings of redemption. We see the course of history changing. Halevi, in contrast, lived at a low point of Jewish history, when Christians and Moslems were at the height of their power. Each ruled over half the world and claimed that their success was an expression of divine blessing. Judaism is Job's great gamble against his friends. It is the gamble that the sufferer takes when redemption is beyond the scope of his horizon. The response of "Job-the Jewish people" is "Even if He slay me, I still trust in Him" (13:15), and, at the same time, "I await the [Messiah's] arrival every day."

Exile and Redemption

Faith in redemption is paramount in our theology. The Torah, stamped with divine truth, foretells the redemption of the Jewish people. God has foreknowledge of world history. Therefore, we pray that he be involved in our redemption.

Halevi teaches us that the process of world redemption goes on, even while the Jews are in exile. Divine providence functions in ways that are mysterious to us and seems to bring about the complete opposite of redemption. Halevi, and Maimonides after him (Laws of Kings, chapter 11), teach that the mysterious workings of divine providence stand behind the success of Christianity and Islam as well. The message of Judaism was spread to the ends of the earth through these messengers. Thus Rabbi Abraham, Maimonides' son, writes in his father's name:

> By keeping my Torah, you will be world leaders. Your relation to them [the nations of the world] will be as that of a priest to his community, the world will follow in your footsteps and imitate your actions and follow your paths. This is the explanation I received from my father of blessed memory. (Rabbi Abraham son of Maimonides, *Commentary on Genesis and Exodus* [5718], p. 202.)

This idea is repeated in Rabbi Bahya ben Asher's Kad *Ha-Kemah*:

> The reason for the dispersion in my opinion . . . is that the Jews be spread among the nations . . . and they will teach them the belief in the existence of God and of the divine providence that hovers over every detail of human existence. (*Kad Ha-Kemah*, s.v. *Geulah*)

Later, this idea was expressed by Rabbi Hayyim ben Betzalel, brother of the Maharal. In his interpretation of the prophecy of Isaiah, the servant of God, he writes:

> We may also explain: God wished to oppress the Jews and disperse them among the nations for the sake of the goodness of the other nations who are also the work of His hands. Through the

Jews who are dispersed throughout the world the true faith will also be spread throughout the world . . . for God desires that the nations also hold the true faith. For this reason they [the Jews] are called children of Yizra'el, ("God will plant," a play on words with Yisra'el), for they are the seed that God planted throughout the world, like the person who plants his wheat and does not throw it down in one place but spreads it to all the edges of the fields, so the Jews were dispersed to the four corners of the earth, so that through them the true faith would spread throughout the world. (*Sefer Ha-Hayyim, Ge'ulah Vi-Yeshu'ah*, chapter 7 [Krakow, 5353], p. 46a)

Exile is a trial, a trial that is part of a divine plan of history. However, the proof of the truth lies also in the ending of the book of Job, which closes, despite everything, with redemption. The key to understanding this ending lies in the verse that tells us that God "restored [*shav et shevut*] Job" (42:10). This verse necessarily evokes other verses with a similar turn of phrase, specifically, those in Psalm 126: "When God shall restore Zion . . . Restore, O God, our exiles." The return of Job's sons and daughters represents the return of the nation after the exile. The end of the book prophesies the redemption, and bears witness that, despite everything, history owes a debt to the Jewish people. Ultimately, history will be altered, and the world will witness the redemption and the return.

We cannot consider the history of our ancestors in exile without being aware of their greatness. But here, too, thank God, our situation has changed. We, the modern successors of the Kuzari, must emphasize different things today. These are the ideas Halevi will teach us at the end of Part V of the Kuzari. We must understand that in our day the exile is a trap, and our attitude towards it must be one of repudiation of the exile and also *aliyyah* to Israel. The status of exile today can be summed up in one sentence: exile today is not a punishment; it is a sin.

The Dry Bones

Halevi discusses the question of the fate of the Jewish people in his discussion of the suffering of the individual (III:11). He teaches that the meaning of suffering for the individual must reflect the meaning of the suffering of the group as well.

For when confused reasoning leads one to think despairingly of
the length of the exile and the dispersion of the people and the
dwindling of their numbers, one must first comfort oneself by
accepting God's justice, as I have said. Then he should consider
the punishment for sin, and then think of the reward and punishment that await in the World to Come, and then cling to the divine
presence in this world.

A third stage is added to the first two responses to suffering. To the
philosophical stage at which we accepted the meaning of evil, we added
the understanding of reward and punishment. To these we add a third
stage, the connection that the sufferings of the past build us up towards the
future. This is true both with regard to the individual and the nation. To
this Halevi adds:

> If Satan brings him to despair by saying, "Shall these bones live?"
> for our imprint on the nations has been greatly diminished and our
> impression is forgotten, as it is said, "Our bones have dried up we
> have lost hope, we are doomed," he must think of the miracle of
> the exodus from Egypt . . . and then it will not seem impossible to
> him that we will return to our former state even when there will
> be only one person left of us, as it is written, "Fear not, worm of
> Jacob." For what is left of man after he becomes a worm in his
> grave?

Here we meet once again with Halevi the daring commentator. There are
many ways that the term "worm of Jacob" is commonly explained.
Particularly well known is the explanation of the Sages that, like the silk
worm, our power is in our mouths. But Halevi makes an amazing leap of
interpretation here, taking the phrase to refer to a worm on a dead body,
the sign of the end of life. Despite it all, we will rise again.

Here we see, regarding both the individual and the nation, that suffering is first and foremost a trial. This is in essence Job's question. Job asks
the question of suffering, and refuses to accept the standard philosophical
answers. Yet, he believes.

Let me explain the meaning of Job's faith by contrasting two situations in modern literature. One is from a short story by Isaac Bashevis
Singer, who inherited the Jewish tradition from his parents' home. The tradition never disappeared despite the power of the evil inclination. Singer

himself, very much aware of the struggle, does not want to lose his Jewish roots. The story, "Zeidlus the Pope," tells of a learned Jew named Zeidel (of which Zeidlus is a Latinized form), whom Satan attempts to lead astray. Satan's initial efforts, involving his regular temptations, fail, but the temptation of pride is too strong for Zeidel to resist. How does one tempt a Jew with pride? If you convert, says Satan, you will go far, You will become Pope Zeidlus the First. Zeidel falls into the trap. But his life does not turn out quite as Satan promised.

We will not go into all of Zeidel's adventures. We will only say that he failed at everything, and when Satan appears at the moment of death to take his soul, and Zeidel sees him, he exclaims,

"Is it you Satan, angel of death?"

"Yes Zeidel," I [Satan] replied, "I have come for you. And it won't help you to repent or confess, so don't try."

"Where are you taking me?" he asked.

"Straight to Gehenna."

"If there is a Gehenna, there is also a God," Zeidel said, his lips trembling.

"This proves nothing," I [Satan] retorted.

"Yes it does," he said. "If Hell exists, everything exists. If you are real, He is real. Now take me to where I belong. I am ready." (Isaac Bashevis Singer, "Zeidlus the Pope," trans. Joel Blocker and Elizabeth Pollet in: *The Collected Stories of Isaac Bashevis Singer* [New York: Farrar, Straus & Giroux, 1982], p. 178)

This idea, the discovery of God beyond evil, is contrary to the message of one of Ingmar Bergman's "philosophical" films, "The Seventh Seal." In the film—which has a Christian background—a knight appears who asks the final questions, and in one of the dialogues of the film someone who has seen the angel of death claims that he looked into his eyes, but beyond them one could see nothing. In contrast to this, the meaning of "Zeidlus the First" is that beyond evil one can see good. This is the great leap that we must take: the leap from the absurd into a meaningful existence.

The Torah concludes with a commandment to study a song and

remember it from generation to generation, so that it will exist forever. This is the song of Ha'azinu. The Torah explains that days will come when,

> I will hide My face from them and they will be prey, and will be beset by many evils and troubles and they will say on that day, "It is because my God is not with me that we have been beset by these evils." . . . And now, write this song for yourselves and teach it to the children of Israel, place it in their mouths, so that this song will be a witness for the Children of Israel. (Deut. 31:17–19)

A time of great suffering will come, and the nation will ask whether God is indeed among us? Or in a more modern version, "Can one believe in God after Auschwitz?" The Torah commanded us to study this song, so that we will know that despite the pain and evil, God is with us. This is the song that comes to teach us that even in the midst of evil, God is with us. How can one [man] chase a thousand and two [men] pursue ten thousand, if their Rock had not sold them, and God had not trapped them. (Deut. 32:30)

Despite everything, the world is not left to its own devices. This is a prophetic promise given to us so that we will not give up hope.

Here I will dare to make the terrible leap, beyond the gaze of the Angel of Death. In our generation we have learned something beyond Halevi's lesson. We can learn about the truth, as Halevi said, from the fact that God revealed himself at Mount Sinai and chose the nation that He loves, the Chosen People, and gave them the Torah. To our sorrow, however, there is another path in history as well. If Satan appeared, and I was indeed certain that he was Satan, I could learn, paradoxically, from him, that the Chosen People are the nation that Satan recognizes and announces to be his enemy. History has shown us many anti-Semites, great and small. However, Satan himself was none other than Nazism. Nazism appeared and, pointing at the Jewish people, announced, "This is my enemy." We have learned that the Jewish people are the Chosen People—from the evidence given by Satan. Satan did not hate the Jews because we were opposed to his political ideas or because we disturbed his plans. The child and the old man, who were powerless to harm anyone, were also Satan's enemies. To some extent, the Holocaust was an encounter at Auschwitz, an "awesome" parallel to the Encounter at Mount Sinai, in which Satan appeared and showed us the way to the great leap, the need to see beyond the empty eyes of the Angel of Death. Beyond them there is something else. It is not emptiness. Zeidlus the First was right: "If you are real, He is real."

The world understands this logic, even if only subconsciously. We can understand this if we analyze different reactions to the Holocaust. The anti-Semite complains that the Nazis did not finish the job. We are also familiar with the attempts of Nazi sympathizers who want to deny the Holocaust, and sometimes we hear both claims at once. This is one side of the range of responses. But we also hear more sophisticated denials. For many years we have been witnesses to an attempt, by Poles for example, to deny that the Jews were the victims of the Holocaust. The most prominent attempt is without a doubt the establishment of the Carmelite monastery at Auschwitz. Here we are faced with an attempt to rewrite history as, for example, in the Church's attempt to make Christianity into a victim of Auschwitz by making a Jewish convert to Christianity, killed because she was Jewish, into a Christian saint. This is because, consciously or subconsciously, everyone whose conscience was not destroyed by Nazism understands that every honest person should have been at Auschwitz. There Satan made the selection, and whomever was not chosen by him to be wiped out, cannot possibly be the chosen one of God.

Cinderella and Her Sisters

Today we can understand this because of our perspective on the first verses of the final chapter of the book of Job. From this perspective, which stems from a sense that we are at the beginning of the Redemption, we ought to reread the end of the Cinderella story. How did Cinderella treat her sisters after her rise to greatness? I leave the reader to do his own homework, but I promise him that a look at the various versions will be very interesting. What God expects from Job is clear. He expects Job to pray for his friends who have constantly directed their arrows at him. This is a very difficult moral paradox, but it helps us understand the secret of the book's ending. The redemption of Job represents the return of the Jewish people to their land. The verse actually uses the phrase "returned his exiles" (42:10), which is essentially a national term. Now we also understand another difficulty. His first children are lost to him, yet Job's comfort—a comfort that does not erase the pain—is in his second children. The Holocaust was an event that can never be forgotten, and we are left with problems that cannot be rationally explained away. But we now see the return of Job's exiles, and the prayer that he wishes for the whole world: may sins, not sinners, be obliterated.

Job's friends, Cinderella's sisters, are the other religions that point an accusing finger at Job: Job, your suffering is proof that you have sinned, that God has rejected you. The book ends with the meeting with the prince: "And God returned the exiles of Job." This is the Redemption.

CHAPTER 50:
SLEEPING BEAUTY

I Believe in Sleeping Beauty

Once upon a time an evil witch cursed the princess. On the princess' fifteenth birthday she climbed up an old tower, pricked her finger on a spinning wheel and immediately fell into a deep sleep. The king and queen fell asleep as well, as did the horses, the dogs, the pigeons on the roof and the flies on the wall. Thorny rosebushes grew tall and spread around the castle, concealing it from view.

One day a prince arrived in the country and heard from an old man about the castle hidden behind the thorny rosebushes and about the beautiful princess who lay sleeping inside it. He also heard that many had attempted to awaken the sleepers and had lost their own lives in the attempt. The prince was not afraid. He reached the castle. The thorns made way for him but closed up after him. The dangers of the enchanted castle threatened him as well, but he was not deterred. He reached the tower and found the sleeping princess. He kissed her and she awoke.

The prince and the princess married and had children. The sleeping beauty is the Land of Israel. During the years of exile, it was asleep, and its castle was overrun with brambles and wasteland. Whoever has read Mark Twain's description of the parched land, so barren that he felt this could not possibly be the land of which the Bible speaks, understands what the renewal and rebirth of the land means. Both vegetation and animals disappeared. Was this indeed the same princess who was described as a land flowing with milk and honey? The prince, the Jewish people, believed in the legend and awakened the slumbering princess.

The Love of the People and the Land

Today we use the term homeland. The Bible and our Sages used another term: "Mother." The Land of Israel, Zion, is a "mother," and our Sages play on this term. But the true relationship between the Jewish people and

235

Zion, as it is expressed in the spirit of the nation, cannot be understood unless we add to the mother relationship a relationship of love, a marriage between Zion and the Jewish people. Abraham reaches Jerusalem led by the heavenly call, "Go . . . to the Land which I will show you" (Gen. 12:1), like one who is unconsciously drawn to a mysterious figure. The yearning, the love whose vague image appeared in our dreams, gave meaning to our lives.

The relationship between the nation and the Land is one of love. This relationship has lasted for over a thousand years, and Jerusalem was and remains at its core. The destruction of the Temple and the years of exile distanced the Jewish people from their land. This was the basic tragedy. But a deeper tragedy took place when the conquerors were not satisfied with separating the lovers and tried to erase the love itself, its remains, its memories, even its name. The Romans were not satisfied with building a shrine to Jupiter in the Holy Temple. They felt the need to change the very name of the land. Referring to the Philistines—a nation then no longer in existence—they called it Palestina.

This name represents the battle against the love between the Jewish people and the Land of Israel. The conflict with the Romans, like the earlier conflict with the Philistines, was at its core a conflict between nations. Judea's rebellion was the uprising of a nation that preferred freedom over the oppressive peace of Rome. Yet even then the conflict had connotations that strayed beyond the political plane. This was a conflict between strangers. When Abraham became the "Father of Many Nations" and his faith spread beyond the boundaries of his nation, even more tragic chapters were added to the annals of this love.

The Scriptures have become, in one way or another, the inheritance of all of humanity. Scriptural terms and concepts became the foundations of both Western and Eastern civilization. Christianity and Islam both see themselves as the ultimate heirs of Judaism, the ones who will fulfill the universalistic ideal.

Christianity and Islam, however, did not battle Judaism from the outside. The tragic irony from the perspective of Judaism lies in the fact that the adherents of these religions did not feel it was enough to establish religious centers in Rome and Mecca. They received much of the content and symbols of their religion from Judaism, but were not satisfied. They saw themselves as legitimate inheritors of the father, and in an oedipal act, wished to ravish the mother, Jerusalem. The murder of the father, the

Jewish people, was carried out in various ways, some biological, some theological. There were those who persecuted the Jews passionately. More tolerant theologians satisfied themselves—like Noah's son Ham in the aggadic account of the episode—as trying to castrate the father. He is allowed to remain alive merely as an aged witness, who cannot even die until he witnesses the success of the son who has risen against him. The political conflicts were supplemented by the most difficult conflict of all, the religious one.

In Genesis 14:18–20, we read of the significant encounter between Abraham and Malchizedek, king of Shalem (understood to be Jerusalem): "Malchizedek, king of Shalem brought out bread and wine, and he was a priest of the highest God. And he blessed him and said, blessed is Abraham of the highest God, ruler of heaven and earth." According to Moshe David Cassuto, the Torah intends to convey "that Jerusalem was a holy city. [This was] an eternal holiness, extending since time immemorial, and even when it was populated by idol worshippers, who were accustomed to worshipping many gods, its inhabitants could not but worship their highest God," who is essentially identical to the one God of biblical monotheism.

Rashi understands this encounter differently. Our rights to the land are not the result of a divine promise accompanied by military conquest. Our Sages emphasized our "historical rights" to the land. Rashi describes how the children of Shem had lived in the Land according to the original division among Noah's sons, and how "The Canaanites were conquering the land of Israel from the children of Shem." Against the background of this unjust conquest, which ended the original harmony among the peoples of the world, Abraham, a descendent of Shem, appears upon the stage of history. He meets with Malchizedek, one of the last Semitic kings of Jerusalem, before they were displaced by the Jebusites. This last remaining Semitic monotheistic priest prophesies that God "will someday return [Jerusalem] to your children, who are the descendants of Shem" (Rashi, on Genesis 12:6).

Maimonides presents an additional unique aspect of Jerusalem. In the *Guide* (III:45) he suggests that the Bible has political reasons for referring to Jerusalem as "the place which the Lord shall choose," without calling it explicitly by name. The name of the place was concealed "lest nations should hold fast to the place and fight for it with great violence, knowing as they do that this place is the final purpose of the Law on earth" (Pines trans., p. 576). Sadly, this effort to hide Jerusalem was not successful, and the struggles over Jerusalem continue to this day. Political struggles have a mechanism of their own. In Jerusalem, a religious struggle exists as well.

The Jewish people are returning to their land with a demand for justice that is beyond law. No one disputes other religions' ownership of their spiritual centers. This is one of the great tests of humanity. Will they recognize the rights of the father, who has returned to life and to youth, to live in his own land?

Jerusalem was conquered by Christians and by Muslims. But Jerusalem is holy to the Jews not because of an event that occurred in it, nor because of a building in it, but because of its very essence. The Temple could burn down, foreign temples could be built in its place, and yet the connection with the land would remain, as though nothing had changed. The Jewish people therefore mourned over Jerusalem, and Halevi expressed the longing of Jerusalem for its people:

> Zion! Wilt thou not ask if peace be with thy captives
> That seek thy peace—that are remnants of thy flocks?
> . . .
> To wail for thy affliction I am like the jackals; but when I dream
> Of the return of thy captivity, I am a harp for thy songs.
> (trans. Nina Salaman, in *Selected Poems of Jehudah Halevi* [Philadelphia: Jewish Publication Society of America, 1924], p. 3)

Nahmanides saw the double tragedy as the symbol of the deepest expression of the love between the people and the land. The nation could not rest peacefully in any other place in the world, and the land would not bear fruit for any foreign conqueror. It patiently awaited the return of its people.

CHAPTER 51:
THE LAND OF ISRAEL

The Paradox and Explanation

We will now return to our discussion of the uniqueness of the Land of Israel, the great paradox we have been living since the birth of Judaism in the first pages of the Scriptures. For God, there are no political or geographical boundaries, no boundaries between nations or countries. Yet, the great message of this universalism is expressed in two particularisms—the uniqueness of the People and the uniqueness of the Land. The paradox teaches that uniqueness is the path to universalism. The uniqueness of the Jewish people is part of a plan that will lead us and the nations of the world to the end of days, a plan for the redemption of the entire world. In this plan, the descendants of the Patriarchs hold a unique position.

This paradox was a focal point of debate with many thinkers, particularly those who drew on Judaism and accepted some of the general principles of our Torah. The Scriptures proclaimed that Abraham would become the father of many nations, and, indeed, many nations have accepted the Torah of the Patriarchs. But many of them wished to accept these principles while erasing the name of the Jews. Sometimes this was done by actually killing Jews. More often, it was done by stealing their identity and claiming to be the true Israel.

Models

The paradox of uniqueness demands an internal explanation as well. Halevi used biological and climatic models to explain his central thesis. The reader, in my view, is free to accept or reject these models as they appear, or to suggest improvements to them. Halevi attempts to analyze a difficult and important issue but lacks the tools for the job. He saw the biological and climatic theories as models that could clarify what he saw. For example, he referred to the fact that certain traits are present in the grandfather, disappear in the father and reappear in the third generation.

In this way, Halevi wished to convey the surprising idea that traits can reappear despite an apparent break in continuity and education. There can be restoration after interruption. What Halevi describes is a return to something that does not come from without but that already exists within. The biological model is wonderful, because it demonstrates that there can be a potential within one's genetic makeup that is not expressed outwardly. The difference in genetics between a genotype and a phenotype is the difference between uniqueness and chosenness. There are traits that remain hidden because of the environment in which the organism develops. However the genotype, the uniqueness, the inner potential, continues to exist. This description is true of the nation as well. This is the essence of the principle of eternal uniqueness in the philosophies of Halevi, the Maharal and Rav Kook.

Territory

This topic brings us to the place of territory in Jewish thought. We are better equipped, thank God, to discuss this question than previous generations, who read Halevi's philosophy regarding the Land of Israel yet were cut off from it. Here in the Land of Israel we face the full significance of Halevi's writings on the subject, as well as the difficult dilemmas that the topic raises.

One can view the Land of Israel as the place where the Jewish state resides. This is an instrumental view, in which territory becomes a vehicle. Like a house, a country is a place in which we live, and it constitutes, in the broadest sense of the word, a vehicle, a tool necessary for our survival. This is a rational approach, and stands as one of the principles of Zionism. This principle implies that Jewish existence in the Diaspora was abnormal and unhealthy, and that the nation must be healed and rehabilitated through Zionism. This can be compared to a disabled person who has lost the use of his hands and legs and hopes for the return of their powers. The hands and legs represent the two central characteristics of political existence in an independent state. The hands represent the nation's ability to defend itself militarily, while the legs symbolize the connection to a territory. If we were to continue in this direction, we would arrive at the territorial basis necessary to justify the Zionist idea, and that might seem enough. But here we must learn the great lesson of the *Kuzari*.

Let us jump to the end of the book, where the *haver* bids farewell to the king and prepares to journey to the Land of Israel. "After these events the *haver* decided to leave the land of the Khazars and journey to Jerusalem" (V:22). The king is astonished:

> The *haver*'s departure was difficult for the Kuzari and he spoke to him of it, saying, "What is there to find in the Land of Israel today, since the divine Presence has left it? Since the closeness of God can be achieved in any location by a pure heart and a strong desire, why should you place yourself at the peril of the deserts and the seas and the hatred of the various peoples?" (V:22).

This king's question must amaze us. Since the very first discourse, Halevi has emphasized the significance of the Land of Israel. His journey to the Land of Israel is the necessary and logical result of all he has been saying and writing. If so, why is the Kuzari king surprised? The answer lies in the recognition of a paradox, which is expressed at the end of the book and sheds a different light on the entire work. The *haver* had built a Jewish state in the land of the Khazars! Furthermore, his place in that state is comparable to the role of the philosopher, who guides the king in his leadership of the ideal kingdom. We can understand the significance of this ideal state when we read the letter that Hasdai Ibn Shaprut wrote to the Kuzari king. He writes:

> If there is a place where there is a beacon and a kingdom for the exiles of Israel and they are not tyrannized or controlled, and if I knew that this was true, I would despise my own honor and depart from my greatness and desert my family and would speedily go up mountains, over land or sea, until I would reach the place where my lord the king rules to see his greatness and his glory and the residence of his subjects and the superiority of his servants and the repose of the exiles of Israel. And upon seeing his greatness and glory, my eyes would alight and my innards rejoice and my lips would praise the One who had not withheld His bounty from my forlorn nation.

Hasdai Ibn Shaprut, a Jewish minister of high personal and political standing in the Caliphate in Cordova, claims that he would abandon all his glory and become a simple subject in the Jewish state in which the Jews have independence. This state has religious significance as well:

For how can I bleed for the destruction of our glorious House and
for the few saved from the sword who went through fire and
water, who are but a small remnant and have lost our glory and
dwell in exile. We lack the power to respond to those who say to
us all day, "Every nation has a kingdom and you have no remembrance in the land."

Behold a Jewish state exists, in the kingdom of the Khazars. But
Halevi instructs us through the paradox of his own life and choices. The
haver abandons a Jewish state, nobility, independence and everything that
goes along with it in order to travel to a place under foreign rule, the Land
of Israel. Therein lies the great lesson. We relate to the Land of Israel not
as a territory in which, by chance, a Jewish state exists. We relate to it as
our destiny and view the encounter with it as part of our essence as Jews.
Jewish sovereignty and independence are significant, but so is our relationship to the Land of Israel. At the end of the book we will learn how
Halevi envisioned the ultimate return to the Land of Israel and the
redemption. It is a mystery and a paradox. The return to the Land of Israel
is not a tool or a means. What we have here is a relationship, an encounter,
a cosmic meeting of those intended for each other from the beginning of
time. Just as every person's marriage partner is announced in Heaven forty
days before his birth, so too it is announced that a particular field in the
Land is intended for a particular person. Our Sages wished to teach us the
romantic idea that the connection between a couple exists before they
meet for the first time, and that their meeting is not a chance occurrence.
So too, the relationship between the People and the Land is more than a
chance occurrence. It was destined from the start.

   What mysterious force underlies the relationship between the People
and the Land? What makes a particular union successful and unique? Here
we enter into the realm of theory. Halevi associates it with the unique climate of the Land of Israel. Maimonides takes a similar approach, though
he moderates it by noting that the climate is not unique to the Land and
characterizes the entire region. Halevi himself says as much. "Ever was
the designated progeny of Shem . . . since his inheritance was the lands of
comfortable climates, at the center of which is placed the coveted land, the
land of Canaan, the land of prophecy" (I:95).

   The climatic condition thus is necessary but not sufficient. The Land of Israel is unique in that its climate integrates heat and cold. In other words, it combines the characteristics of those places lacking the conditions for creating a great civilization and a sophisticated culture. Indeed, both the inception and the development of civilization took place in the temperate climates.

Beyond the geographical conditions, however, there is a mystical reality, a spiritual uniqueness, which makes the Land a place where prophecy can become a reality. The Land of Israel is the destined location of the ultimate encounter between the Jewish nation and God, the place destined for prophecy and redemption.

This approach to the Land of Israel may be understandable only in terms of love. A person can assess a prospective mate according to the size of the dowry or other monetary interests, as a means to advance one's career or one's social status, or on the basis of other purely rational considerations. But we all know that this is not enough, nor should it be. Beyond these things we expect something more, something non-rational and emotional, something we can only describe as love. The word love describes the relationship between the People and the Land. The book of Genesis describes how the Great Matchmaker, the Creator himself, took Abraham, the father of the Jewish nation, and brought him to the Land of Israel. There he would establish His nation, and there the great encounter between the Jewish people and God would ultimately take place. The encounter between the People and the Land is also a condition of redemption.

Thank God, for us no contradiction exists between the instrumental approach and what we might term the romantic approach. We must realize how fortunate we are to live in an age when, after so much trial and suffering, these points of view finally merge. The distinction between the two approaches to the People and the Land was illustrated through a historical dilemma: Uganda or Palestine? The instrumental approach demanded that territory be sought somewhere. This territorial stance contrasted with the position that stressed the Land of Israel. Both are important, and the Kuzari state and the other Jewish states that arose in the Diaspora involved no transgression. But neither did they bring salvation. There were also many Jews who did not think it a crime to live in the Diaspora but who considered the creation of a Jewish state in the Diaspora a betrayal of their allegiance to the Land of Israel.

These issues are important because of their current implications. We are faced with dilemmas that center on the ideals of the redemption of the People and of the Land. We will not enter into politics here. Politics means solving these dilemmas in a particular way. But understanding the dilemmas is beyond politics. We must always be aware of the two-sidedness of our relationship to the Land. On the one hand, there is the instrumental relationship to a home. On the other hand, there is an absolute relationship to something irreplaceable. This relationship is represented in the Scriptures and in later literature by the classic image of the relationship to a mother. The Land is perceived as a mother to some individuals, and as a wife to the nation. We express this relationship through loyalty, love and respect.

The Land of Israel

As we have seen, we can view the content of Jewish thought as focused on three central points: Creation, Revelation and Redemption. History is a process with many twists and turns, but it ultimately leads from Creation, through Revelation, to Redemption.

The Land of Israel symbolizes creation. The Land of Israel is also the land of prophecy.

The binding of Isaac is tied to the second point, Revelation. There is a striking resemblance between the wording of God's command to Abraham to go to the Promised Land and His command that Abraham sacrifice his son. Just as Abraham is told "Go . . . to the land that I will show you" (Gen. 12:1), so is he told "Go . . . to one of the mountains that I will show you" (id. 22:2).

In the latter case like the former, Abraham follows the call to go to a place that he does not know. Only when he reaches it does God inform him that this is the place destined for the great drama of the sacrifice of Isaac. Abraham's going shows the holiness within the holiness. Abraham learned to recognize the holiness of the Land of Israel when he reached it. The holiness of Jerusalem had to be revealed much later, at the final trial.

The mount of the sacrifice, say the Scriptures, is the "mountain where God appeared," the place of revelation, of the encounter with God. On this mountain the Temple will be built, the Temple in which man will encounter the divine Presence. The Scriptures themselves are aware of the paradox in this claim. In his prayer, King Solomon says, "For can it be that

God reside on the earth? For all the heavens contain You; how can this House I have built [contain You]?" (1 Kings 8:27). But divine transcendence left room for the immanence that is associated with "this place . . . and You will hearken from the heavens" (ibid. 8:29–32).

Revelation is expressed in two ways: in the personal encounter and in the collective revelation of the Torah. Next to the Temple sat the High Court, whose role was to teach Torah to the entire people of Israel.

The third point that is encompassed in Jerusalem is connected to the future: the Redemption. This idea means the triumph of good in the various circles of human activity: the national, the human-universal and the cosmic.

National redemption is the return of the Jewish people to their Land. When the Jew prays for redemption, he prays to the God who "will rebuild Jerusalem," and adds, "May our eyes witness Your merciful return to Jerusalem. Blessed are You God, who will return His Presence to Zion." The redemption is the renewed meeting of the three: the People, the Land and the divine Presence, the divine immanence.

Jerusalem is also the axis on which human-universal redemption turns as well. The mountain that was the center of spiritual ascent for the Jewish people will become a center of inspiration and education for the entire world.

> And in the end of days the mount of the house of God will be placed above all mountains and rise above all hills and all the nations will swarm towards it. And many nations will go, saying, come let us go up to the mountain of God, to the House of the God of Jacob, and He will teach us of His ways and we will follow in His paths, for Torah will go forth from Zion and the word of God from Jerusalem. (Isaiah 2:2–3)

The particularism of a chosen People and Land is thus merged with absolute universalism. The People and the Land preserved the Torah so that it would be spread among all the nations, spreading its key notion of universal peace: "And they shall beat their swords into plowshares and their spears into pruning hooks; nation shall not lift up sword against nation, neither shall they study war any more" (id. 2:4).

In Jewish tradition, Jerusalem is also the center of the cosmic redemption. Isaiah's vision of the wolf dwelling with the lamb (11:6) is certainly an allegory for the ideal international relations that will reign in the messianic era. But it hints as well at a religious utopia, in which even the natural reality will change.

Various verses in Ezekiel likewise hint at future changes in Jerusalem. A spring will gush from it, and from it powerful rivers will stream forth, which will even cure the Dead Sea. Clearly, these are references to the ancient Garden of Eden.

Indeed certain commentators understood it in this way. According to their interpretation, the Garden that God planted in Eden underwent a catastrophic change as a result of the sin. With the advent of the redemption, however, it will revert to its original state. The Garden of Eden is the Land of Israel, and its center is Jerusalem.

If this motif exists in the Scriptural tradition, then the symbolism of the Holy Temple can be understood in its light as well. At its center, as in the Garden of Eden, the *keruvim* protected the Tree of Life, which is none other than the Torah—the word of God.

CHAPTER 52:
THE UGLY DUCKLING

I Believe in the Ugly Duckling

The eggs have just hatched and the ducklings have clambered out, quacking together—all but one, an odd looking duckling whose egg hatched late.

"What an ugly duckling! Look at his hawk nose, his curly feathers . . . "

"He is so strange and odd. We must beat him into shape."

"I hope a cat pounces on you, you disgusting thing!"

Hans Christian Andersen did not tell you the whole story. If I were to try to complete it, my pen and ink would not suffice. Andersen did not say that the ugly duckling met chickens that strutted like geese. Nor did he tell us that on the way he met an insect, whose story was told by Kafka. "Once I was a man, my name was Gregor Samsa," said the insect to the ugly duckling, "but the Nuremberg laws transformed me into an insect."

The Scriptures tell of the ugly duckling. Halevi puts it this way:

Said the *haver*: [In Isa. 52–53, the Jews are] likened to one who "has no beauty and no glory," "people hide their faces from him." That is, they are like a person whose odd appearance and ugly image are so filthy that a refined soul avoids gazing upon and hides his face from them. They are; "despised and rejected; a man of sorrow and acquainted with grief." (Isa. 53, 3)

Said the Kuzari: And how is it possible to see this chapter as referring to the Jewish people? For it says there, "Indeed he carries our illness," but the Jews suffer for their own sins.

Said the *haver*: For the Jewish people among the nations are like a heart among the other organs, which has both more illness and more fortitude than all the others.

The rest of the story of the ugly duckling is well known. One evening, a flock of beautiful large birds appeared. The ugly duckling had never seen anything so beautiful. He discovered that he was in fact a swan. The ugly duckling is the Jewish people. His fate is exile. Zionism was the realization that he is not a duck but a swan.

My awareness that I am a swan is Zionism.

CHAPTER 53:
A COVENANT OF FATE AND DESTINY

Anti-Semitism and Zionism

The ugly duckling's life is deeply affected by his encounter with anti-Semitism. Indeed, anti-Semitism and the Holocaust are very basic components of our identity. For many of our brethren, this is the starting point of Jewish and Zionist awareness. Must this be the case? We must answer in the negative, and emphasize that this popular position expresses only a partial truth, and therefore is erroneous, even harmful.

The picture must be rounded out. We will do so using the concepts laid down by Rabbi Joseph B. Soloveitchik in his important work, *Kol Dodi Dofek* (trans. David Gordon, [New York: Yeshiva University Press, 2006]).

Rabbi Soloveitchik's system of ideas encompasses a wonderful synthesis of classical Jewish thought and modern, particularly existentialist, philosophy. *Kol Dodi Dofek* is a summary of Rabbi Soloveitchik's approach to contemporary history. The work itself is divided into two parts —a direct analysis of the events that led to the establishment of the state of Israel and a more general analysis of Jewish history.

The work is unique in its style. Continuing, in effect, the method of classical midrashic literature, Rabbi Soloveitchik makes use of biblical figures to represent various contemporary Jewish characters. The Scriptures provide a source of inspiration to help us relate to the world around us, but also offer a terminological framework for use in expressing our responses to our experience of the world.

The ugly duckling faces the problem of his identity. Rabbi Soloveitchik points out a biblical character who faces the same situation:

> And they cast lots and the lot fell upon Jonah. And they said to him, please tell us, you on whose account this evil befallen us, what is your trade and from where have you come, what is your country and of what nation are you? And he said to them, I am a

Hebrew and I fear the God of the heavens, who created the sea and the land." (Jonah 1:8–10)

Rabbi Soloveitchik sees Jonah as representing the Jew who is faced with the question of his identity. He is the Jew trying to run away from God, trying to escape his fate and be "swallowed up" in a different reality outside of it. But he cannot do so. The storm brings him back. The storm is anti-Semitism.

Jonah is commanded to identify himself, to recognize his Jewish identity. He must decide about his future. The modern Jewish reality in which we live is the result of the coalescence of two similar decisions. These decisions are expressions of two covenants that have been with us since the birth of the Jewish people. The first is the Covenant of Egypt, based on the verse, "And I will take you to be My nation and I will be your God." The second is the Covenant of Sinai, based on the verse, "And he took the Book of the Covenant . . . and he said here is the blood of the Covenant which God has established with you." These two covenants correspond to two types of reality, both in the individual and in the nation. The first is a covenant established in the wake of a new reality that is beyond man's control: "the Covenant of Fate." The second is established out of desire and choice: "the Covenant of Destiny."

The Covenant of Fate

What is the meaning of this sense of loneliness? Jonah experienced what the Maharal writes of the Jewish fate. Rabbi Soloveitchik writes of it as follows:

> The historical loneliness of the Jew percolates from a feeling of compulsive fate. He is as alone in his life on earth as in his death. The concept of *kever yisrael* emphasizes the Jew's strange detachment from the world. Sociologists and psychologists may say what they wish about the inexplicable isolation of the Jew. Their explanations are nothing more than barren speculation, incapable of rationally describing the phenomenon. Jewish separateness belongs to the framework of the Covenant of Fate that was concluded in Egypt. In truth, Judaism and withdrawal from the world are synonymous. Even before the exile in Egypt, separateness descended upon our world with the appearance of the first Jew, our father Abraham. Abraham the Hebrew (*ivri*) lived apart. "The

whole world was on one side (*ever*), and he on the other side" (*Bereshit Rabbah* 42:8). Balaam, when he gazed upon the Israelite camp, understood the wonder of the experience of Jewish separateness and proclaimed with amazement: "They are a nation dwelling alone and shall not be reckoned among the nations" (Numbers 23:9). Even if a Jew reaches the pinnacle of social and political accomplishment, he will not be able to free himself from the chains of isolation. (pp. 52–53)

Jewish history is mysterious. The explanations for the unique Jewish sense of loneliness are, in the final analysis, useless. Nevertheless, let us engage a bit with the explanations offered by psychologists and sociologists. We have much to learn from them, although the problem itself will remain unsolved.

Anti-Semitism and Its Causes: The Psychological Background

Anti-Semitism is a multi-faceted phenomenon, which lends itself to various analyses. Its various dimensions, however, are complementary rather than contradictory, as we shall show.

We begin with the first level, the psychological dimension. To explain it I will use a simple analogy. In the Rorschach Test often used by psychologists, the patient is asked to look at a series of pictures and explain what he sees. These pictures have no intrinsic meaning. They are simply ink blots on paper, symmetrical designs created when the paper was folded in two. People nevertheless explain them, offering explanations that exist only in the person's mind. This is an opening through which the psychologist tries to enter the inner world of the patient, who "projects" what is inside himself onto the pictures.

This mechanism, according to many psychologists, can shed light on the phenomenon of anti-Semitism. The anti-Semite sees in the Jews negative qualities that threaten and endanger him. These characteristics do not exist in the "picture." They exist only in the mind of the beholder. They are the projections of the anti-Semite, who uses the Jew as an ink blot of his own making, onto which he projects the dark sides of his inner world.

This, in very general terms of course, refers to the psychological background of anti-Semitism. The fact that the Jew is a minority, a foreigner who is relatively easily identified, was a psychological factor that contributed to the choice of the Jew as the screen upon which the anti-Semites projected their fears and hatred. This is actually the explanation for a number of noticeable characteristics of anti-Semitism. We find many types and forms of attacks on Jews. In one place the Jew is described as having one trait, and in another place he is accused of the opposite characteristic. This is true regarding both his personal traits and his social and political traits. Thus, for example, the Jew is portrayed as the capitalist trying to take over the world, and on the other hand as the revolutionary, who is attempting to weaken the power of wealth and utterly abolish personal ownership. The fact that we are faced with a psychological phenomenon means that we must not search for logic here. All anti-Semites project their various and contradictory fears upon the Jew.

Anti-Semitism and Its Causes: The Social Basis

Anyone who thinks that the foregoing analysis exhausts the matter is mistaken. Anti-Semitism is a social, not an individual, phenomenon. In addition to its psychological aspects, we must study anti-Semitism from its social and general perspectives as well. A view of history and philosophy in recent generations will help in our attempt. Let us therefore move on to the second level of our analysis, the collective, political and social level.

Leading thinkers of the last century had already expressed the psychological account just noted. They viewed anti-Semitism under the rubric of xenophobia, as an aspect of the much broader phenomenon of inter-group tensions—those between majority and minority or between various races who live together within one society. From this perspective there is no essential difference between the hatred of Jews and the hostility that exists towards others, such as blacks. But this is only one level of the explanation—the roots of the problem and its individual expressions.

If anti-Semitism were only an individual psychological phenomenon, it would indeed be similar to other forms of discrimination and hostility. In the modern world, however, anti-Semitism has taken on a different hue, as various groups have used it for political purposes. We can trace clear attempts to use psychological hostility—which, it seems, has deep religious roots—to advance political aims. Thus modern anti-Semitism was born, and acquired a more and more tragic and satanic form. The widespread use of this technique began in Czarist Russia, in the struggle to suppress the revolutionary attempts that finally toppled the Czarist rule. The Czarist regime, especially through its secret police, sought to equate revolutionary action with Jewish wrongdoing. In fighting against various trends, the rulers of Czarist Russia created a sort of equation, supposedly proving their claims. The Czarist secret police produced a document that became an anti-Semitic classic, *The Protocols of the Elders of Zion*. This forgery supposedly reveals the so-called secret plan woven by the leaders of the Jews to take over the entire world. *The Protocols of the Elders of Zion* became sacred writ among anti-Semites.

The Protocols of the Elders of Zion was simply a rewriting of a French book that attributed ambitions of world conquest to Emperor Napoleon III. This tract was called "A Dialogue in Hell between Machiavelli and Montesquieu" or "Politics of the Nineteenth Century." Although its accusations were not at all directed towards the Jews and Judaism, the dialogue was adapted and transformed into the protocols of an imaginary group whose members were the world leaders of Judaism, attempting to take over the politics of various European countries.

Even the Czar himself, Nicholas II, although far from bearing the Jews any fond feelings, saw that the book was a fake and opposed its publication. Despite this, the first Russian edition appeared in 1905. A number of years later, other editions began to appear. Some of the editions were altered and corrected in order to make it possible to accuse the Jews of various catastrophes, which took place between one edition and another. At various opportunities it became the topic of public court cases, in which the book was proved to be a forgery. That, of course, did not check the book's growing popularity, particularly in the wake of Nazi influence. The book influenced various writers, who were mistakenly taken in and convinced of its authenticity. Thus, for example, Henry Ford was inspired by *The Protocols of the Elders of Zion* to write "The International Jew," in which he continued these accusations. Various other books were written in its wake until recent years.

This is an example of a lie and forgery that influenced the course of history, but which the power of truth could not effactually surmount. This abominable book became a justification of Nazism and the ensuing genocide. In this way, forgeries spread throughout the world and people are convinced by them. The process is difficult to deal with, but deal with it we must.

The Mystery of the Covenant of Fate

But enough of smokescreens. The rational explanations try to obliterate the powerful impact of the paradox, but they cannot do so:

Our neighbors perpetually blame us for the transgressions of our
co-religionists, and they turn the Talmud's rhetorical question of,
"[If] Tobias sins; should Zigud be whipped?" (TB Pesahim 113b),
into an everyday reality that no one questions. The identification
of the activities of the individual with the deeds of the nation is a
fundamental truth of the history of our people. Our enemies do
not allow the individual Jew to remain alone in his own confines.
They take him out of his own four cubits into the public domain
and there harshly criticize the [entire] community because of him.
This "standard" is only employed in relation to Israel and not with
respect to other nations (pp. 59–60).

Once again, the explanations of the experts for this phenomenon are not satisfactory. It makes no difference whether the
causes are found in the realm of psychopathology or in the sphere
of social history. Scientific classification is beside the point; the
phenomenon remains obscure and inaccessible. We Orthodox
Jews have one solution to this riddle: the hand of the Covenant of
Fate, which was concluded in Egypt on the basis of the absolute
uniqueness of the nation, is revealed amidst such an unintelligible
reality (pp. 60–61).

Rabbi Soloveitchik speaks of two explanations: the psychological and
the political-historical. They are more or less parallel to the two levels of
explanation we described earlier. Rabbi Soloveitchik regards them as unsat-
isfactory. They offer only a sort of scientific organization of the phenomena,
which cannot really explain them: "The phenomenon remains obscure and
inaccessible." Anti-Semitism is connected to the "Covenant of Egypt,"
which was made with our nation, and which still applies to us. This is the
loneliness expressed in the term *ivri*: "All the world was on one side
[Hebrew: *ever ehad*] while he [Abraham] was on the other side [*ever ehad*]."

Cain and Anti-Semitism

Halevi relates to anti-Semitism in the framework of his approach to the
"divine element," which refers to the relationship between man and God.
The appearance of the *inyan e-lohi*, the divine element, also means the
beginning of the tension that came into being because of our people's
uniqueness.

Beyond the political, economic and social hostility of anti-Semitism, there lurks a metaphysical principle. The prototype of this tension, according to Halevi, is the conflict between Cain and Abel (I:95). To understand this, we must explain the concept of the *benei ha-elohim* [lit, "sons of God"] referred to in the Torah. The "children of God" are people possessed of a special quality. Abel is one of them, and he attains the divine element. Cain does not, and religious envy, more powerful than economic envy, is thus born. That enmity was why Cain killed Abel. Maimonides would reiterate this idea in his "Epistle to Yemen."

The Four Principles of the Covenant of Fate

Loneliness is expressed in anti-Semitism, yet it is also present in "the individual's embrace of the group," an emotion that connects the Jew to the nation, "and in the sense of severance which cannot be explained from the foreign world." It takes place in Egypt, and the exile of Egypt becomes a kind of model for the future. It is in Egypt that the congregation of Israel rises to the level of a nation. Rabbi Soloveitchik defines the word nation, *'am*, as "togetherness" (from the Hebrew word *'im*, meaning "with"). This is an etymological interpretation, which claims that the Hebrew word *'am* points to the unity among brothers, and what was for Abraham the destiny of the individual now became the destiny of the nation. Most interesting is the fact that this destiny follows the Jew even when he abandons his religion, "Even if he desecrates his Shabbat, defiles his table and his bed," meaning even if he abandons the commandments connected with forbidden foods and family purity, even if he "denies his identity," despite all this he cannot abandon the God of the Hebrews.

Jewish law expressed this separateness with a symbol, which was intended to stay with the Jew even after death: the concept of a Jewish burial. Thus Joseph made his brothers swear an oath that was intended to be passed on from generation to generation, so that the grandchildren would take Joseph's bones with them when they left Egypt.

Jewish burial is an example of the fact that we must study not only the reasons for the commandments, but also their effects. Like circumcision, Jewish burial is a commandment that was maintained even after many other commandments were abandoned, and in many cases, even after the entire religious system was discarded. It was a commandment that even Jews whose lifestyles were far from traditional tried to keep. This can be demonstrated in the histories of various Jewish communities in the world, particularly in South America, that were born as a result of the struggle to maintain Jewish burial. Paradoxically, it was the *Hevrah Kadisha*—the burial society—that led to the birth of communities.

The Covenant of Fate symbolizes the Zionist response to anti-Semitism. Zionism means overcoming the negative through a positive response. Rabbi Soloveitchik enumerates four expressions of this awareness:

1. Awareness of a common fate. The first component is our sense that we have a common history.

> We are all in the realm of a shared fate that binds together the different *strata* of the nation and does not discriminate between classes and individuals. Fate does not distinguish between nobility and commonfolk, between rich and poor, between a prince dressed in royal purple velvet and a poor man who goes begging from door to door, between a pious Jew and an assimilationist. Even though we may speak a mix of different languages, even if we are citizens of different lands, even if we look different (one being short and black, the other tall and blond), even if we live in different economic systems and under different living conditions (the one living in a royal palace, the other in a humble cave), we have but one fate. When the Jew in the cave is attacked, the security of the Jew standing in the courtyard of the king is jeopardized. "Do not think in your soul that you, from all the Jews, [will escape and] shall flee to the palace of the king" (Esther 4:13). Queen Esther robed in majesty and Mordechai wearing sackcloth were situated in the same historical nexus. . . . We are all persecuted, or we are all saved together (pp. 55–56).

This unity of fate is represented by biblical heroes. A good example is the Scroll of Esther, in which two characters act—Esther and Mordecai. Mordecai, who knows of Haman's evil plan, wears sackcloth, while Queen Esther is dressed in royal clothing. Yet they are connected. Whether in a cave or in a royal court, Jews have a common future of danger or ultimate salvation.

2. An awareness of shared historical experiences leads to an experience of **shared suffering**.

> A feeling of empathy is a basic fact in the consciousness of shared Jewish fate. The suffering of one segment of the nation is the lot

of the entire community. The scattered and separated people mourns and is consoled together. Prayer, the cry, and the consolation were formulated, as I emphasized above, in the plural. Supplications that emerge from the depths of travail are not confined to the suffering and affliction of the groaning individual. They encompass the needs of the entire community. When there is a sick person in one's house, one prays not only for that person but for all the sick of Israel. When one enters the house of a mourner to comfort him and to wipe the tear from the bereaved's sad face, he directs his words of condolence to "all the mourners of Zion and Jerusalem." The slightest disturbance in the state of an individual or a sector of the people should trouble all segments of the nation throughout their dispersion. It is forbidden and it is impossible for the individual to isolate himself from his fellow and not participate in his suffering. If the assumption of shared historical experience is accurate, then shared suffering is its direct corollary. (pp. 56–58)

This phenomenon brings about the experience of shared suffering. The pauper must experience the suffering of his brethren. The third element is a corollary of the preceding one. It involves mutual involvement, obligation and responsibility. From here comes the concept of *areivut* (mutual responsibility), a legal term.

3. Joint suffering creates a feeling of **joint obligation and responsibility**. "Sharing of responsibility is not simply a halakhic-speculative notion, but a central fact in the history of Israel's relations with other nations." The third dimension is connected to the concept of *kiddush ha-Shem*—a life lived in sanctification of God's name. Rabbi Soloveitchik treats the issue primarily in its sense that the individual is not alone. His actions are recorded on the roster of the nation. In other words, he does not act as an individual, an anonymous person, but as a representative of the nation at every moment, and thus also of God, who is connected to the nation. This is a serious responsibility. At the same time, it makes the life of the Jew into something unique and full of significance. We will discuss *kiddush ha-Shem* further in the next section. Rabbi Soloveitchik writes:

The commandment to sanctify God's Name and the prohibition against desecrating it are clear in light of the principle of shared

responsibility and obligation. The activity of the individual is deb-
ited to the account of the many. Every wrong committed by an
individual stains the name of Israel throughout the world. The
individual is responsible not only for his own conscience but also
for the collective conscience of the nation. If he conducts himself
properly, he has sanctified the name of the nation and the name of
the God of Israel; if he has sinned, he causes shame to befall the
nation and desecrates its God. (p. 61)

4. The fourth element is **cooperation**. This is expressed in one of the
most important phenomena in Jewish tradition: actions, mutual help and
charitable works that help overcome suffering and which express participation in the suffering of the other. Here we should pay attention to the
historical phenomenon of the wide variety of Jewish charitable institutions throughout Jewish history:

> Fourth, shared experience is expressed by cooperation. The obli-
> gation to perform acts of charity (*tzedakah*) and loving-kindness
> (*hesed*) is derived from the experience of unity that is so all-per-
> vading and encompassing. When the Torah deals with these pre-
> cepts it uses the term "brother" rather than "friend."
>> And if your *brother* shall become impoverished . . . you
>> shall support him . . . and he shall live among you.
>> (Leviticus 25:35, emphasis added).
>> Do not harden your heart, and do not shut your hand against
>> your needy *brother* . . . open your hand to your poor and des-
>> titute *brother* in your land.
>> (Deuteronomy 15:7,11, emphasis added)
> Confrontation with the fateful reality of the nation in all of its
> strangeness instills the Jew with his common awareness in the
> realm of social activism.The shared situation of all Jews, whether
> in the objective realm, as an event, or in the subjective realm, as
> suffering, taps the sources in the individual's soul for loving-kind-
> ness and pity for his brethren, who are in trouble and that in a
> roundabout way touches him as well. Maimonides formulated this
> idea in his laconic but content-filled manner.
>> All Jews and those attached to them are like brothers, as it is
>> said, "You are sons to the Lord your God" (Deut. 14:1), and

if a brother will not show mercy to his brother, then who will have mercy on him? And to whom can the poor of Israel look for help—to those other nations who hate and persecute? They can look for help only to their brethren. (*Hilkhot Matnot Aniyyim* 10:2)

From [both] the midst of a heritage which is compulsive and fateful and a terrible aloneness which are the source of the unity of the nation, issues forth the attribute of loving-kindness which summons and drives the fateful collective to imbue their unity with positive content by means of the constant participation in events, suffering, consciousness and acts of mutual assistance. The isolated Jew finds his solace in his active adhesion to the whole and by tearing down barriers of egotistical-separatist existence, and by joining his neighbors. The oppressive experience of fate finds its connection in the coalescing of individual personal experiences into the new entity called a nation. The obligation of love for another person emanates from the self-awareness of the people of fate, which is alone and perplexed by its uniqueness. For this was the Covenant of Egypt concluded. (pp. 61–63)

Identity and Essence

To this point, we have discussed the "Covenant of Fate" that, through the generations, united all Jews, including those far removed from their religion. This covenant of fate expresses a coerced existence. But there is more. In his "Meditations on the Jewish Question," Sartre, the great existentialist philosopher, writes of the Jew:

What is it, then, that serves to keep a semblance of unity in the Jewish community? To reply to this question, we must come back to the idea of *situation*. It is neither their past, their religion, nor their soil that unites the sons of Israel. If they have a common bond, if all of them deserve the name of Jew, it is because they have in common the situation of a Jew, that is, they live in a community which takes them for Jews . . . . The Jew is one whom other men consider a Jew: that is the simple truth from which we must start . . . . [I]t is the anti-Semite who *makes* the Jew. (Jean-Paul Sartre, *Anti-Semite and Jew: An Exploration of the Etiology of Hate* [Schocken, 1948, 1976], pp. 67–69)

Indeed, this conclusion was correct with regard to the assimilated Jews who had abandoned their Jewishness and thought that they had achieved complete integration into gentile society. They discovered the essence of Judaism against their will, and their Judaism was expressed only through their being the object of anti-Semitic hatred. Sartre was not acquainted with the believing Jew, living the Covenant of Destiny. Here we must return to a basic concept in Jewish identity.

To illuminate the relationship between the influence of anti-Semitism and the Jew's Jewishness from a somewhat different perspective, we may use a few concepts developed by the late Professor Shimon Herman in his studies of Jewish identity. When he speaks of the identity of the Jew, Herman suggests that we distinguish between the concepts of "salience" and the concept of "valence." Though Herman defined the concepts with precision, we here simplify them for ease of presentation. "Salience" describes the relation between a particular element within consciousness and overall consciousness itself. Salience varies between "zero" and "total." But salience says nothing about worth. Thus, there may be a person who is very uninterested in his Jewishness yet thinks that Jewishness is a positive thing. Someone else, on the other hand, may be very interested in his Jewishness, allowing it a prominent place within his consciousness, yet take a negative attitude toward it.

It follows that we can identify assimilated Jews who nevertheless identified with their Jewishness, such as Einstein, Freud and Buber, as well as others who tried to erase every last remnant of their Jewish identity. At times, historical events, such as outbreaks of anti-Semitism, will highlight the salience of the Jewish phenomenon. This was the situation of the assimilated Jews at the time of Hitler, when they were suddenly forced to recall something they had always tried to forget—their Jewishness.

Such an assimilated Jew could find himself confronted with severe anti-Semitism. In that context, his Jewishness becomes especially prominent, consuming his entire life, but it does not on that account necessarily increase in worth for him. In fact, self-hatred and hatred of Judaism may often result. *Kiddush ha-Shem*, in contrast, is a phenomenon of maximal worth and maximal salience.

Taken together, salience and valence can define the intensity of an individual's Jewish identity. Anti-Semitism can alter salience, but it generally does not alter valence. The assimilated Jews whom Sartre described are a tragic example of people for whom the valence of Jewishness was and remained zero, while its prominence was impelled to its zenith because of historical events and anti-Semitism.

If, God forbid, there were nothing more to Judaism, Sartre's analysis would be correct. He reached his conclusions through extrapolation. Of course, he had not truly analyzed Judaism, and his misperception is not only false. It is dangerous. We do not view ourselves merely as an object for the projections of strangers. We see ourselves first of all as having an essence, and a goal, as fighting for our existence, and discovering our identity and the meaning of our own existence. We encounter anti-Semitism and try to fight against it, but this is a tragic phenomenon outside of us, and we do not construct our identity based upon it. Fate affects prominence, while destiny affects worth. We believe in both the Covenant of Fate and the Covenant of Destiny. Only Jewish destiny adds the essential meaning and significance to our identity.

The Covenant of Destiny

The difference between the Covenant of Fate and the Covenant of Destiny can be understood with the aid of a simple analogy. An automobile consists of a number of different systems: one steers the car, another generates the energy needed for movement and still others start the car or stop it. If we compare the movement of the Jewish people to the movement of a car, we may say that anti-Semitism was often the starter, and sometimes the energy, but never the steering wheel. Like an old car that is stuck, we must sometimes be pushed. To our sorrow, anti-Semitism was the push that stirred many Jews into action. But if the push is applied without the use of the steering system, the car may roll off a cliff. This is true regarding anti-Semitism as well. Anti-Semitism can bring the Jews to deterioration, insanity, despair and even self-loathing. Paradoxically enough, however, anti-Semitism sometimes became a source of positive energy, which has brought many Jews to do great things.

Anti-Semitism alone, of course, could never be an answer or a direction. To find direction one needs other sources. To see this, consider the Dreyfus Affair: Dreyfus's trial spurred Herzl towards his Zionist viewpoint, but it did not alter the beliefs of Dreyfus himself, who died far removed from Judaism despite having been the Affair's protagonist. If one studies Herzl's biography, it becomes clear that the source of his Jewish and Zionist position was not the Dreyfus trial. Its roots were much deeper, and various events in his life foreshadowed the change that was to take place. These examples show that anti-Semitism can spur us on but cannot solve problems. These must come from a different place, from an inner source. Zionism is not a result of anti-Semitism. It is a modern expression of the eternal desire to return to Zion and resurrect the Nation and the Land.

Zionism organized the political means that made this return possible. The activism that arose in reaction to anti-Semitism was an expression of the Jewish Covenant of Fate. In contrast, the Zionism rooted in the sources of Judaism is the Covenant of Destiny. There is no better way to present the Covenant of Destiny than the words of Rabbi Soloveitchik:

> What is the Covenant of Destiny? In the life of a people (as in the life of an individual), destiny signifies an existence that it has chosen of its own free will and in which it finds the full realization of its historical existence.

> What is the content of the Covenant of Sinai? It is a special way of life that directs the individual to the fulfillment of an end beyond the reach of the man of fate—the striving of man to resemble his Creator via self-transcendence. The creative activity that fulfills the Covenant of Destiny flows from a totally different source, from man's rebellion against an "as is," factual existence, and from the longing that impels him to more enhanced and sublime forms of existence. Acts of loving-kindness and fraternity, which are integrated into the framework of the Covenant of Sinai, are motivated not by the strange sense of loneliness of the Jew, but by the sense of unity experienced by a nation forever betrothed to the one God. The absolute oneness of God is mirrored in the unity of the nation that is eternally bound to Him. "You are One, and Your name is One, and who is like Your people Israel, One nation." The essence of Jewish fellowship on this level is a byproduct of the father-son relationship between the members of the nation and God. . . .

> How does destiny differ from fate? In two respects: fate means a compelled existence; destiny is existence by volition. Destiny is created by man himself, who chooses and makes his own way in

life. Fate is expressed in an ideological sense, in a denuded existence, whereas destiny embodies purpose and objectives . . . . Shared Destiny means having free will to strive for a goal (a decision freely willed to be sanctified to an ideal) and a yearning and longing for the Master of the Universe. Instead of the blind fate that pursued him, Jonah in the end chose the exalted destiny of the God of Israel. "I am a Jew, and I fear the Lord, the God of the heaven" (Jonah 1:9).

Albeit, even in the experience of Shared Destiny there is an element of separateness, but the apartness of destiny is totally different both in character and experience. It is not the negative sentiment that Balaam foresaw in his prophecy of "they are people which dwells alone" (Numbers 23:9), but rather the special awareness that Moses promised Israel in the last few hours before his death: "And Israel shall dwell in safety [separate and secure] by the fountain of Jacob" (Deuteronomy 33:28). In truth, this self-isolation is nothing but the aloneness of a glorious, strong, holy, and sacred existence. It is the isolation expressed in the singularity of a people, in its holy self-image and unique existential experience . . . . It is the solitude of which Abraham spoke to his attendants when he said, "You sit here with the donkey, and the lad and I will go to *that* place, and we shall worship" (Genesis 22:5, emphasis added). While man's isolation is a destructive feeling of inferiority that expresses self-negation, the solitude of man testifies to his greatness and sanctity—the greatness contained within himself and the sanctity that hovers in the recesses of his unique awareness. Isolation robs man of his inner peace; loneliness bestows upon man security, self-esteem, significance, and confidence—"separate and secure" (Deuteronomy 33:28).

Judaism has always believed, as we said at the outset, that man has it within his power to take fate into his own hands and shape it into the destiny of a free life, a life full of meaning and saturated with the joy of living turning isolation into aloneness and disparagement into significance. For this reason Judaism places so great an emphasis on the principle of free will. [And] for this reason [Judaism] so appreciates the human intellect, which has it within its power to free man from his enslavement to nature and allow him to rule over his environment and its blind circumstances and subjugate it to his will. The Community of Israel is obligated to use this free will in all facets of life, and especially for the good of the State of Israel. If secular Zionism, in the end, comes to understand that the establishment of the State of Israel has not weakened the paradoxical fate of Jewish alone-ness, but, on the contrary, that the incomprehensible state of, "I shall take you unto Me as a people" (Exodus 6:7) has become even more pronounced in the international arena, it must ask itself the age-old question: "What is your occupation; from where do you derive . . . and from what people do you come?" (Jonah 1:8). The question is asked in any event; if not by the Jew, then by the gentile. We must answer with pride that, "We fear the Lord, the God of the heavens" (Jonah 1:9). Our historic obligation today is to raise ourselves from a people to a holy nation, from the Covenant of Egypt to the Covenant of Sinai; from a compelled existence to an original way of life, permeated with morality and religious principles, that transcends history. We must go from being an Encampment to being a Nation (pp. 65–66, 85–88).

CHAPTER 54:
IN RABBI JUDAH HALEVI'S FOOTSTEPS

Kol Dodi Dofek (II:24)

Halevi gave us a new perspective on life in the Diaspora, but also taught us how to interpret the historical process of awakening. Halevi read the Song of Songs, as did our Sages of blessed memory, as a dialogue between the Jewish people and God. But he went further and found within the book the secret of our national rebirth. He reveals that secret to us in the conversation between the King and the *haver* in Part II (II:24).

Halevi has the King speak accusingly: why did the Jews not return to the Land of Israel when they had the opportunity? The *haver* answers honestly: the King has indeed identified our shame.

In the days of the Second Temple, "The divine element was going to descend among them as of old, if they had all heeded the call and returned to the Land of Israel with a willing spirit." Only a few returned, however, and most, among them the most prominent, remained in Babylon. Here Halevi adds an interpretation of some additional verses in the Song of Songs: "This may be what king Solomon was alluding to when he said, 'I am asleep but my heart is awake.' In other words, the nation in exile slept while 'The voice of my beloved knocked'—God called them to return to the Promised Land. 'My head is covered in dew'—this is the Divine Presence coming out of the Temple and calling the exiles to return to their Land. And the people answer, 'I have removed my gown.' They are too lazy to get up and go. In the end only a portion of the nation returns, and therefore the divine promises are only partially fulfilled, in accordance with their limited response. For the Divine Element rests upon a person only in accord with his preparedness."

This is the secret of *Kol Dodi Dofek*—"The voice of my Beloved knocketh"—which Rabbi Soloveitchik would later develop.

In the end, history is a question of partnership. If we do not join forces with Divine Providence, the promises will not be fulfilled. In a sense, this is the basic reality of every love relationship—the blending of caution with the need not to lose the moment, which may never recur. In history the situation is much more serious, and Halevi exhorts us not to miss our opportunity. History is knocking at the door, but we must be the ones to open it.

Partnership Between the People and God

The same demand that we act at the right moment is clear from another biblical book: Esther. This book teaches us, as Martin Buber has pointed out, that Divine Providence is the partnership between man and God. When we read the story of Esther we already know the ending. We are witnesses to the process of Divine Providence preparing all the mechanisms by which we solve the problems and emerge from danger. For example, consider the conspiracy of Bigtan and Teresh. Mordecai discovers their plot, passes the information on to Esther, who passes it on to the king in Mordecai's name. This is an incidental story, clearly one of many intrigues in Ahasuerus' court. But the story of Bigtan and Teresh will attain its full significance only later, when it is read to the insomniac king precisely when Haman appears before him. The entire book is written as a sort of puzzle, in which the meaning of the early episodes becomes clear only at the end. The end is predestined from the beginning. The means for survival are put in place in advance.

On the surface it seems that the story is rigidly controlled, with everything established from the start. Yet, in the midst of the story, at a decisive moment, Mordecai says to Esther, "Do not imagine that you will save yourself in the King's palace . . . for if you are silent at this time, salvation will come to the Jews from another source" (4:13–14). In other words, if Esther had declined to act, all the divine preparations would have gone to waste and God would have had to find himself another way to save the Jews. God prepared the ground, but He needs a partner in carrying out His plan. Here, at the decisive point in the book, Mordecai tells Esther that she must take decisive and dangerous action and appear before the King without having been called to his presence: "Who knows, perhaps for this moment you became queen?"

The historical progress of Divine Providence is a dialogue between God and man. God prepares the ground, but the process is never necessary, but rather contingent. God and man must work together to bring about human salvation.

In the Footsteps of Halevi and Maimonides

Modern Zionism arose under the influence of Halevi and Maimonides.

What is our attitude towards the process of redemption? How do we translate the historical partnership we spoke of earlier into practical terms? It seems to me that a synthesis of Halevi's and Maimonides' viewpoints leads to what may be called an activist position.

To understand this position, we will contrast it to another, which sees the redemption as an event that is not at all dependent upon human activity. Redemption is, rather, the result of historical processes in the hands of God, over which man has no control. This position, which has many variations, may be termed "apocalyptic." On this view, the end of the processes of redemption is not in our hands. It constitutes a revelation of a hidden reality marked out in advance.

In contrast, the position we call "activist" claims that the redemption will occur as the result of human action. This position, too, can be understood in various ways, but we refer here to rational activism. It unites two principles:

1. The approach of Maimonides, who perceived the movement into the Messianic era not as a miraculous event but as the result of the actions of the Jewish people.

2. Halevi's ideas about *aliyyah*, which he believed would bring about the redemption. We must reach the Land of Israel before the Messiah, not after him.

Maimonides dismissed the theory that miraculous events are prerequisite to the Messianic era and clear signs that the Messiah is on his way. He taught, rather, that the transition to the Messianic era would occur through rational means. An interesting detail of this approach is the possibility of reestablishing the Sanhedrin naturally, given the consent of the Sages of the Land of Israel. We saw this type of activity during the sixteenth century in the activities of Rabbi Jacob Berab and his supporters, who wanted to re-institute classical *semikhah* (rabbinic ordination) and again in the nineteenth century, at the dawn of modern religious Zionism. This was rational activism intended to bring about the redemption. This is the vision of the precursors of Zionism.

Rabbi Zvi Hirsch Kalisher writes, for example:

[Regarding] the redemption of Israel that we await, one must not think that God, may He be blessed, will suddenly descend from the heavens to the earth and tell His people "Go," or that He will send His Messiah in an instant from the heavens to blow the great trumpet to the dispersed of Israel and gather them to Jerusalem. Rather the redemption of Israel will come about slowly . . . for the beginning of the redemption will come through the awakening of philanthropists and the desire of the kingdoms to gather some small portion of the scattered people of Israel to the Holy Land.

The term "precursors of Zionism" in my opinion works an injustice to these pioneers. While Herzlian Zionism is made to seem modern and practical in its intention to provide an answer to modern anti-Semitism, we are, paradoxically enough, closer to the "precursors of Zionism." For us, Zionism is not an answer to the problems of anti-Semitism; it is a national liberation movement. Rabbi Zvi Hirsch Kalisher saw this clearly, writing at the conclusion of his book *Rishon Le-Tziyyon*:

It is wondrous and glorious for the nation of Jeshurun who turn to the love of the Land of their forefathers . . . . For are we less than other nations, who consider their blood and possessions as nothing compared with the love of their country and their people? Pay heed to what the Italians, the Poles, the Hungarians have done for the sake of territorial inheritance.

Jewish thought encompasses several positions regarding the relationship between redemption and rational political activity. As we have seen in our discussion of the concept of redemption, their common denominator is the basic premise that the two do not contradict each other—in other words, the reverse of the approach we earlier termed "apocalyptic." We have seen the position of Rabbi Zvi Hirsch Kalisher. Let me present three others.

Rabbi Samuel Mohliver originated, or at least emphasized, the distinction between two possible types of redemption: *be-ittah* ("at its time") and *ahishenah* ("I will hasten it"). (The formulation plays on Isa. 60:22, which concludes, using the Hebrew terms here, "I the Lord will hasten it in its time.") Completely miraculous redemption—"I will hasten it"—is one possibility. But since we had not been worthy of that, the second, more naturalistic possibility—"at its time"—is now underway. He writes:

In my opinion we have hinted at a wondrous idea regarding the future redemption, which we await. It is well known that many of the great sages and most of the populace believe that the redemption will occur through a wondrous miracle that is high above the ways of nature. But there are also those among the great sages who tend to think that the redemption, or at least the beginning of the redemption, will be natural, as is explained in the Jerusalem Talmud, in the first chapter of tractate *Berakhot*, "Just as the dawn appears bit by bit," . . . so does the redemption of Israel. My opinion also tends in this direction, following two statements of our Sages in Tractate *Sanhedrin* [98a] . . . "Rabbi Joshua ben Levi asks: it says 'at its time' and it says, 'I will hasten it.' If they are worthy, 'I will hasten it.' If they are not worthy, 'at its time.'" Rabbi Joshua ben Levi also asks there, "It says, 'with heavenly clouds' and it says, 'as a pauper riding a donkey.' If they are worthy—'with heavenly clouds.' If they are not worthy—'as a pauper and riding on a donkey.'" In my opinion, the two statements of Rabbi Joshua ben Levi are quite similar, and they reflect what we have found in many sources: that the redemption will be on a lower level and in a natural way. For this reason he says that if they are worthy, "I will hasten it." He means that if they are not yet ready for redemption by natural means, [God] will hasten it miraculously and it will take place on a very exalted level. But if they are not worthy [of such miracles], it will take place "in its time," in other words naturally.

God promised us in our Torah that, "Also when they are in the land of their enemies I will not be repulsed by them nor will I be disgusted by them [to the extent that] I will destroy them." Thus our hopes will not be dashed that in the end of days we will take our stand as an independent nation in our Holy Land and that this will occur naturally, as we have seen. For the glimmerings of dawn have already begun to shine for us, and we have achieved rights and freedom. There are those of us who stand at the highest levels in wisdom, wealth and position. This is the meaning of "If they are not worthy it will be at its time." In other words that we will slowly rise higher and higher until we return to our Land . . .

Although the redemption will occur naturally, it will not,

heaven forbid, be by chance, for there is no such thing as chance in the universe, and who is the controller of nature if not God alone? But in any case it must occur naturally, meaning that when we ourselves are ready for it, we will try to convince all the kings and rulers to agree to be kind to our people because of the troubles and trials their forefathers imposed upon our forefathers.

A third opinion was that of Rabbi Reines, who sharply distinguished between Zionism and Messianism. Yet, his positions requires clarification. Some see apologetics in his position. Yet his view is not a response to the ultra-orthodox attack, which claims that Zionism transgressed the messianic idea by its belief in human action. It is, rather, a response to the claim that Zionism itself is the true Messianic national idea, which has now been cleansed of all the illusions that were added to it over the generations in religious contexts. In other words, Reines saw a need to protect the messianic idea against the danger of becoming solely a political matter. The person who expressed the latter idea explicitly was Max Nordau, and it was repeated with the birth of the state in the writings of Ben Gurion. In Rabbi Reines' period ideas such as these were expressed by itinerant Zionist orators. A nicely worded statement on the matter is that of Rabbi J. L. Zirelson, in his article "*Kotz she-ba-Ketz*," *Ha-Meilitz*, 1898:

> It is truly a great mistake to equate Zionism with that approach. It is possible for those who are faithful to the faith of Israel . . . to believe that just as the beginning was through miracles, without any natural preparation on our side . . . so, too, God's power is strong enough to create new wonders for those who look to Him for salvation this time as well . . . . At the same time [people will continue] loving Zionism with all their heart and might, a natural love and not an artificial love born of the outburst of anti-Semitism, just as a person who seeks medical help does not damage his faith or make a sham of his prayers for God's healing.
>
> When we consult with doctors or travel for trade, we do not thereby act contrary to our prayers for health and wealth, whose delivery we thank God alone for. Even as we involve ourselves with all these, we believe that all of man's endeavors at salvation are as naught, and only . . . [God] can make our endeavors bear

fruit. Accordingly, our actions are not sinful at all. On the contrary, we gain from them, for we will develop and thereby fulfill God's desire of us. Thus, from this perspective, when we turn to build the ruins of our Holy Land with our hands, not only will we not impair the twelfth [Maimonidean] principle [which declares that God will send the Messiah to redeem us]. In fact, we will gain much from a religious perspective: the settling of the Land (itself a constant commandment that applies even when we are in exile); keeping the commandments that are dependent upon working our Holy Land; working the fields and plowing . . . as a source of livelihood for many people who are now idle and starving, so that we will no longer be a confirmation of the Gentiles' view of our poverty as just punishment for being merchants and moneylenders. Above all [another positive element will be] the unification of all of our parties, which are very far from each other, in focusing upon one general ambition, in which much good is contained for the Jewish people. This is the spirit of the rule that our Sages expressed in their interpretation of the verse, "At its time, I will hasten it": "If they are worthy, 'I will hasten it'; if they are not worthy, 'in its time.'"

Let us hope that the resultant gain will be one of the two: if our actions on Mount Zion will be desirable before the Lord, He will hasten our redemption. If this merit does not tip the scales, the redemption will take place whenever it will, at its time, and we will receive merit for all our good actions.

The National Answer

We learn this from Halevi's approach. Moving to Israel is a prerequisite for redemption, and it teaches us that exile is no longer a punishment but a sin. Our national and political identity owes a great debt to Halevi. If exile is a sin, then the repentance for it will bring about the redemption, and this redemption is first of all the return to the Land. "But the beginning of the redemption is not dependent upon repentance but upon return to the Land" (Rabbi Zvi Hirsch Kalisher, *Derishat Tziyyon* [1919], 18a).

The return to the Land and its settlement are prerequisites for redemption. A well-known motif in Jewish tradition is that redemption depends upon keeping the commandments. Here we find a revolutionary idea:

bringing the redemption is not connected with the commandments in general, but first and foremost with the commandment to settle in the Land. This new emphasis is also connected to Halevi's approach. At the end of the *Kuzari*, Halevi refers to the custom among sages to kiss the earth and stones of the Land of Israel. The sages based this custom on a verse from Psalms, which has been quoted hundreds and perhaps thousands of times. Halevi, however, gives it a new reading, connecting it to the preceding verse: "You will arise and have mercy upon Zion. for it is time to pardon her, for the time has come. For Your servants fulfilled [the punishment] of her stones and have pardoned her dust" (Ps 102: 14–15).

The *haver*'s meaning is clear:

> In other words, Jerusalem will indeed be rebuilt when the Jewish people will long for her with a great yearning, until they will bring about the pardon of her stones and dust (V:27).

Subject Index

NAME INDEX